CAREER PATTERNS
of LIBERAL ARTS
GRADUATES

by Robert Calvert, Jr.

Revised Edition

The research reported herein was supported by the Cooperative Research Program of the U.S. Office of Education, U.S. Department of Health, Education and Welfare.

THE CARROLL PRESS
Publishers

43 Squantum St., Cranston, R. I. 02920

About the Author:

Dr. Robert Calvert, Jr., has been active in guidance and placement for twenty years as administrator, lecturer, consultant and teacher.   He has served with the Peace Corps as Director of the Career Information Service and, later, as Director of the Office of Volunteer Support. Prior to accepting his Peace Corps assignment, Dr. Calvert was Manager of the Student and Alumni Placement Center at the University of California in Berkeley, one of the largest university placement organizations in the U.S. At Berkeley, he was also an Associate Research Analyst for the Survey Research Center.

With John E. Steele of the Harvard Business School as co-author, Dr. Calvert wrote *Planning Your Career,* a widely used guide for graduating students. This book and another book by Robert Calvert, *How to Recruit Minority Group Students,* were listed among the best books in the field of guidance in 1963. His name appears frequently in professional periodicals to which he has contributed over forty articles. He is often a featured speaker at professional meetings. Dr. Calvert earned his Bachelor of Arts degree in economics from Oberlin College, a Master of Arts and a Doctor of Education in guidance from Columbia University.

Library of Congress Catalog Card Number: 73-84568
Clothbound (SBN 910328-00-5) $10.00

Printed in the UNITED STATES OF AMERICA by The Alpine Press, Inc., South Braintree, Mass.

Cover design by Julius Spakevicius and staff.

To My Father

ROBERT CALVERT

CONTENTS

LIST of TABLES

LIST of TABLES — continued

PREFACE

During the past three decades, a college degree was more or less a guarantee of employment. Now suddenly in the 1970's the tide has turned. School systems report more good teaching applicants than they can use. Government agencies are faced with executive mandates ordering retrenchment or taxpayer revolts, inhibiting expansion. Business firms are more concerned with cost-cutting and profit margins than with continued recruitment of new college trainees. The once-glamorous space industry has turned into a sickly giant.

The change in the demand for its graduates has forced colleges and universities to re-evaluate their programs. Nowhere is this re-evaluation process more crucial than for the liberal arts college — already concerned about its role in what has been labelled the "Age of Specialization." The future of liberal education may be at stake — possibly through over-reaction, based upon the employment plight of the newest graduating class.

Useful in appraising the merits of general education today are opinions from liberal arts alumni commenting upon their careers and the adequacy of their own college training. For this reason, attention has been focussed upon a national study of liberal arts graduates conducted in the mid-1960's. The results of this survey were published in 1969 under the title, *Career Patterns of Liberal Arts Graduates.* The impact of the findings revealed in this report have increasing relevance to the problems facing liberal arts graduates in the current employment market. This second edition of the report is being issued with new conclusions appropriate to the changing economic environment.

The study reported on these pages was conducted through the Survey Research Center at the University of California in Berkeley. Key to the successful execution of this project was the strong support and leadership offered by the then Director of the Center, Charles Y. Glock.

The original support for this research was furnished through the Cooperative Research program of the U. S. Office of Education.

Later, a supplementary grant by the Carnegie Corporation supplied additional resources. Their generous support made a comprehensive study possible.

A number of colleagues at the University of California provided help at different stages of the project. Robert E. Mitchell and Joseph Speath helped to conceptualize the project and design the questionnaire. Technical advisor on the selection of the sample of participating colleges was William L. Nicholls, II. Mrs. D. J. Miller supervised the early stages of the project aided by Ann and Jim Burk and Ann Stoops.

Mrs. Beth Huttman supervised the project in its middle stages and played a major role in the development of the analysis plan. Working with her were coding supervisors, Peg Templeton and Judy Muhlfelder. Virginia Norris helped in the editing of the final report.

Final responsibility for the content of any report rests with the author. In this project, however, so many able people worked so hard that their efforts merit special recognition.

Robert Calvert, Jr.

Garrett Park, Maryland
August, 1973

INTRODUCTION

The Study Design

The primary objectives of this study were to examine the career patterns of liberal arts alumni and their roles in a society marked by a heavy emphasis on science and specialized skills. For these purposes, a national sample of graduates was surveyed, with special emphasis on their occupational experiences and satisfactions and on their evaluations of their college training as seen from current perspectives. Such information, it was felt, would prove valuable to college officials who develop or revise liberal arts programs, to high school and college counselors who advise students regarding educational and career plans, to employers who hire (or specifically avoid hiring) liberal arts graduates, and to national leaders concerned with the utilization of manpower resources. Judging from individual comments on the questionnaires, the information would also prove of special interest to the graduates themselves.

Since a primary focus was to be on occupational adjustment, an early decision was made to restrict the survey to male graduates. Virtually all would be engaged in, or preparing for, full-time careers, and this would provide a common base of experience and interest about which they could be questioned. While a comparable study of women graduates would undoubtedly have proved interesting, its greater complexities suggested that it should not be attempted in the same survey.[1]

The study was further limited to graduates of the post World War II period. Many changes had occurred during the war both in the occupational structure and in the vocational significance of higher education, thus making the experiences of earlier graduates less relevant to present day concerns. Very recent graduates, those who had been out of college less than five years also were excluded, as large numbers would be in graduate or professional school or in temporary military service.

Since the study was to be conducted in 1963, this narrowed the relevant classes to those between 1948 and 1958. Three classes spanning this period were chosen for study, those of 1948, 1953, and 1958. Five, ten, and fifteen years after graduation, they would provide cross-sections of alumni from early to middle stages of career development. [2]

To make comparisons between these classes most meaningful, however, it was necessary to insure at least some rough comparability in the type and quality of education they received. Between 1948 and 1958, several new colleges emerged, some formerly technical institutions established liberal arts programs, and existing liberal arts colleges grew at differing rates. Thus, if a separate sample were drawn for each year, each fully representative of all male liberal arts graduates in that year, the three samples would differ not only in number of years since graduation but also in the institutions where they were trained. To overcome this problem, only those colleges and universities which granted liberal arts degrees in all three years were included. The 1953 sample was then chosen to be representative of all male liberal arts graduates of those institutions in that year, and the 1948 and 1958 samples were selected solely for comparability as explained in the description of sampling below.

This design has important consequences for the interpretation of tables presented in this report. First, it must be recognized that none of the three samples is wholly representative of all male liberal arts graduates in that year. In particular, each omits graduates of emerging and submerging institutions and of those which established or abolished liberal arts programs during this period. Second, trends observed over the ten-year period must be recognized as trends within comparable samples of graduates from the same set of institutions. These need not correspond to trends among all male liberal arts graduates since the latter also would reflect changes in the population of institutions offering liberal arts degrees as well as differential growth rates among those granting liberal arts degrees throughout the period.

Definitions of the Population

The population of liberal arts institutions was first restricted to accredited colleges and universities within the continental United States, Alaska excluded, which awarded bachelor's degrees to men in each of the academic years 1947-48, 1952-53, and 1957-58. Then liberal arts institutions were identified within this set. [3]

Liberal arts institutions were identified by their awarding of bachelor's degrees in distinctively liberal arts subjects rather than by the occasionally misleading self-descriptions contained in college catalogs and announcements.[4] Six subject matter fields were selected as readily identifiable as part of a liberal arts curriculum: (1) English; (2) fine and applied arts; (3) foreign languages and literature; (4) philosophy; (5) psychology; and (6) social science, here defined as history, sociology, or political science. Degrees in science and mathematics were not considered, since they are frequently granted by purely technical institutions. Only colleges and universities which awarded bachelor's degrees in at least three of the six designated fields were counted as liberal arts institutions, and a school had to qualify in 1947-48, 1952-53, and 1957-58 to be included.[5] In total, 412 colleges and universities were identified which satisfied all criteria for the study.

The population of liberal arts graduates also was delineated in two steps. Initially, this population was defined as all males who graduated from the 412 liberal arts institutions in the three selected academic years with majors in the following subjects:

Anatomy	Mathematics
Anthropology	Music or music history
Art or art history	Physics
Biology and other bio-science fields	Philosophy or logic
	Physiology
Botany	Pre-medical or pre-dental
Chemistry	Political science
Economics	Psychology
English	Religion
Foreign languages and literature	Sociology
	Speech or drama
General programs in humanities social sciences or science	Zoology
	Other interdisciplinary majors
Geography	which are combinations of
History	the above

February and August graduates as well as those who received their degrees in June were included.

When additional information was received from the sample of schools and from the graduates themselves, the definition was further refined to exclude: (1) foreign students no longer living in the United States; (2) graduates whose degrees clearly were obtained in a non-liberal arts program, such as chemistry graduates of an engineering curriculum; and (3) persons who died before the summer of 1963. Graduates who completed a double major in a liberal arts subject in combination with a non-liberal arts field, such as economics and business administration, were included unless their questionnaires reported the non-liberal arts field as their primary field of training.

An Overview of the Population

Before presenting sampling and field work methods, a brief overview of the total male liberal arts population is appropriate. This analysis, which is based on information available from *Earned Degrees Conferred* and similar published sources, serves three related purposes. First, it introduces several distinctions among the schools which are employed throughout the analysis. Second, it provides more complete information about the proportion of liberal arts degrees granted by various types of institutions than is available from the sample data analyzed in the remainder of the report. And third, it identifies trends in the populations which were intentionally removed to provide a comparable sample in each year.

In total 59,291 liberal arts bachelor's degrees were granted to men in 1948 by the 412 institutions in the school population. In 1953, the number of such degrees declined slightly to 56,075, but it rose sharply to 71,925 in 1958. This represented a 21 percent increase over the ten-year period. The pattern of growth did not proceed evenly in all types of schools, however. Important trends summarized in Table 109 are found by type of administrative control, school size, and academic quality. (Table 109 is in Appendix A, page 210.)

Administrative control was determined by reference to *Education Directory, Part III, Higher Education* for the appropriate years.[6] Five types of control were distinguished: state, municipal, Roman Catholic, Protestant, and private secular. For most of the analysis, however, these are grouped into broader categories of public (state and municipal), Roman Catholic, and private (Protestant and private secular).

One major trend observed in Table 109 is the growing importance of public institutions (state and municipal) in the preparation of liberal arts graduates. In 1948, they accounted for 40 percent of the liberal arts degrees received by men, but in 1958 their proportion of the total had increased to 44 percent. Roman Catholic institutions also increased their proportion of the total between these two dates, from 8 percent to 10 percent, while the private colleges and universities experienced a relative (and absolute) decrease, from 52 to 43 percent. A closer look at the figures indicates that the increase in public school graduates is explained by the rapidly expanding state colleges and universities, while the declining production of the private institutions occurred in the private secular schools.

The size of an institution may be measured in a variety of ways, depending upon one's purpose. In this study, size was taken primarily as an indicator of the total social and intellectual climate of a campus, and, for this purpose, total student enrollment seemed the best measure. The count included, therefore, part-time as well as full-time students, and both those at the undergraduate and graduate levels. All classifications by size in this report refer to the fall enrollment for 1952-53, the middle year of the three chosen for investigation.[7] In some tables, a six-level classification is presented, but in most only three levels of size are employed: small (under 2,500 students); medium (2,500 to 9,999 students); and large (10,000 students or more).

When this trichotomy is employed, 30 percent of the 1948 male liberal arts graduates are found to have received their degrees from small institutions, 38 percent from medium-sized schools, and 32 percent from large universities. In 1958, the proportions graduating from small and medium-sized institutions had increased to 34 and 41 percent, respectively, while the large universities now accounted for only 25 percent of the total. The greatest relative decline occurred among the very largest schools, those with enrollments of 14,000 or more. Their proportion of the total male liberal arts graduates decreased from 23 percent in 1948 to only 16 percent in 1958.

A similar trend was observed by academic quality. This was measured by an index originally developed by Lazarsfeld and Thielens and modified here for a somewhat different time period and population of institutions.[8] While full details have been deferred to the Appendix, it may be sufficient here to note that the index is based on six factors: (1) total number of volumes in the school library; (2) number of library books per student; (3) total annual budget per student; (4) percentage of Ph. D. 's on the faculty; (5) tuition charges, with separate scales for public and private institutions; and (6) proportion of alumni who received selected academic distinctions. The resulting index scores generally have been grouped into three categories, labeled high (27 to 30 points), medium (19 to 26 points), and low (less than 19 points). Since the cutting points were chosen simply for convenience of analysis, the resulting categories must be seen merely as arbitrary groupings on a continuous scale, not as synonyms for more than adequate, adequate, and less than adequate quality.

As measured by this index, low-quality institutions increased their production of male liberal arts graduates most. In 1948, they accounted for 32 percent of the total; in 1958, they accounted for 38 percent, reflecting major policy decisions by several first-rank universities to restrict their growth during this period. While this and the foregoing trend might differ somewhat if changes in quality and size during the ten-year period were taken into account, they do suggest that the most rapid growth during this general period of expansion was taking place among institutions at the lower ends of the quality and size spectrums.

As would be expected, control, size, and quality proved to be related characteristics. Since the same relationships appear in the sample, it is important to remain aware of them in drawing interpretations from tables where they are employed. As shown in Table 110, for example, none of the Catholic schools was classified as "large" or of "high" quality by the procedures just described, and of the remaining colleges and universities, the private institutions tend to be smaller than the public institutions.

Perhaps the most important relationship, however, is that between size and quality shown in Table 111. Although there are exceptions, the larger schools generally are higher in quality. As a result, when graduates of large schools are compared with graduates of small schools, it must be recognized that they also tend to differ in the quality of the institutions where they were trained.

Sampling Methods

The sampling methods were designed to meet several objectives. First, the sample was to include approximately 100 of the 412 liberal arts institutions in the school population. Second, approximately 6,000 male liberal arts graduates of these schools were to be drawn for each of the three years selected. Third, the sample of graduates for the middle year (1952-53) was to be representative of all graduates in the student population of that year. Fourth, the samples for the remaining two years were to be drawn for comparability with this middle year, each containing approximately the same numbers of graduates from the same 100 institutions.

The initial sampling ratios were intentionally set higher than required, aimed at securing 105 schools and approximately 7,400 graduates in each year. This was done to allow flexibility in drawing the final sample in accordance with the last objective, and in anticipation that some schools might refuse to cooperate and that some graduates might prove unreachable because of a lack of current addresses.

The 412 institutions in the population were first divided into two main groups, those with more than 100 liberal arts graduates in 1952-53 as reported in *Earned Degrees Conferred* and those with 100 or less. Both the large and the small schools were then stratified by their control (public, private, and Catholic) and by their quality scores. The divisions by strata are described in Appendix A.

Sampling within strata proceeded differently for the small and large schools. The small institutions were chosen by simple random sampling with equal probability per school until the desired number of graduates was reached. All graduates of the chosen schools in each of the three years were then included in the preliminary sample.

The large schools were drawn by systematic random sampling with probability porportionate to their numbers of liberal arts graduates in 1952-53. Then approximately equal numbers of graduates in each year were selected from each school, 68 from each Roman Catholic institution and 75 from the others. When the procedure designated the same institution twice, a double sample of its graduates was taken in each year. This method of sampling insured that all schools with large numbers of liberal arts graduates were included while the representativeness of the sample was maintained.

Of the 105 colleges and universities selected by the foregoing methods, 98 agreed to participate. Of the seven which declined, two did so early enough that a randomly chosen alternate from the same stratum could be drawn and contacted. Only one of these two alternates agreed to participate at this late date, bringing the total to 99 institutions. One additional college, a Roman Catholic institution, was initially invited as a replacement for a school which later agreed to participate in the study. While the alternate might then have been dropped, preliminary returns indicated that a somewhat smaller response rate might be expected from the graduates of Catholic institutions. Final returns proved this to be true. The alternate, therefore, was retained in the sample to bolster the number of graduates of Catholic institutions, thus bringing the final total to 100 institutions.

Administrative details of the selection of alumni from the co-operating colleges and universities varied but generally took one of two courses. Either information was requested for all liberal arts graduates of the three selected years or a list of such graduates was first requested, a systematic random sample of the required size drawn from this list, and the same information requested for those sampled.

Five pieces of information were requested for each graduate: (1) his name; (2) his last known address; (3) his undergraduate major or majors; (4) his undergraduate cumulative grade point average; and (5) his overall percentile score on the American Council on Education Psychological Examination or the Ohio State Psychological Examination. Majors were carefully reviewed to determine eligibility for inclusion in the study, and an attempt was made to eliminate foreign students no longer living in the United States by excluding alumni with both a foreign address and a name identifiable with the country in which they resided. Scores on the two psychological tests were available on so few graduates (12 percent) that no use was made of them in the study.

As expected, some losses were incurred at this point through the absence of current addresses. Among the oversample of 29,582 names provided by the schools, 4.3 percent were lost for this reason. This ranged from 5.1 percent of the 1948 graduates to 3.2 percent of those of 1958. Wherever possible, graduates with known addresses were used as replacements, but for some small colleges, where all alumni were to be included in the sample, this was not possible.

As previously noted, the initial sample was overdrawn to anticipate such losses and to provide flexibility in selecting the final sample of 18,000 graduates in accordance with the study's objectives. Reductions in the sample size were accomplished by randomly eliminating cases within selected strata and years to increase the proportionality of each year's sample with the population of the central year, 1952-53. For the large schools, these adjustments were made by modifying the constant number of graduates sampled per school per year. For the small schools, they involved taking standard proportions of the available cases in each year and strata to achieve the desired numbers. For some strata, the ideal numbers were not obtainable with the numbers available. Additional cases then were generally drawn from adjacent strata.

Field Operations

In mid-November of 1963, a questionnaire (see Appendix C) and a covering letter were mailed to each of the 18,004 persons in the final sample. A prepaid envelope was enclosed. Second and third mailings included a fresh copy of the questionnaire followed in January and March of 1964 to those who had not responded to earlier requests.

Two special steps were taken to reach alumni whose addresses were no longer current. First, all questionnaires were sent by return requested mail. More than 3,000 address corrections were obtained in this manner and the questionnaires were remailed to the new addresses. Second, when a questionnaire was returned without a forwarding address, the school was contacted to learn if a more recent address, or the address of the graduate's parents, was available. An additional 1,250 remailings were made.

Returns were accepted through June 18, 1964, when 10,877 completed and usable questionnaires had been received. The overall, crude return rate was 60.4 percent of the 18,004 mailed. Based on evidence described in Appendix A, on page 205, it is estimated that of the eligible subjects who received a copy of the questionnaire, 70.2 percent replied.

The Completed Sample

A detailed evaluation of the final sample of completed questionnaires is presented in Appendix A, pages 206-208 and Table 117 on page 216. Here we will merely summarize its conclusions.

First, two of the major sampling aims appear to have been achieved in the completed sample. The individual samples for the three selected years are found to be closely comparable to one another, at least in their distributions by type of control, school size, and academic quality. In addition, these three samples also are found in at least general correspondence with the 1953 population on these same characteristics, as was the intention. Graduates of public institutions and of schools with less than 1,000 students are slightly under-represented, but these discrepancies are not of sufficient size to greatly affect tables presented in this report.

Second, when a follow-up study was undertaken with a sample of non-respondents to the main questionnaire, those who were reached proved to be remarkably similar to the respondents on a wide range of characteristics — including undergraduate major, undergraduate grades, occupational satisfaction, income, and attitudes towards liberal arts education. The non-respondents were, however, disproportionately employed in the private non-manufacturing sector of the economy, typically in such professions as law, medicine, dentistry, and fiscal management. Apparently, the survey was somewhat less successful in reaching such professionals than those employed in the public or private manufacturing sectors of the economy. Large numbers in these occupations, however, did respond and are included in the tables which follow.

Third, it should be pointed out that one potential and essentially unassessable bias in the reported tables still remains. This derives from the inability of the survey to locate approximately one-tenth of the total sample from the addresses provided by the cooperating institutions. Since they appear to have ceased contact with their alma maters and to have moved repeatedly since their last known address, it seems unlikely that any effort short of a census would succeed in locating a substantial number of them. Whether they differ appreciably from those who could be located must remain unknown.

Methods of Presentation

In the chapters which follow, several measures have been taken to avoid overwhelming the reader with a plethora of detail. Several major classifications have been defined in this introduction, so that they need not be explained in succeeding use.

Numbers of graduates in each category have been eliminated from the tables to reduce their detail. Variations between total number of graduates responding to individual items were statistically insignificant.

In selecting tables and cross-classifications for presentation, a general policy was followed of including only those containing a difference of at least 5 to 10 percentage points except when the information, even if a full finding, appeared to have intrinsic interest or to contradict a commonly held belief. This policy explains apparent inconsistencies in variables studied in related sequences of tables.

Finally, two definitional points should be stressed as important to a general understanding of many of the tables. First, all characteristics of the colleges, such as size and quality, describe them as they were in 1952-53, the middle of the three years selected for study.

Second, all references to colleges and universities, except where specifically noted to the contrary, are to the single undergraduate institution from which the alumnus received his bachelor's degree.

FOOTNOTES

1. Havighurst, Robert J., *American Higher Education in the 1960's.* Columbus, Ohio, Ohio State University Press, 1960, p. 37. In his analysis of college alumni, for example, Havighurst found it necessary to treat economic and educational data for men and women separately.

2. Procedures for selection of the sample of graduates were developed by William L. Nicholls II of the Survey Research Center of the University of California at Berkeley. Portions of this Introduction and most of Appendix A (Technical Notes) were written by him.

3. *Education Directory, Part III: Higher Education,* for 1947-48, 1952-53, and 1957-58. Washington, D.C., U.S. Office of Education, U.S. Government Printing Office, 1948, 1953 and 1957.

4. As one illustration of disagreement between a formal statement and actual practice, one of the schools which subsequently declined to participate in the study wrote explaining that it granted a substantial number of liberal arts degrees but that its role in liberal arts education was not countenanced by the state legislature which supplied its funds.

5. *Earned Degrees Conferred by Higher Educational Institutions* for 1947-48, 1952-53 and 1957-58. Washington, D.C., U.S. Office of Education (Circular Nos. 247, 380 and 570), U.S. Government Printing Office, 1948, 1953 and 1959.

6. This proved more complex than one would suspect. For example, Cornell University, described as a combination private and public institution in each year, was considered a private university since its liberal arts program appeared to be privately financed. Rutgers University, which was described as both public and privately supported in 1948 and 1953 and classified as a public school in 1958, was treated as a public school.

7. *Educational Directory,* 1952-1953, *op. cit.*

8. Lazarsfeld, Paul F. and Thielens, Wagner, Jr., *The Academic Mind.* Glencoe, Ill., The Free Press, 1958, p. 460.

CAREER PATTERNS
of LIBERAL ARTS GRADUATES

1

The CHANGING ROLE of LIBERAL EDUCATION

For colleges and universities in the United States, conditions have seldom been more favorable. Their financial problems are being met by increasing billions of dollars of state and federal support, aid from private foundations, rising returns on endowments, and the economic benefits of operating with near-maximum enrollments. Their academic standards are aided by the bins full of applications from young men and women who from early childhood have been engaged in a great national competition to gain admission to the best possible college. Their faculty and staff recruitment benefits from a new mood of respect for the academic life, aided no little by full professorships which pay near Madison-Avenue-level salaries.

Where time can be spared from actions necessary to operate the basic educational program and from essential public contacts, the presidents of our colleges and universities and their top assistants focus attention on new building programs, on development of new research or service institutes, on complying with reports to account for funds received in the past and stimulating awards of new monies in the future or on attempting to analyze the student mores of today.

The colleges are concerned about what happens after graduation to their alumni, but this concern has a low action priority. Furthermore, so little research has been done in this area that substantive discussion, let alone action, is difficult. Their students, in turn, have been so preoccupied with the frenzied dash to gain admission to college that often little thought has been given to the life which follows. Here, too, planning is handicapped by lack of knowledge.

3

Interest is developing in the use made of the national manpower resource represented by the college graduate, but this interest is more a tide than a torrent. In *The American College*, Sanford pointed out that "there is a remarkable discrepancy between the wide public acceptance of the value of college education and the paucity of demonstrated knowledge that it does some good."[1] A foundation official cited better measurement and documentation of the outcomes of college education as one of four areas now most appropriate for foundation support. He noted: "In promotional literature, colleges and universities boast about the achievements of their alumni, but rarely are the claims supported by more than conjecture or piecemeal data."[2]

Even professional schools collect little meaningful information about the subsequent activities of their graduates. Gordon and Howell have pointed out: "Relatively few business schools know very much about the careers their graduates follow, and they lose contact with students very quickly after graduation."[3]

Historically, liberal education has been the cornerstone of American higher education. Even today, three-fourths of all colleges and universities offer degree programs in liberal arts, and approximately 40 percent of all male baccalaureate graduates receive their degrees in the liberal arts.

The career patterns of liberal arts alumni present more of an enigma to the concerned educator than do the career patterns of graduates from professional programs. Obviously, the liberal arts graduate finds no clear career pattern laid out before him. Thus it is in this area, where information is most needed, that this survey seeks to make its contribution.

The Historical Role of Liberal Education

The term "liberal arts" is derived from the Latin *artes liberales*, the higher arts, which in early Roman times were accessible only to freemen (*liberi*). But the tradition of liberal education dates back at least to Greece, to Plato and his Academy with its devotion to truth and learning for their own sake. Even then, there were parallel and often competing ideas of the goals of learning. Pythagoras and his followers were concentrating upon the study of mathematics and astronomy, while the Sophists were concerned with instructions in such useful subjects as rhetoric. As Clark Kerr points out —

> The modern academician likes to trace his intellectual
> forebears to the groves of Academe; but the modern uni-
> versity with its professional schools and scientific insti-
> tutes might look equally to the Sophists and the Pythag-
> oreans. ... The "Two Cultures" or the "Three Cultures"
> are almost as old as culture itself. [4]

The great medieval universities of Europe helped to perpetuate
these diverse educational outlooks. The University of Paris became
a leader in the study of the classics, philosophy, and theology, and
established a pattern for the early development of Oxford and Cambridge along the lines of the liberal arts tradition. Salerno and Bologna
were the professional centers, excelling in medicine and law.

In England, Francis Bacon argued for a utilitarian approach to
education and decried the pursuit of learning for its own sake. This
attitude was later strongly opposed by one of history's most eloquent
defenders of liberal education, Cardinal Newman, who declared:
"Knowledge is capable of being its own end. Such is the constitution
of the human mind, that any kind of knowledge, if it really be such,
is its own reward." [5] University education, Newman said —

> ... aims at raising the intellectual tone of society, at
> cultivating the public mind, at purifying the national taste,
> at supplying true principles to popular enthusiasm and
> fixed aims to popular aspirations at giving enlargement
> and sobriety to the ideas of the age, at facilitating the
> exercise of political powers, and refining the intercourse
> of private life. ... It prepares a man to fill any post
> with credit, and to master any subject with facility. [6]

The nine colleges of Colonial America strongly reflected the
views of Newman and of the Oxford of his times. "They offered little
or no opportunity for specialization, taught little science, and their
faculty members engaged in little research." [7] When modern languages and natural sciences entered the curriculum in the early part
of the nineteenth century, many students avoided them as inferior
substitutes for Greek, Latin, mathematics and philosophy. Almost
all the students used college as a gateway to careers in the ministry,
law, and medicine.

In the last half of the nineteenth century, a number of factors
influenced higher education. The scientific revolution was having
its effect upon the university curriculum and upon the development

of research, first in the German universities and then elsewhere. In America, the great liberal arts institutions such as Harvard and Johns Hopkins broadened their scope and developed facilities for professional specialization. The agrarian concerns of the country and the interests of both federal and state governments in expanded educational opportunity culminated in the passage of the Morrill Act in 1862, laying the foundation for the great network of land-grant colleges and universities across America. Agriculture, engineering, and mining took their place in the curriculum beside liberal arts.

The new segment of the population attracted by higher education clearly contemplated using college as the basis for a career. The college, or more particularly the university, responded to an increasingly complex social and economic order by further specialization through course work in such fields as theatre arts, accounting, and public health.

While elementary and secondary school teachers first prepared at special two-year normal schools, before long many colleges, including liberal arts institutions, were devoting a considerable portion of their energies to students seeking preparation for teaching careers. Even traditional liberal arts fields underwent transformation.

The natural sciences — zoology, geology, botany — were added to the classical fields of mathematics and astronomy. The social sciences — political science, economics, psychology — developed as distinct disciplines instead of components of philosophy or history. The days were gone when one broadly-educated professor could teach courses in philosophy, mathematics, and biology. Specialization and achievement within a single field became increasingly important for faculty appointment and promotion. As Schmidt observed: "The Yale catalog for 1829 managed to include the entire four-year course of study in one page; in 1955 it took two hundred pages to list the undergraduate fields of study." [8]

Despite these changes, the liberal arts continued as the cornerstone of American higher education. In 1955, John Millett was saying:

> Not in nearly one hundred years has the appreciation of
> the need for a liberal education been more widespread in
> education circles. ... Today there is a new desire to
> make a liberal education meaningful. Scientific inquiry
> has had its field day. [9]

Around the same time, President Kappel of the American Telephone and Telegraph Company was speculating: "It seems to me almost certain that a great expansion of liberal arts education lies immediately ahead." [10]

Before the end of 1957, Russia had launched both Sputnik and the Space Age. The resultant enormous spurt in emphasis on science and technology affected the liberal arts. By 1963, IBM's Thomas Watson was warning:

> ... The events of the past six years have had an impact on education which should concern us all; in the blazing light of man-made comets, the continuing need for an appropriate balance between science and humanities has been blotted out. [11]

What, then, is the role of the liberal arts college in the modern world? How will general education evolve in the years ahead? It is hoped that studies such as this one will help provide accurate information on the present-day relevance of liberal education and a basis for more informed speculation about its role in future American history.

Today's liberal arts college is beset by many pressures for more (or less) general education, for the need to combine in a single curriculum both pre-professional and terminal education, and by demands of society that liberal education be concerned at one and the same time with national survival, more equal education for all citizens, and a general increase in our cultural level. Reports from college alumni can assess the contribution of the college in the past and point out guidelines for the future.

The Sheepskin Explosion and the Liberal Arts

In an era of rising graphs (population, automobiles, polluted rivers, and prices paid for TV rights for professional football games), a most spectacular rise has occurred in both college enrollment and annual graduates. While our national population tripled between 1870 and 1940, the number of college students jumped 19 times.

Between 1940 and 1962, the median years of education completed by men between 18 and 64 years old rose from 7.7 to 12.1, [12] and twice as many men 25 years and older had completed four years of college.[13] Moreover, these trends appear likely to continue well into the future. Statistical projections suggest that between the years 1960 and 2000, the percentage of 22-year olds with bachelor's degrees will double, while the percentage of 25-year olds with master's degrees will triple, and the percentage of 28-year olds with doctorates will quadruple.[14]

The data in Table 1 show that enrollments in liberal arts fields have remained remarkably constant over the past six decades. The percentage of college graduates with liberal arts majors dropped from 42.7 percent in 1901-05 to a mid-period 36.7 percent in 1931-35 and then climbed back up to 44.6 percent in 1961-62. The sharpest losses occurred in the humanities and arts, which declined over the period from 25.3 percent to 14.5 percent, with foreign languages showing the greatest loss in these disciplines (12.2 to 2.1 percent). The greatest gains occurred in the social sciences, up from 3.8 per cent to 15.2 percent. The natural sciences held fairly steady, with a decline in chemistry counterbalanced by an increase in other physical sciences and mathematics.

Fields outside the liberal arts remained relatively constant in total enrollments (down from 57.3 to 55.4 percent) but exhibited sharp shifts by subject area. Education climbed from 0.4 to 25.4 percent, business and commerce from 0.2 to 12.9 percent, and engineering from 3.3 to 8.6 percent. The sharpest declines were in health fields, from 33.2 to 3.0 percent, and law, from 11.2 to 0.1 percent. Projections to 1975 suggest that these major trends will continue over the next decade.[15]

One can only conclude that enrollment in liberal arts fields has held up surprisingly well in the first six decades of the twentieth century. Despite the introduction of city planning, police administration, and other specialized fields and active recruitment by them for students, liberal arts programs continue to attract 40 percent of all students. As an aside, one might feel compassion for national manpower planners in a free society. Despite fiercely attractive salaries, outspoken national concern about need in the field, and extensive support, the percentage of students majoring in engineering actually declined for several recent years.

While maintaining its relative position within the academic community, liberal arts education faces a number of problems pertinent to this study of its graduates.

Current Problems in Liberal Education

Liberal arts education, while it continues to attract 40 percent of all undergraduate students, faces a number of problems which prompted this inquiry.

1 Conflict between general and scientific education.

The most obvious problem is the still vigorous conflict between professional and general education. Clearly, these two positions compete for students, resources, and status with no less energy than Detroit automakers use to gain acceptance for their products.

In his controversial 1959 Rede lecture at Cambridge, C. P. Snow pointed out that the "intellectual life of the whole of western society is increasingly being split into two polar groups ... at one pole we have the literary intellectuals (and) at the other scientists, and as the most representative, the physical scientists." [16]

The polarization affects the sometimes uneasy union of the sciences with other majors within the liberal arts college. The Dean of that unstable campus federation known as the College of Arts and Sciences often looks upon the Chairman of the powerful Department of Chemistry with the same deference which the President of a land-grant university pays to the Dean of the College of Agriculture. Conflicts between the science and the other segments of the College may arise over the relative emphasis of scientific subjects in the curriculum, over basic courses provided for non-majors, and over the depth required in programs for majors, not to mention the inevitable competition for space, faculty, and research funds.

2 Pressure for early specialization.

Barzun notes:

> ... the best colleges are being invaded, not to say dispossessed, by the advance agents of the professions, by men who want to seize upon the young recruit as soon as may be and train him in a "tangible salable skill" ... The undergraduate who can assist his instructor in the instructor's research, the youth who can get an essay published in a journal, the senior whose program is half made up of graduate courses — these are the models for envy and emulation. The liberal arts college ... will find that the secondary school has added a year or two to its present curriculum; that the graduate school has kidnapped

all the college juniors and seniors into its departments.
All that will be left in college is the dean, and he is the
most expendable of creatures. [17]

This is not a new problem. In 1947, a Presidential Commission
on Higher Education noted that "the unity of liberal education has been
splintered by overspecialization." [18]

Some have assumed that specialization and general education can
be combined without loss to either. For example, Gordon and Howell
say:

Business looks to the colleges to give it generalists and
specialists, if possible, embodied in the same person. ..
If these courses are properly planned and well taught, no
liberal arts college should be reluctant to accept them in
partial fulfillment of the requirements for a liberal arts
degree. [19]

Many skeptics, however, feel it is impossible to add both breadth
and depth to the curriculum without expanding its length.

3 Withdrawal of faculty members from students.

The increased availability of research funds from the federal
government and the foundations during the past two decades has tended
to shift the focus of much university activity from undergraduate
teaching to sponsored research. The separation of students and faculty is accentuated also by the large classes used to cope with the
related problems of rapidly-increasing enrollments, higher faculty
salaries and fewer teaching hours per week. The gulf between undergraduate student and researcher-teacher is most marked in the liberal arts college. In many scientific and professional fields faculty
are somewhat closer to undergraduate students who are viewed as
future colleagues in a close professional fraternity.

Faculty focus on research has obvious effects upon the liberal
arts curriculum. Cowley wonders where the liberal arts colleges
will obtain teachers broad enough in their outlook to teach within a
general education program.[20] Columbia College reports it is "difficult to persuade enough young faculty members to devote time — let
alone enthusiasm — to the teaching of an important part of the 'Contemporary Civilization' course." [21]

Liberal arts faculty members often are less close to their students than professors with specialties in accounting, social welfare, and engineering whose own professional involvement helps to link academic work and student career interests. One placement officer complained that she wrote the chairman of each of the 30 liberal arts departments on her campus asking for an appointment to discuss career opportunities for graduates and to report on the status of the last graduating class. Only three departments even acknowledged the letter and none desired an appointment. The lack of interest seems to be increasing. The faculty members most interested in students often are the older, retiring members. Too many of their younger colleagues aspire to eminence within their academic field, not with their students.

4 <u>The emphasis on the public service role of higher education.</u>

Involvement in the economic development of the state is a relatively new departure for colleges and universities. Some university presidents take almost a chamber-of-commerce pride in the industries which now fringe the borders of their campus. Many members of state legislatures are clearly more impressed with excellence in training for animal husbandry, highway design, and electronics than in early English dialects, woodwind harmony, or non-western languages. This emphasis detracts from the status of liberal arts and its own long-range contribution to society.

5 <u>The poor quality of many liberal arts colleges.</u>

As the president of one top-flight institution said, "There is nothing quite as bad as a poor liberal arts college." Unfortunately, no college program is easier to administer, finance, equip, and house than liberal arts. The bottom several hundred liberal arts colleges in the United States demand a "raison d'etre." They offer a program with little of the intellectual atmosphere essential for a liberal education. Their faculty lacks real capacity to teach in the great tradition of liberal education, their curriculum is unimaginative, and their libraries are small or inappropriate. Even their teacher preparation programs often are vastly inferior to similar curricula at the frequently-damned, used-to-be teachers' colleges. These weak liberal arts institutions find it difficult to improve and almost as impossible to die.

6 <u>Liberal arts useful only as a pre-professional education.</u>

In 1964 the Office of Graduate and Career Plans at Harvard University reported that more of its senior class entered graduate school than went directly into business and industry. This highlights the growing tendency to consider liberal arts training as preliminary in nature, rather than as terminal education. If this judgment becomes more universal, it will have a profound effect on the design of liberal education.

The value of liberal arts as preparation for nonprofessional positions remains a puzzle which existing information does not solve. It appears that some employers who favor "liberal arts graduates" actually mean that the particular job requires no special training. In a book extolling the merits of liberal education, the head of a major corporation was quoted as saying: "... the real professional school of business is found directly in the field of industrial and commercial life."[22] Yet this president's corporation recruited only business school graduates at a university in which the author served as placement officer.

The civil service director of one of the larger states recently confided that each year the number of liberal arts graduates applying for state employment increases and the number of suitable openings declines. Faced with this problem, the director would like to increase specific course requirements (such as requiring the candidates for jobs as parole officers to have taken at least two courses in criminology), but admits that he is prevented from doing this by pressure from the liberal arts colleges. The liberal arts graduates, however, often must take a standard civil service test. Their classmates in engineering, home economics, and accounting need only to fill out an application blank.

Even where employers are on record as favoring "liberal arts graduates," they usually mean that no specific training is required. Many would just as soon hire a physical education major as a graduate in English.

7 <u>Long-range employment demand for college graduates.</u>

During the years that our alumni respondents were students, dire predictions were made about future employment prospects for college graduates.

We are likely to educate, particularly in the post-graduate area, many more men and women than can earn a living in the field in which they have chosen to be educated, and too often anywhere also, and we shall find that, embittered with their frustration, these surplus graduates will turn upon society and the Government, more effectively and better armed in their destructive wrath by the education we have given them. [23]

Seymour Harris noted that the economy had absorbed only 2.7 million college graduates between 1870 and 1940 and concluded that it could not assimilate 10 million more between 1940 and 1968. [24]

It is essential that the promised excess of supply of educated men and women over demand in the desired positions be advertised widely and the serious political, social, and economic repercussions be generally known. Otherwise, our country will suffer greatly both from unemployment and low income in the learned professions. [25]

If the output of the colleges is to be absorbed, the graduate will have to be satisfied with openings not formerly acceptable. ... It will require a revolution in attitudes of college-trained men and women if the occupational downgrading of college-trained personnel is not to have serious social and political effects. [26]

Ten years later, Havighurst noted "the fact that there have been more jobs for college graduates than there have been qualified young people to fill those jobs has had the effect of expanding enrollment." [27] He predicted a surplus of college graduates beginning in 1960, however, and estimated the oversupply by 1980 at between 10 and 50 per cent.

It is too early to assess Havighurst's conclusions, but those of Harris have proven pessimistic. He failed to anticipate the marked increase in business recruitment and the utilization of college alumni in sales and administrative positions, the growth of schools and educational techniques which required many new cohorts of teachers, and the manpower implications of the national defense effort including the wars in Korea and Vietnam and the Race for Space. In all fairness to Harris, it should be pointed out that the availability of college graduates has itself created an increase in demand: As employers sensed they could hire college graduates, more job openings were stamped "college degree required."

The unexcelled employment conditions of the past few decades have provided an ideal economic climate for the alumni included in this study. So much, in fact, that many observers feel that recent graduates have been spoiled. Experience working with several generations of college students, however, leads the author to the conclusion that the newer graduates have not been spoiled by the climate of their times any more than the alumni who finished in the rugged economic conditions of the 1930's became unspoiled for life.

These, then, are some of the problems facing general education today. The purpose of this report is to provide background to aid in their solution.

FOOTNOTES

1. Sanford, Nevitt, editor, *The American College*. New York, John Wiley and Sons, 1962, p. 805.

2. Pattillo, Manning M., "Foundations and the Private College," *Liberal Education*, Vol. 51, No. 4, December 1965, p. 511.

3. Gordon, Robert A. and Howell, James E., *Higher Education for Business*, New York, Columbia University Press, 1959, p. 44.

4. Kerr, Clark, *The Uses of the University*. Cambridge, Mass., Harvard University Press 1963, pp 9—10.

5. Newman, Cardinal John Henry, *The Idea of a University*. New York, Longmans Green and Co., 1947, p. xxvii.

6. *Ibid.*, p. 157.

7. Cowley, William G., "Three Curricular Conflicts," *Liberal Education*, December, 1960, p. 467.

8. Schmidt, George P., *The Liberal Arts College: A Chapter in American Cultural History*. New Brunswick, N.J., Rutgers University Press, 1957, p. 186.

9. Millett, John E., *Financing Higher Education in the United States*. New York, Columbia University Press, 1952, pp. 14—15.

10. Goldwin, Robert A. and Nelson, Charles A., editors, *Toward the Liberally Educated Executive*. White Plains, N.Y., The Fund for Adult Education, 1959, p. 68.

FOOTNOTES - Continued

11. From a speech delivered by Thomas J. Watson, Jr., at the forty-sixth annual meeting of the American Council on Education held in Washington, D.C., October, 1963.

12. Johnston, Denis F., "Uptrend of Worker's Education," *Occupational Outlook Quarterly,* Vol. VII, September, 1963, p. A—5.

13. Miller, Herman P., "Annual and Lifetime Income in Relation to Education: 1939—1959," *The American Economic Review,* Vol. 50, December 1960, p. 968.

14. *Comparison of Earned Degrees Awarded 1901—1962 with Projections to 2000.* Washington, D.C., National Science Foundation, NSF 64—2, pp. 7, 53, 54.

15. Fullam, Marie G. and Ryan, Frances E., *Earned Degrees by Field of Study and Level Projected to 1975,* U.S. Office of Education Bulletin No. 31. Washington, D.C., U.S. Government Printing Office, 1964.

16. Snow, C.P., *The Two Cultures and the Scientific Revolution.* New York, Cambridge University Press, 1959, p. 4.

17. Barzun, Jacques, "College to University — and After," *The American Scholar,* Vol. 33, Spring, 1964, pp. 214—218.

18. *Higher Education for American Democracy: A Report of the President's Commission on Higher Education.* Washington D.C., U.S. Government Printing Office, 1947, p. 47.

19. Gordon, Robert A. and Howell, James E., *op. cit.,* p. 143.

20. Cowley, William G., *op. cit.* pp. 467—483.

21. Hechinger, Fred M., "End of an Era?" *New York Times Education Section,* Section E, December 15, 1963, p. 7.

22. Goldwin, Robert A. and Nelson, Charles A., editors, *Toward the Liberally Educated Executive, op. cit.* p. 112.

23. Wallin, William J., Chancellor of the New York State Board of Regents, in a speech reported in *The New York Times,* March 29, 1950.

24. Harris, Seymour E., *The Market for College Graduates.* Cambridge, Mass., Harvard University Press, 1949, p. 97.

25. *Ibid.,* p. 13.

FOOTNOTES - Continued

26.   *Ibid.*, p. 65.

27.   Havighurst, Robert J., *American Higher Education in the 1960's*. Columbus, Ohio, Ohio State University Press, 1960, p. 37.

TABLE 1

Trends in Bachelor's and First Professional Degrees, 1901 - 1962

	1901-05	1931-35	1961-62
Natural Science	13.3%	10.4%	12.4%
Chemistry	3.7	2.9	2.1
Physical science	3.7	3.0	5.5
Earth science	1.1	10.0	0.4
Biological science	4.8	3.5	4.4
Psychology	0.3%	1.3%	2.5%
Social Science	3.8%	8.9%	15.2%
Economics	1.0	3.2	2.2
History	2.4	2.9	4.6
Other Social Science	0.4	2.8	8.4
Humanities and Arts	25.3%	16.1%	14.5%
English	7.0	6.2	6.9
Foreign Language	12.2	5.3	2.1
Philosophy	4.9	1.8	2.0
Fine arts	1.2	2.8	3.5
Sub-total for Liberal Arts	42.7%	36.7%	44.6%

─────────────────────── TABLE 1 - Continued ───────────────────────

	1901-05	1931-35	1961-62
Engineering	3.3%	8.0%	8.6%
Applied Biology	0.2%	4.2%	2.7%
Agriculture	0.2	1.9	1.6
Home Economics	--	2.3	1.1
Health Fields	33.2%	7.0%	3.0%
Medicine	18.6	3.6	--
Dentistry	8.0	1.4	--
Other Health Fields	6.6	2.0	3.0
Business and Commerce	0.2%	6.9%	12.9%
Education	0.4%	20.1%	25.4%
Other Fields	20.0%	17.1%	2.8%
Law	11.2	6.1	0.1
Other professions	0.1	2.2	0.2
All other	8.7	8.8	2.5
Sub-total for Non-Liberal Arts	57.3%	63.3%	55.4%
TOTAL	100.0%	100.0%	100.0%

SOURCES

Wolfe, Dael, *America's Resources of Specialized Talent*. New York, Harper and Bros., 1954, pp. 292–293.

Earned Degrees Conferred, 1961–1962, U.S. Office of Education Circular, No. 719. Washington D.C., U. S. Government Printing Office, 1963.

2

The EDUCATION of LIBERAL ARTS GRADUATES

As three quarters of all our colleges and universities award degrees in liberal arts fields, a review of the education of liberal arts alumni moves us quickly into the heart of American higher education. As represented by the graduates included in our sample, this chapter describes the educational background of today's liberal arts alumni. It discusses in turn their undergraduate institution, college major, graduate study, factors related to academic work, influence of extra-curricular activities and sources of financial support.

Type of College Attended

Contrary to the myth that most liberal arts alumni come from small campuses, almost equal numbers graduated from institutions with enrollments over 5,000 as did from those with enrollments under 5,000. (TABLE 2)

Thirty-five percent received their degrees from relatively small institutions with total enrollments under 2,500, 39 percent graduated from medium-sized institutions with enrollments from 2,500 to 9,999, and 26 percent from larger institutions.

Since the sample for each of the three classes was drawn for comparability with the 1953 population, no trends, of course, are apparent. Eleven percent were graduates of Catholic schools, 37 percent of public institutions, and 52 percent of private colleges and universities. Among the private college graduates, 17 percent at-

18

tended church-related institutions. Since the cutting points on the quality index were largely arbitrary, the proportions receiving their degrees from "high," "medium," and "low" quality schools have little meaning in themselves and are included only for the sake of completeness.

Relationships between size and quality and control and quality are shown for the entire population in Appendix A. When any of these three variables is considered singly, it must be recognized that its effects are likely to be intermixed with those of the other two.

Undergraduate Major

While the percentage of alumni electing individual undergraduate majors varied sharply according to year of graduation (TABLE 3), the distribution of majors remained remarkably constant among broad categories of science and mathematics, social sciences, and humanities. (For a description of the components of these categories, see Appendix.) The greatest fluctuation occurred within the social sciences, where economics majors declined from 16.8 percent to 12.0 percent while majors in the remaining social sciences rose from 30.1 to 35.9 percent. Despite several decades of concern about our national dependence upon science and technology, during the period the percentage of students electing majors in science and mathematics actually declined.

Type of college or university attended has a marked relationship to college major. Graduates of Roman Catholic colleges are more likely to have studied one of the humanities, particularly English or philosophy. A significantly higher percentage of public school graduates majored in science (both physical and biological). Almost half of all private college alumni majored in a social science. Where double majors were reported, the field of greatest concentration was used for analyses dealing with college major. When this was not designated, the first listed field was taken. Surprisingly, science and mathematics graduates were more likely to come from low quality institutions, 33.4 percent as contrasted with 26.3 percent for the high quality and 36.4 percent for the medium quality schools.

Attributes of social science majors offer interesting contrasts: Alumni from high-quality colleges were more likely to elect a social science major, but for all types of institutions the poorest students were the most likely to major in the social sciences. The percentages majoring in both the humanities and science and mathematics increase with academic records. It should be noted here that data in this study are based on grade point averages provided by the institution, where available, rather than those recalled by the graduates.

The alumnus tends to view himself as a better student than can be verified by the registrar at his Alma Mater. For the purpose of this study, where available, the actual grade point average provided by the institution was used. The rosy hue through which the alumni view past academic prowess shows that among graduates who reported their record as "B", 50.7 percent actually made "C's" in contrast to only 1.1 percent "A's".

Students often are not required formally to declare a major until the end of their sophomore year, so that all changes of major, official and unofficial, may not have been considered when alumni were asked this information. Yet, 38 percent of the graduates reported a change of major.   (TABLE 4)

Most shifts were within the liberal arts curriculum, particularly away from original science subjects. For students changing from outside the liberal arts college, the greatest movement was away from engineering. While the data are not shown, the results show little deviation by year of graduation or by control, quality, and size of college.

Graduate Study

One goal of liberal education has been to provide a sound foundation for graduate study. Half of the alumni in the survey hold a graduate degree. (TABLE 5) Another sixth took some graduate work; only a third of the alumni stopped at the baccalaureate. Many, as will be shown later, anticipate receiving an additional degree in the future. While older alumni report the highest rate of advanced education, it should be noted that some in the younger classes have not yet finished their graduate education.

As expected, the greatest incidence of graduate study was reported by students with the highest undergraduate academic records: 43.0 percent of all graduates held master's or professional degrees; 7.1 percent acquired doctor's degrees; in contrast, 55.9 percent of the master's degree holders and 19.6 percent of the doctor's degree recipients were in the "high" academic record group. Over twice as many doctor's degrees were awarded in the science and mathematics disciplines (11.5 percent as compared to 4.6 in social sciences and 5.4 percent in the humanities).

Unexpected, however, was the fact that quality of college attended had relatively little relationship to advanced education. Almost as many graduates of the weakest colleges went on for postgraduate training as did men from the high-quality schools. Social science majors were the most likely to report a bachelor's degree as their highest, and majors in science and mathematics were the most inclined to earn doctorates. Graduates of high-quality schools are more likely to have gone on to study law and medicine.

Looking toward the future, 21 percent of the graduates in our study say they will (and another 18 percent say they may) receive yet another degree in the next few years. (TABLE 6) More than half of the men who finished five years earlier say they may receive another degree, and a quarter of the 15-year alumni say they may receive one. The field of study proposed most often is education.

Among fields of graduate study selected by the alumni, the most popular were law, education, and medicine. (TABLE 7)

Factors Related to Academic Work

The graduates were mobile over their total undergraduate and graduate years, less than a third having attended only one institution. Graduates of high-quality schools and larger institutions were somewhat less mobile.

When the data are limited to undergraduate studies, however, mobility drops sharply. Three-fourths of all alumni attended only one undergraduate college, and less than six percent attended more than two: 75.0 percent, one college; 18.6 percent, two colleges; and 5.6 percent three or more colleges. The graduates of 15 years ago were significantly more mobile than the other two classes, undoubtedly reflecting educational programs interrupted by military duty or attendance at a college during military service. Students with high academic records were somewhat less mobile than those with low records.

How seriously did these alumni, as undergraduates, take their education? Three-quarters said that they were "deeply" or "quite a bit" concerned about how well they were doing academically. (TABLE 8)

Less than two percent were "not at all concerned." Students with high academic records were markedly more concerned than those with lower academic records. Science and mathematics majors reported somewhat more concern about their academic performance than did social sciences or humanities majors. While not shown, size of college, type of control, and quality of the institution seem to have made little difference in attitude toward academic success.

Among the best students, 76 percent felt they worked harder than their classmates. (TABLE 9) In contrast, only 23 percent of the poorest students felt they worked harder than the others. While not shown, there are no particular differences in impressions of hard work between the older and younger alumni, between those from large and small schools, or between graduates of institutions of high and low quality. Graduates in humanities and science and mathematics recall working somewhat harder than did those in the social sciences.

An analysis of contact with faculty members shows that, while the overwhelming majority (71 percent) of the graduates had "some contact with faculty," fewer (24 percent) would describe it as a "great deal." (TABLE 10) As expected, graduates of smaller institutions are more likely to report "a great deal of contact" with faculty members as shown below:

      13 percent of graduates of large institutions;
      19 percent of graduates of medium-sized institutions;
      37 percent of graduates of small institutions.

Although not shown, very little variation was reported by year of graduation, contradicting the common contention that students and faculty members have had increasingly less contact with each other in recent years.

The influence of fellow students is seldom assessed. Certainly, stimulation from other students enriches education and encourages deeper thinking. Table 11 shows the extent to which alumni recall participating in intellectual discussions with their fellow students and indicates that more than half spent "a lot of time" discussing issues with their classmates. This was particularly true of the better students, of those who majored in the humanities, and of those from high-quality colleges. While not shown, there were only slight variations by year of graduation and by size and control of college.

The alumni also were asked the extent to which they gave academic assistance to their classmates and received help from them. (TABLE 12)

While nearly half the graduates could recall providing help, only a quarter remembered asking for assistance. The best students recalled providing the most assistance, and the poorer students recalled receiving the most aid from classmates.

Our study also explored the extent to which alumni participated in senior seminars or advanced Reserve Officer's Training Corps, received academic honors or membership in Phi Beta Kappa, or wrote a thesis in their major field. These responses were reported:

43 percent took a senior seminar course;

25 percent wrote a thesis in their major field;

12 percent completed an advanced ROTC course;

5 percent received membership in Phi Beta Kappa;

17 percent received academic honors.

As might be expected, those who completed advanced ROTC were much more likely to have graduated from a large university. Recent graduates were more likely to have participated in a senior seminar than were earlier graduates; the figures show 49 percent for graduates of five years ago and only 36 percent for graduates of 15 years ago. Graduates from high-quality institutions were considerably more likely to have participated in senior seminars than were those from poorer institutions (52 percent vs. 37 percent), and to have completed a thesis in their major field (32 percent vs. 22 percent).

Financial Support During College

Today, financial assistance is regarded as a key to expanded educational opportunity. For this reason, it is interesting to note that 90 percent of the alumni earned at least some of their college expenses. (TABLE 13) Alumni who finished 15 years ago reported the least amount of self-support. It should be noted that almost 80 percent of them benefitted from the G.I. Bill of Rights and may not have included this support in their earnings. The questionnaire erred in not making clear whether G.I. Bill income was to be classed as "earnings." Graduates of high-quality colleges were less likely to have been self-supporting than alumni from low-quality schools.

While not shown in the tables, the highest self-support was reported by men who attended public institutions and those who studied either social sciences or humanities as their major subject.

A wide variety of sources helped finance college education. (TABLE 14)   The contribution of parents to educational expenses is much less than anticipated.   It seems difficult, however, to accept the premise that only a quarter of the graduates received any financial help from their parents. Perhaps support from family was assumed and many alumni checked the remaining special sources.

The most frequently cited source of financial assistance was self-support, both part-time employment and summer earnings. In addition, almost half (80 percent of the class which graduated 15 years ago and 23 percent of the class of five years ago) utilized the G. I. Bill of Rights to help finance education. These graduates were among the 2,000,000 veterans who took advantage of the educational provisions of this bill.

Trends in the sources of financial assistance show an increasing reliance on scholarships, summer employment, loans, and support from parents, and less upon the G. I. Bill.

Extra-Curricular Activities

Despite the fact that many of our alumni were quite literally descended from the highly-publicized, racoon-coat "College Life" students of the 1920's, the graduates of the 1940's and 1950's displayed a moderated attitude toward extra-curricular activities. Among the typical activities offered on most campuses, intramural sports were the most popular among our alumni, with almost 60 percent of them reporting some participation. (TABLE 15)   More than half of the alumni took some part in social fraternities and slightly less than half participated in departmental clubs.

As almost half of all fraternity men held a major office, employers who may value this experience should, at the same time, discount its uniqueness.

Examining the academic backgrounds of students who participate in extra-curricular activities shows that social fraternities and intramural sports are the only areas in which more low students participate than top students. The greatest participation in fraternities and intramural sports also was reported by alumni who stopped at the bachelor's degree rather than going on for the doctorate.

Despite highly publicized exceptions and the classical Greek theory which links mental and physical prowess, our survey showed that varsity athletes were more likely to come from among the poorer students. Three-quarters of all students, however, took no part in varsity athletics.

An analysis of type of residence during college shows that approximately half of the graduates lived with other students in a school dormitory, a boarding house, or a fraternity. Another sixth lived in a room or apartment, perhaps with other students; and the final third lived with their parents or in their own residence.   (TABLE 16) Small institutions were much more likely to provide dormitory quarters than were large institutions. While not shown, twice as many graduates of private colleges (34 percent) lived in school dormitories as alumni of public institutions (15 percent). Sharp variations in number living in fraternities characterized different types of control: Roman Catholic (1 percent), public (15 percent), and private (18 percent). Over half (52 percent) of those who attended Catholic colleges lived in their parents' home, in contrast to 27 percent of the public and 23 percent of the private school alumni.

Graduates of smaller institutions report much greater involvement in extra-curricular activities and in student housing.

Percent who -	*Size of College Attended*	
	Large	*Small*
Held major student government office	7.1	13.2
Earned varsity athletic letter	7.5	20.9
Lived in student housing	28.2	56.8

--- TABLE 2 ---

Types of Colleges Attended

| | | Years Since Graduation | | |
Size of College	All Graduates	Fifteen	Ten	Five
Under 1,000 students	12.8%	12.4%	12.9%	12.9%
1,000-2,499	22.2	23.2	21.6	21.8
2,500-4,999	16.3	15.3	17.1	16.5
5,000-9,999	22.7	22.8	22.5	22.7
10,000-13,999	8.0	8.5	8.4	8.0
14,000 and over	17.0	17.8	17.5	18.1
Total =	100.0%	100.0%	100.0%	100.0%

Control

Roman Catholic	11.2%	1.03%	11.8%	11.7%
Public	36.8	36.2	36.2	38.2
Private	52.0	53.5	52.0	50.1
Total =	100.0%	100.0%	100.0%	100.0%

Quality

High	21.2%	21.2%	21.5%	20.9%
Medium	45.4	44.5	45.4	46.2
Low	33.4	34.3	33.1	32.9
Total =	100.0%	100.0%	100.0%	100.0%

▷ More than half attended private colleges and universities.

A larger proportion attended small institutions, under 2,500, than attended institutions with enrollments over 10,000.

Three-fourths attended only one school during their undergraduate studies.

High school background influenced both the quality and the control of the college attended.
    Parochial school graduates were the most likely to attend Catholic colleges, but they were also the most likely to attend low-quality colleges.
    Public high school graduates, who make up the great majority of the sample, were much more likely to attend public colleges and were least likely to attend Catholic colleges.

—————————————— TABLE 3 ——————————————

Undergraduate Majors

		Years Since Graduation		
Major	All Graduates	15	10	5
Chemistry	8.1%	9.8%	7.9%	6.7%
Other Physical Sciences	6.6	5.3	6.1	8.3
Biological Sciences	13.4	15.0	13.1	12.1
Mathematics	5.2	4.7	5.1	5.7
Sub-Total: Science and Math	33.3%	37.8%	32.2%	32.8%
Economics	13.8	16.8	12.7	12.0
Other Social Sciences	33.4	30.1	34.1	35.9
Sub-Total: Social Sciences	47.2	46.9	46.8	47.9
English and Speech	11.7%	10.8%	12.7%	11.6%
Foreign Languages	1.9	1.8	1.7	2.2
Philosophy and Religion	3.7	3.6	4.0	3.6
Fine and Applied Arts	2.0	1.8	2.4	1.9
Sub-Total: Humanities	18.1	18.0	20.8	19.3
No Answer		0.3	0.2	
Totals	100.0%	100.0%	100.0%	100.0%

▷ Almost half majored in a social science.

Significantly fewer majored in sciences and mathematics or humanities.

Distribution among these general fields remained almost constant but there were some shifts within fields; for example, majors in economics declined while majors in other social sciences increased markedly.

The percentage of alumni majoring in science and mathematics actually declined during the period under study.

Social science majors were more likely to have been the weakest students.

—————————————TABLE 4—————————————

Changes in Major During College

<u>Made no change in major</u>   62.1%

<u>Changed from these liberal arts majors:</u>

Chemistry	3.3%	
Other Physical Science.	1.8	
Biological Science	7.5	
Mathematics	1.3	
		13.9
Economics	1.0	
Social Science	4.1	
		5.1
English and Speech	2.5	
Foreign Languages	0.4	
Philosophy and Religion	0.9	
Fine and applied arts	0.9	
		4.7

<u>Changed from these non-liberal arts majors:</u>

Business administration	3.4	
Education	1.6	
Engineering	7.4	
Architecture	0.2	
Accounting	0.7	
Other fields	0.9	
		14.2

Total   100.0%

▷ During college, more than a third of the alumni changed their majors.

TABLE 5

Highest Level of Education Completed

Highest Level of Education Completed	All Graduates	Years Since Graduation		
		15	10	5
Bachelor's	31.6%	31.5%	30.0%	33.4%
Some graduate work (no degree)	15.7	12.3	14.1	20.4
Master's	21.6	22.5	21.8	20.5
Bachelor of Divinity	3.8	3.7	4.4	3.3
LLB	8.2	7.9	9.3	7.3
MD, DDS, Etc.	9.4	8.4	10.6	9.2
PhD, EdD, Dsc, etc.	7.1	10.5	7.4	3.5
Other	1.3	1.0	1.4	1.4
No Answer	1.3	2.2	1.0	1.0
Total	100.0%	100.0%	100.0%	100.0%

TABLE 6

Additional Degrees Anticipated

Plans for Additional Degrees:	All Graduates	Years Since Graduation		
		15	10	5
Yes	20.8%	10.2%	17.3%	34.5%
Maybe	18.2	12.8	19.0	22.6
No	60.5	76.5	63.3	42.4
No Answer	0.5	0.5	0.4	0.5
Total	100.0%	100.0%	100.0%	100.0%

▷ Graduate training was almost the norm.

───────────────── TABLE 7 ─────────────────

Fields of Graduate Study

No Graduate Training   31.6%

Graduate Field

Law	10.0%	
Education	8.1	
Medicine	8.1	
Social Sciences other than Economics	7.9	
Philosophy and Religion	5.2	
Business Administration	4.2	
English	3.6	
Physical Sciences other than Chemistry	3.6	
Chemistry	3.0	
Biological Sciences	2.3	
Mathematics	2.1	
Dentistry	1.6	
Economics	1.3	
Engineering	1.1	
Fine and Applied Arts	1.0	
Social Work	1.0	
Foreign Languages	0.9	
Accounting	0.5	
Architecture	0.3	
Pharmacy	0.3	
Other Fields	0.8	

Sub-Total   66.9

No Answer   1.5

Total   100.0%

―――――――――――――――――――― **TABLE 8** ――――――――――――――――――――

Concern About Grades

*To what extent were you concerned about how well you
were doing academically?*

	Deeply Concerned	Quite a Bit	Little	Not at All	No Answer	Total
All Graduates	24.4%	54.1	19.5	1.5	0.5	100.0%
Academic Record						
High	52.5%	38.4	7.4	1.6	0.1	100.0%
Average	23.7%	58.9	15.3	1.5	0.6	100.0%
Low	16.2%	51.2	30.9	1.1	0.6	100.0%
Type of Major						
Science and Math.	28.8%	53.4	16.0	1.4	0.4	100.0%
Social Sciences	21.5%	55.1	21.3	1.5	0.6	100.0%
Humanities	23.8%	52.9	21.3	1.6	0.4	100.0%

▷ Three-quarters of the alumni said they were "deeply" or "quite a bit"
concerned about how well they were doing academically.

―――――――――――――――――――― **TABLE 9** ――――――――――――――――――――

How Hard Alumni Studied

*Compared to other students in your class in college,
how hard would you say you worked on your studies?*

	Considerably Harder than Average	Somewhat Harder	Same	Somewhat Less than Average	Considerably Less	No. Answer	Total
All Graduates	9.8%	32.8	35.0	16.6	5.4	0.4	100.0%
Academic Record							
High	28.2%	48.2	15.5	6.0	2.0	0.1	100.0%
Average	9.5%	37.7	34.3	14.3	3.9	0.3	100.0%
Low	4.9%	19.1	42.8	24.4	8.4	0.4	100.0%
Type of Major							
Science and Math	10.7%	36.8	34.0	14.0	4.3	0.2	100.0%
Social Science	8.6%	30.6	36.1	18.1	6.2	0.4	100.0%
Humanities	11.2%	31.5	34.0	17.5	5.6	0.2	100.0%

TABLE 10

Contact with Faculty Members

How much personal contact did you have with faculty members?

	A Great Deal	Some	Very Little	None	No Answer	Total
All Graduates	23.7%	47.1	24.8	4.1	0.3	100.0%
Academic Record						
High	38.7%	45.3	14.3	1.5	0.2	100.0%
Average	26.3%	47.7	22.4	3.5	0.1	100.0%
Low	18.0%	47.6	29.1	5.1	0.2	100.0%
Size of College						
Small	36.8%	47.8	14.2	1.0	0.2	100.0%
Medium	19.2%	49.0	27.2	4.3	0.3	100.0%
Large	13.0%	43.4	35.2	8.1	0.3	100.0%
Quality of College						
High	17.0%	46.9	30.3	5.6	0.2	100.0%
Medium	22.8%	46.2	26.0	4.7	0.3	100.0%
Low	29.2%	48.5	19.6	2.4	0.3	100.0%

△ The majority reported some contact with faculty members; twice as much in the smaller colleges.

Less than a quarter of the students recalled "a great deal" of contact with faculty members.

———————————— TABLE 11 ————————————

Extent of Intellectual Discussions During College

To what extent do you agree or disagree: "I spent a lot of time discussing intellectual issues with my classmates."

	Strongly Agree	Agree	Disagree	Strongly Disagree	No Answer	Total
All Graduates	15.7%	43.6	36.3	4.0	0.4	100.0%
Academic Record						
High	18.6%	47.4	31.2	2.5	0.3	100.0%
Average	16.2%	44.2	35.4	3.8	0.4	100.0%
Low	12.4%	41.6	40.8	4.8	0.4	100.0%
Type of Major						
Science and Math	10.8%	40.7	43.8	4.5	0.2	100.0%
Social Sciences	16.0%	44.7	34.8	4.0	0.5	100.0%
Humanities	23.5%	46.1	26.9	3.2	0.3	100.0%
Quality of College						
High	19.6%	45.5	30.8	3.8	0.3	100.0%
Medium	15.0%	42.1	38.2	4.4	0.3	100.0%
Low	14.3%	44.4	37.2	3.7	0.4	100.0%

▷ More than half reported spending "a lot of time" in intellectual discussions with their classmates.

———————————— TABLE 12 ————————————

Assistance Given or Received from Fellow Students

To what extent do you agree or disagree . . . .

	"My classmates often asked me for help in their studies."		*"I often asked my classmates for help with my studies."*	
	Strongly Agree	Agree	Strongly Agree	Agree
All Graduates	5%	43	1%	22
Academic Record				
High	13%	54	1%	13
Average	5%	47	1%	21
Low	2%	34	1%	28

▷ Half said they often gave academic help to fellow students, but only a quarter remembered asking their classmates for help.

——————————————————— TABLE 13 ———————————————————

Extent of Self-Support in College

What portion of your total expenses at college did you earn yourself?

	None	1-25%	26-50%	51-75%	76-100%	No Answer	Total
All Graduates	9.5%	36.9	21.4	14.8	17.1	0.3	100.0%
Years Since Graduation							
Fifteen	11.6 %	40.0	20.3	13.3	14.3	0.5	100.0%
Ten	9.4 %	37.3	21.6	14.6	16.9	0.2	100.0%
Five	7.6 %	33.5	22.3	16.3	19.9	0.4	100.0%
Quality of College							
High	14.7 %	45.8	18.5	9.1	11.4	0.5	100.0%
Medium	9.2 %	38.2	21.7	15.4	15.0	0.5	100.0%
Low	6.5 %	29.4	22.8	17.5	23.4	0.4	100.0%

——————————————————— TABLE 14 ———————————————————

Sources of Financial Support During College

Which of the following contributed to your expenses while you were in college? (Check all that apply.)

	Scholar-ships	GI Bill	Summer Employment	Part-time Emp.	Loans	Parents Funds	Wife's Earnings	Employer Paid	Saving	Full Time Employment
All Graduates	29.2%	42.5	67.3	64.8	10.3	27.5	2.2	1.4	3.6	2.7
Years Since Graduation										
Fifteen	24.8%	79.5	51.4	63.8	6.4	18.1	2.6	2.9	4.7	2.3
Ten	29.6%	26.7	73.5	66.1	10.0	31.2	2.1	0.7	3.2	2.5
Five	33.1%	22.6	76.4	64.4	14.4	32.8	1.9	0.8	3.0	3.2
Academic Record										
High	54.1%	38.6	70.3	63.4	7.4	30.3	2.8	1.6	4.8	1.5
Average	30.7%	41.7	68.5	65.7	10.4	26.6	2.7	1.3	3.6	2.7
Low	20.5%	42.8	66.0	64.2	10.4	28.4	1.4	1.5	2.9	2.6

Note: As alumni checked all applicable sources, totals add up to over 100.0%.

———————————————— **TABLE 15** ————————————————

Extent of Participation in Extra-Curricular Activities

*How would you classify your participation in each of the
following extra-curricular activities?*

	None	Some	Active, but no major office	Active and held major office	No Answer	Total
Social Fraternity	46.1%	12.7	15.5	22.2	3.5	100.0%
Editorial staff of student publication	69.8%	7.9	3.2	7.3	11.8	100.0%
Student government	61.0%	13.6	5.1	9.4	10.9	100.0%
Dramatics or debating	66.8%	10.9	5.1	4.7	12.5	100.0%
Choral, orchestra or band	66.2%	7.8	10.1	4.1	11.8	100.0%
Departmental clubs	43.4%	24.0	11.6	10.6	10.4	100.0%
Political clubs or organizations	65.0%	13.2	5.2	4.2	12.4	100.0%
Religious clubs or organizations	53.7%	18.7	8.7	7.7	11.2	100.0%
Intramural sports	36.2%	26.8	21.9	9.4	5.7	100.0%

▷ Two-thirds of the graduates participated in intra-mural
    sports in contrast to only a third in student government
    or student publications.

TABLE 16

Type of Residence During College

As an undergraduate student where did you live for the longest period of time while in college?

	School Dorm	Boarding House	Fraternity	Parent's Home	Room or Apt.	Coop Housing	Vet's Housing	Own Home	No Answer	Total
All Graduates	26.5%	5.1	15.1	28.1	15.7	0.7	3.8	3.0	2.1	100.0%
Quality of College										
High	41.6%	5.5	19.3	10.3	15.6	0.8	2.6	1.8	2.5	100.0%
Medium	22.4%	5.2	20.9	25.4	16.0	0.9	4.3	2.8	2.2	100.0%
Low	22.1%	4.8	4.3	43.1	15.3	0.3	3.7	4.2	2.2	100.0%
Size of College										
Small	33.5%	4.0	19.2	18.9	13.2	0.2	5.4	2.8	2.8	100.0%
Medium	31.0%	5.0	13.6	26.2	15.1	0.8	3.1	3.4	1.8	100.0%
Large	9.9%	6.8	11.5	43.2	20.0	1.2	2.5	2.8	2.1	100.0%

Δ Approximately half of the graduates lived in college-related housing.

HOW LIBERAL ARTS GRADUATES APPRAISE
THEIR EDUCATION

The voices best able to testify concerning the values of liberal education are seldom heard. Most public evaluations come from speeches of college presidents, statements of businessmen being honored at commencement, or defenses presented by college professors themselves. Seldom are opinions of alumni collected to provide a tested-by-time measure of liberal education.

Major attention in this study is focused upon alumni attitudes toward their collegiate preparation. This chapter examines their judgments about college purposes, their conclusions about how well these purposes were actually fulfilled, their appraisals of various aspects of the academic experience, and their second thoughts about their choices of college and courses.

Appraisal of the General Program

Before reviewing their evaluation of liberal education, it is essential first to discover what liberal arts alumni hoped to obtain during their college preparation. The objective selected as most important was that of providing a broad fund of knowledge about different fields. (TABLE 17)

Clustered in a secondary position were the objectives of developing ability to get along with different types of people, developing moral capacities, ethical standards and values, providing a fund of knowledge useful in later life, and training a person in depth in at least one field. Ranked considerably less important was the development of social poise.

37

The alumni then were asked how well their own education had achieved each of these goals. (TABLE 18)   A comparison of expectations and achievements shows a fairly high degree of alumni satisfaction. Yet each objective fell somewhat short of accomplishment in the views of alumni. The widest gap between expectation and achievement came in the areas of providing of a broad fund of knowledge about different fields and developing of moral capacities and ethical standards.

The survey questionnaire did not ask for opinions about the total length of the liberal arts program, but comments volunteered by the alumni suggest that this is a topic of at least some concern.

> Liberal arts education should be extended to a five year
> program and students should take a wide variety of elec-
> tives before choosing a major field of study.
> *Arizona State University*

> Today's industry demands a minimum of five years of
> study.   *University of Arkansas*

> We need a longer college course. Five or six years is
> not too much. I would like to begin with two or three
> years of electives and then take the last three years in
> my specialized field.   *Louisiana State University*

More than four-fifths of the graduates agree that their college courses, on the whole, were "quite challenging and interesting." (TABLE 19)   , Here, alumni with the highest academic records, those from the high-quality institutions, those from private institutions and those majoring in one of the humanities were the most satisfied. There was a slight tendency for majors in science and mathematics to express more satisfaction with their courses. While not shown, year of graduation did not produce differences in satisfaction. It should be noted that Table 19 reveals that graduates were relatively but not completely satisfied with courses. While 86 percent of the respondents generally agreed courses were challenging and interesting, only 18 percent were willing to express strong agreement.

Some alumni comments indicate that the graduates, at least in retrospect, place a high value on demanding programs and faculty:

> While I spent a lot of time in an academic environment,
> I did not really receive a sound basic education: not in

the liberal arts nor in the sciences. I consider much of
this my own fault, but also the fault of the environment
itself — which was anything but demanding. It was frankly
easy, and the whole experience was soft. As much as
possible, take courses from the most challenging professors regardless of the field and seek their personal
advice on their fields and their appraisals of you.
                                    University of California, Los Angeles
Students should pick demanding teachers, no matter what
the subject.   *Boston College*

Alumni satisfaction with the extent of their undergraduate training in the important area of self-expression is shown in Table 20.
Seventy percent of the graduates agree that they received good training in the means of expressing their ideas, but a significant 30 percent express disagreement. Logically, humanities majors are the
most satisfied with this training and science and mathematics majors,
the least.

In reporting on the balance between academic and extra-curricular
activities on their campuses, only 16 percent of the alumni feel their
college education placed too much emphasis on outside activities.

Alumni tend to place their own final stamp of approval on liberal
education when nearly four out of five agree with the statement, "I
would advise a high school graduate to take a liberal arts major."
(TABLE 21)   Some who disagree said that they did so because any such
blanket advice might not be appropriate to all individuals. Humanities
majors and graduates of high-quality colleges are the most loyal to
liberal arts. Alumni who attended private colleges or small institutions, or who earned the highest grades are also more likely to en-
dorse liberal education.

Appraisal of College Major

The best evaluation of a college major may be whether its graduates would repeat it. Overall, 49 percent of the respondents would
major in the same subject — ranging from 55 percent of the science
and mathematics graduates to 44 percent of the social science alumni.
(TABLE 22)   Another 32 percent would switch majors, but within the
area of liberal arts.

The least loyalty to original major (less than 40 percent would repeat) was shown by those who majored in general science, geography, economics, general social science, sociology, speech, religion, and general humanities. The greatest loyalty (more than 60 percent would repeat) is reported by those who studied physics, premedicine, art, and music. Those who would switch within the liberal arts are most likely to elect either science and mathematics or social sciences rather than the humanities.

Where majors in science and mathematics would now choose a non-liberal arts field, it is usually engineering. Those from the social sciences or humanities who would now elect a non-liberal arts subject most frequently favor business administration. Still, over 80 percent of the graduates, it should be emphasized, would repeat a liberal arts major.

Appraisal of Individual Courses

The range of courses taken by liberal arts alumni is formidable.
(TABLE 23)   Since some graduates selected courses outside the traditional liberal arts program, the list of subjects taken includes accounting, agriculture, business administration, engineering, journalism, physical education, and ROTC. Reflecting basic college requirements, almost all alumni took some courses in English, foreign languages, history, and mathematics. More remarkable is the variety of the curricula followed.

The graduates also were asked now whether they wished they had taken more, the same, or fewer courses in each field. Here the desire to take individual courses exceeds the normal capacity of the college program. In only five fields out of 31 would alumni take less rather than more course work, and four of the five are non-liberal arts fields: agriculture, education, physical education, and ROTC. As many as 40 percent or more of the respondents wish they had taken more course work in nine fields: art or art history, economics, English, foreign languages, history, mathematics, philisophy, political science, and speech.

Each graduate was asked to list the subject which was the most enjoyable, the best taught, the most difficult, and the most useful in his career.

Adjusting for exposure in terms of both original major and extent of individual course work, their reactions may be summarized:

Most Enjoyable Courses	*Least Enjoyable Courses*
Philosophy or Religion	Economics
English	
Foreign Language	

Most Difficult Courses	*Least Difficult Courses*
Mathematics	Social Science
Foreign Language	Fine and Applied Art
Chemistry	Biological Science
Physical Science	

Most Useful Courses	*Least Useful Courses*
English	Fine and Applied Art
Mathematics	Economics
Psychology	Social Science

Best Teaching	*Poorest Teaching*
Foreign Language	Economics
English	Fine and Applied Art
Philosophy and Religion	

For each type of major, respondents found their most enjoyable courses within their own general major fields. (TABLE 24) Humanities majors are the most likely to enjoy courses in their own area, more than three-fourths of them listing a humanities course as the most enjoyable.

Majors and non-majors generally agreed on subject preferences both within and outside their own fields. All three types of majors selected courses in biology and mathematics as two of the three most enjoyable subjects in science and mathematics. All three named history and psychology as two of the three most enjoyable subjects in the social sciences. And all three agreed upon philosophy, English and foreign languages as the three most enjoyable subjects in the humanities area.

Considerable unanimity also was displayed in rating the most difficult courses. (TABLE 25) Regardless of type of major, the majority of all graduates found their most difficult subject within the sciences and mathematics — usually specifically mathematics. Almost a third of the majors in each general category identified a humanities course as the most difficult, particularly a foreign language. Relatively few (8 to 12 percent) named social science courses as their hardest.

Enjoyment of a course seems closely related to good teaching. The courses previously mentioned as the most enjoyable (TABLE 24) were frequently credited with the best teachers. (TABLE 26)   Regardless of the type of original major, there was general consensus that history was the best taught among the social sciences and that English was best among the humanities. Within the area of science and mathematics, the three subjects which appeared at the top of all the scales were chemistry, biology, and mathematics. Majors in science and mathematics rated chemistry as having the best teachers; social science and humanities students felt the best instructors were in biology.

The most useful courses developed quite a different set of nominations. Psychology received little mention as the most difficult, the most enjoyable, or the best taught, but was cited by all types of majors as the social science most useful in their careers. Within the humanities, English was picked by all types of majors as the most useful in their careers. In science and mathematics, majors within the area said chemistry had been the most useful course. Persons who majored outside the area, rated mathematics the most helpful. (TABLE 27)

How do alumni feel about required courses against which freshmen usually rebel? These include English, foreign language, a laboratory science, a social science, mathematics, or psychology at most institutions. Church-related schools may prescribe a course or two in religion.

The graduates, themselves, were satisfied with the basic required courses. In fact, many commented on them more favorably than upon electives.

> Take plenty of mathematics and other courses it would be difficult to pick up without instruction.
> *Rutgers University*

> My curriculum in college included too many science courses for pre-medical students which were taught over again in medical school. This didn't permit important courses in English, speech, business, art, and the humanities which are important in insuring a fruitful and rich life.   *San Jose State College*

Appraisal of Alma Mater

Given a second chance, somewhat more than half the graduates would attend the same college. (TABLE 28)   Recent graduates and those who originally went to high-quality institutions are more likely to repeat their original choice. While not shown, size and type of control of college, academic record, and type of major seem to have little effect on the desire to attend the same institution.

Loyalty to institution of original choice is influenced to a substantial degree by the amount of faculty contact experienced by the alumni during their undergraduate years. (TABLE 28)   Highest degree earned and leadership in student activities bear little relation to the decision whether to choose the same institution a second time.

The alumni portrait of faculty members becomes clearer and shows that 23 percent of the graduates "agreed strongly" and 62 percent "agreed" that their faculty members were really interested in their students.

Two typical comments on faculty members were as follows:

> Develop a close relationship with the faculty member most competent in the fields related to the career you contemplate. Seek his advice.   *Colgate University*

> Biased professors should be fired.   I listened to economics professors who were so far left that I entered my first job with a chip on my shoulder. As a result of my remarks about profits, I was fired.
> *Denison University*

Appraisal of Graduate Education

Most alumni evaluate graduate training positively.   (TABLE 29) Responses here are limited to those who attended graduate school. While attitudes differ, most graduates feel that they benefitted more from graduate than undergraduate education and that graduate school was more difficult.   They feel their graduate education was valuable in helping to complete their education, but at the same time, they acknowledge that liberal arts was valuable in itself.   For the most part, they took advanced training for career purposes rather than to pursue intellectual interests.

──────────────────────── TABLE 17 ────────────────────────

Evaluation of Objectives of a Liberal Education

Liberal arts education should . . .

	Very Important	Fairly Important	Fairly Un- Important	Not Important at All	No Answer	Total
...provide a fund of knowledge about different fields"	66.7%	29.0	3.4	0.5	0.4	100.0%
...develop ability to get along with different types of people"	49.5%	33.8	12.2	4.1	0.4	100.0%
...develop a fund of knowledge useful in later life"	47.1%	39.8	11.1	1.4	0.6	100.0%
...train a person in depth in at least one field"	40.9%	33.2	18.8	6.4	0.7	100.0%
...develop social poise"	20.5%	43.7	26.8	8.2	1.8	100.0%
...develop moral capacities, ethical standards and values"	56.8%	31.1	8.6	3.0	0.5	100.0%

──────────────────────── TABLE 18 ────────────────────────

Appraisal of Liberal Arts Education in Meeting Selected Objectives

Did your education . . .

	Yes	No	No Answer	Total
...provide a broad fund of knowledge about different fields"	79.6%	15.0	5.4	100.0%
...develop moral capacities, ethical standards and values"	68.3%	25.9	5.8	100.0%
...develop ability to get along with different types of people"	72.2%	22.2	5.6	100.0%
...develop a fund of knowledge useful in later life"	80.0%	14.1	5.9	100.0%
...train a person in depth in at least one field"	58.6%	35.6	5.8	100.0%
...develop social poise"	53.2%	40.6	6.2	100.0%

▷ The goals of liberal education were rated to be: (1) To provide a broad
fund of knowledge about different fields; (2) to develop moral capacities
and ethical standards; (3) to cultivate the ability to get along with
different types of people; and (4) intensive training in at least one field.

TABLE 19

Extent of Challenge and Interest in Courses

The courses I took were, on the whole, quite challenging and interesting.

	Strongly Agree	Agree	Disagree	Strongly Disagree	No Answer	Total
All Graduates	18.3%	68.0	12.2	1.0	0.5	100.0%
Academic Record						
High	20.8%	68.2	10.0	0.6	0.4	100.0%
Average	19.4%	68.0	11.2	1.0	0.4	100.0%
Low	14.9%	68.5	14.9	1.1	0.6	100.0%
Type of Major						
Science and Math.	18.0%	69.9	10.8	0.9	0.4	100.0%
Social Sciences	17.5%	68.0	13.0	0.9	0.6	100.0%
Humanities	20.6%	64.9	12.6	1.4	0.5	100.0%
Quality of College						
High	25.1%	65.4	8.5	0.6	0.4	100.0%
Medium	16.9%	68.0	13.4	1.1	0.6	100.0%
Low	15.9%	69.8	12.8	1.1	0.4	100.0%
Control of College						
Catholic	15.9%	66.6	15.2	1.6	0.7	100.0%
Public	16.2%	69.1	13.0	1.3	0.4	100.0%
Private	20.3%	67.6	11.0	0.7	0.4	100.0%

TABLE 20

Extent to which Graduates Received Good Training in Self-Expression

I received good training . . . how to express my ideas clearly.

	Strongly Agree	Agree	Disagree	Strongly Disagree	No Answer	Total
All Graduates	15.4%	53.2	27.5	3.4	0.5	100.0%
Type of Major						
Science-Math	9.5%	52.7	33.3	3.9	0.6	100.0%
Social Sciences	16.5%	53.3	26.3	3.4	0.5	100.0%
Humanities	22.6%	53.5	20.5	3.6	0.8	100.0%

——————————————— **TABLE 21** ———————————————

Extent to Which Alumni Would Now Recommend a Liberal Education

I would advise a high school graduate to take a liberal arts major.

	Strongly Agree	Agree	Disagree	Strongly Disagree	No Answer	Total
All Graduates	33.6%	43.9	15.6	4.7	2.2	100.0%
Years Since Graduation						
Fifteen	30.9%	45.3	16.6	4.7	2.5	100.0%
Ten	33.8%	44.1	15.3	4.6	2.2	100.0%
Five	36.0%	42.2	14.8	4.7	2.3	100.0%
Type of Major						
Science and Math.	28.3%	44.8	18.9	5.6	2.4	100.0%
Social Sciences	34.7%	44.2	14.8	4.5	1.8	100.0%
Humanities	40.2%	41.6	11.9	3.5	2.8	100.0%
Academic Record						
High	39.0%	45.1	11.4	2.1	2.4	100.0%
Average	34.4%	44.1	15.1	4.1	2.3	100.0%
Low	30.4%	43.6	18.0	6.1	1.9	100.0%
Quality of College						
High	40.8%	40.8	12.1	3.4	2.9	100.0%
Medium	31.0%	44.2	17.2	5.4	2.2	100.0%
Low	32.5%	45.4	15.7	4.5	1.9	100.0%
Size of College						
Small	37.4%	44.4	12.8	3.4	2.0	100.0%
Medium	33.4%	43.6	16.0	4.5	2.5	100.0%
Large	28.8%	43.6	18.7	6.6	2.3	100.0%
Control of College						
Catholic	33.5%	46.5	14.2	3.8	2.0	100.0%
Public	26.7%	45.5	20.0	5.6	2.2	100.0%
Private	38.6%	42.2	12.8	4.1	2.3	100.0%

▷ In general, alumni are satisfied with their liberal arts education.
Most would advise today's high school graduate to take liberal arts.

TABLE 22

Original and Present Choice of Major Field

Original Major	Would Repeat Major	Would Change Major to Another Liberal Arts Field in . . .			Would Change Major to a Non-Liberal Arts Field			Other or No Answer	Total
		Science & Math	Social Sciences	Humanities	Business Admin.	Engineering	Education		
All Graduates	49.4%	11.8	11.5	8.9	7.3	5.0	1.9	4.2	100.0%
Chemistry	54.5%	21.6	5.1	4.5	3.5	7.2	0.8	2.8	100.0%
Physics	69.1%	12.4	3.9	2.8	3.4	6.2	0.6	1.6	100.0%
Geology	43.0%	17.7	11.2	4.9	4.5	14.0	1.7	3.0	100.0%
Biology	48.7%	20.4	8.0	9.0	4.9	4.1	0.9	4.0	100.0%
Pre-Med	68.5%	7.0	7.0	6.6	4.0	4.6	1.2	1.1	100.0%
Math	56.9%	10.1	5.2	4.5	5.3	14.2	0.9	2.9	100.0%
Gen. Science	12.3%	38.5	6.2	10.8	1.5	15.4	3.1	12.2	100.0%
Total Sci-Math	54.9%	16.5	6.6	5.8	4.3	7.7	0.9	3.3	
Economics	39.0%	8.7	12.3	9.4	15.5	6.8	2.2	6.1	100.0%
Anthropology	53.1%	14.3	12.2	6.1	2.0	5.1	2.0	6.2	100.0%
Gen. Soc. Sci.	37.0%	10.9	19.0	7.6	14.2	1.4	5.3	4.6	100.0%
Geography	35.7%	15.7	12.8	5.7	8.6	11.4	1.4	8.7	100.0%
History	49.2%	8.9	14.5	10.8	7.9	2.1	2.6	4.0	100.0%
Poli. Sci.	48.0%	7.9	14.6	11.8	8.9	2.7	1.3	4.8	100.0%
Psychology	39.0%	9.5	22.3	8.6	18.6	3.5	4.1	4.4	100.0%
Total Soc. Sci.	43.9%	10.2	13.9	10.3	10.3	4.2	2.3	4.9	
English	58.1%	6.4	14.5	9.9	4.2	2.7	1.5	2.7	100.0%
Speech	38.1%	8.2	14.2	15.7	14.2	2.2	3.7	3.7	100.0%
Philosophy	58.4%	6.5	15.1	11.7	4.5	0.3	1.7	1.8	100.0%
Religion	37.9%	6.9	18.1	16.4	3.4	2.6	9.5	5.2	100.0%
Art	60.8%	3.3	10.0	8.3	5.8	5.0	2.5	4.3	100.0%
Gen. Humanities	31.5%	11.0	24.4	11.0	5.5	2.4	3.1	11.1	100.0%
Music	66.7%	6.9	4.9	6.9	3.9	4.9	4.9	0.9	100.0%
Languages	43.5%	11.1	13.9	13.9	9.6	3.4	1.4	3.2	100.0%
Total Humanities	53.2%	7.1	14.8	11.1	5.6	2.1	2.1	4.0	

△ Over 80 percent would major in a liberal arts subject if they were beginning college again.

Approximately half would repeat their original major.

―――――――――――――――――― TABLE 23 ――――――――――――――――――

Courses Taken in Each Subject and Present Evaluation of Each

*Here is a list of subjects which may have been offered in your
undergraduate college. To the best of your memory, how many
courses did you take in each subject, and how do you now feel
about them?*

*How many undergraduate courses
did you take in each subject?*

*Do you wish now that you
had taken more, the same,
or less courses in each
subject?*

	None	One	Two-Three	Four or More	No Ans.	Total	Less	The Same	More	No Ans.	Total
Accounting	70%	15	9	2	4	100%	4%	53%	35%	8%	100%
Agriculture	91%	1	1	1	6	100%	6%	76	5	13	100%
Anthropology	73%	15	5	1	6	100%	4%	52	34	10	100%
Art or Art History	60%	22	10	3	5	100%	4%	46	41	9	100%
Biology	34%	23	22	18	3	100%	8%	59	26	7	100%
Business Admin.	69%	8	9	8	6	100%	4%	48	38	10	100%
Chemistry	37%	18	19	22	4	100%	11%	58	24	7	100%
Economics	31%	28	21	17	3	100%	5%	45	44	6	100%
Education	66%	8	8	14	4	100%	15%	63	14	8	100%
Engineering	78%	5	6	6	5	100%	7%	64	18	11	100%
English	1%	8	43	48	-	100%	3%	53	41	3	100%
Foreign Lang.	10%	16	42	31	1	100%	12%	45	40	3	100%
General Human.	38%	17	26	14	5	100%	4%	58	30	8	100%
General Science	63%	17	11	3	6	100%	4%	71	15	10	100%
Gen. Soc. Sciences	46%	18	21	10	5	100%	5%	70	17	8	100%
Geography	69%	19	6	2	4	100%	4%	61	26	9	100%
Geology	68%	16	7	5	4	100%	6%	62	24	89	100%
History	10%	17	40	32	1	100%	5%	47	45	3	100%
Journalism	85%	5	3	1	6	100%	5%	65	21	9	100%
Mathematics	19%	20	33	26	2	100%	7%	47	41	5	100%
Music or Music Hist.	63%	22	8	3	4	100%	4%	54	34	8	100%
Physical Education	32%	15	28	22	3	100%	13%	70	11	6	100%
Physics	41%	25	22	9	3	100%	6%	56	31	7	100%
Philosophy	29%	27	25	17	2	100%	5%	42	48	5	100%
Pre-Medical	74%	2	4	14	6	100%	9%	74	7	10	100%
Political Science	30%	26	24	17	3	100%	4%	49	42	5	100%
Psychology	20%	31	31	16	2	100%	7%	50	39	4	100%
Religion	50%	18	15	15	2	100%	7%	63	23	7	100%
ROTC	64%	6	10	16	4	100%	20%	67	4	9	100%
Sociology	39%	31	18	9	3	100%	8%	59	24	6	100%
Speech	38%	36	17	6	3	100%	4%	46	44	6	100%

▷ Some wish they had taken more courses with job implications.

The subject the greatest number of alumni wish they had taken more of,
interestingly, is non-vocational: philosophy.

--- **TABLE 24** ---

Most Enjoyable Course During College

Most Enjoyable Course Was in:	Major		
	Science and Mathematics	Social Sciences	Humanities
Science and Mathematics	67.8%	8.3%	5.8%
	(Biology: 18.9) (Chemistry: 17.0) (Mathematics: 14.7)	(Biology: 2.6) (Mathematics: 2.2) (Geology: 1.5)	(Mathematics: 1.8) (Biology: 1.6) (Geology: 0.9)
Social Sciences	11.9	66.6	14.7
	(History: 4.6) (Psychology: 2.5) (Anthropology: 1.3)	(History: 23.9) (Pol. Sci.: 11.7) (Psychology: 10.8)	(History: 6.2) (Psychology: 3.1) (Pol. Sci.: 1.6)
Humanities	16.7	18.3	76.4
	(Philosophy: 4.9) (English: 4.0) (For. Lang.: 2.5)	(English: 5.4) (For. Lang.: 2.2) (Philosophy: 4.8)	(English: 34.0) (Philosophy: 12.0) (For. Lang.: 7.5)
Other	3.6	6.8	3.1
Total:	100.0%	100.0%	100.0%

(Note: Entries in parentheses were the most frequently mentioned courses in each area, with the percentages selecting those courses.)

▷ Graduates tend to nominate a subject from their own general major field as "the most enjoyable".

The same pattern prevails for the selection of "the best teachers".

Half or more of all graduates name a subject in the science and mathematics field as "the most difficult".

When asked what subject they would now like to take, the graduates nominate more of almost everything.

—————————————————— TABLE 25 ——————————————————

Most Difficult Subjects During College

Which subject did you find the most difficult?

	Major		
Most Difficult Subject in:	Science and Mathematics	Social Sciences	Humanities
Science and Mathematics	58.1%	50.6%	52.0%
Social Sciences	8.3	11.3	12.1
Humanities	29.5	30.6	29.5
Other	4.1	7.5	6.4
	100.0%	100.0%	100.0%

—————————————————— TABLE 26 ——————————————————

College Courses with the Best Teachers

	Major		
Subject with Best Teachers in:	Science and Mathematics	Social Sciences	Humanities
Science and Math	66.0%	10.1%	6.7%
Social Sciences	10.1	61.7	15.9
Humanities	18.6	22.5	73.9
Other	5.3	5.7	3.5
	100.0%	100.0%	100.0%

TABLE 27

College Courses Most Useful in Career

Subject Most Useful in Career:	Major		
	Science and Mathematics	Social Sciences	Humanities
Science and Mathematics	77.7%	6.3%	5.8%
	(Chemistry: 21.4) (Biology: 19.3) (Math: 15.3)	(Math.: 3.5) (Biology: 0.9)	(Math.: 2.9) (Biology: 1.1) (Pre-Med: 0.7)
Social Sciences	4.4	47.9	10.2
	(Psych.: 2.3) (Economics: 0.9)	(Psych.: 12.5) (Economics: 11.7) (History: 9.6)	(Psych.: 4.2) (pol. Sci.: 1.7) (Economics: 1.5)
Humanities	10.6	27.3	74.8
	(English: 6.6) (Phil.: 1.2)	(English: 17.4) (Speech: 3.3) (Phil.: 3.0)	(English: 39.8) (Phil.: 8.8) (Speech: 7.0)
Other	7.3	18.5	9.2
	100.0%	100.0%	100.0%

(Note: Entries in parentheses were the most frequently mentioned courses in each area, with the percentages selecting those courses.)

▷ Three-quarters of all science and mathematics majors and all humanities majors name a subject within their own major area as "the most useful" in their own careers.

Less than half the social science majors consider a subject in the social sciences as the most useful.

────────────── **TABLE 28** ──────────────

Would Graduates Attend the Same College Again?

*If you could start college all over again, would you still attend
the same college you earned your degree from?*

	Yes	Not Sure	No	No Answer	Total
All Graduates	56.9%	29.3	13.5	0.3	100.0%
Years Since Graduation					
Fifteen	52.4%	32.0	15.1	0.5	100.0%
Ten	57.9%	28.4	13.5	0.2	100.0%
Five	60.4%	27.5	11.9	0.2	100.0%
Quality of College					
High	70.5%	20.6	8.5	0.4	100.0%
Medium	54.7%	30.4	14.5	0.4	100.0%
Low	51.4%	33.2	15.3	0.2	100.0%
Highest Degree Earned					
Bachelor's	56.7%	30.0	13.0	0.3	100.0%
Master's or Prof.	58.6%	27.8	13.3	0.3	100.0%
Doctor's	50.7%	31.5	17.6	0.2	100.0%
Student Government Leader					
Yes	59.6%	28.6	11.6	0.2	100.0%
No	56.6%	29.3	13.7	0.4	100.0%
College Editor					
Yes	55.6%	28.6	15.7	0.1	100.0%
No	57.0%	29.3	13.3	0.4	100.0%
Amount of Contact with Faculty Members					
Great Deal	64.2%	25.6	9.8	0.4	100.0%
Some	58.1%	29.2	12.5	0.2	100.0%
Very little	50.2%	32.9	16.5	0.4	100.0%
None	43.0%	29.3	27.1	0.6	100.0%

▷ Only 14 percent would not attend the same college again. The keys to
satisfaction include the quality of the college and the extent of
faculty-student contacts.

————————————————— **TABLE 29** —————————————————

Evaluation of the Role of Graduate or Professional Education
(7,350 alumni who attended graduate or professional school)

Extent of agreement or disagreement with . . .

	Strongly Agree	Agree	Disagree	Strongly Disagree	Total
"Without graduate school, I would feel that my education was not complete"	46.0%	33.4	16.0	4.6	100.0%
"Graduate or professional school was more difficult than undergraduate education"	27.6%	35.6	30.4	6.4	100.0%
"Liberal arts was essentially preparation for graduate school, rather than training useful for my field"	16.2%	33.0	39.4	11.4	100.0%
"On balance, I benefitted more from my undergraduate education than from graduate or professional school"	14.1%	26.5	38.8	20.6	100.0%
"I took graduate study primarily to follow my own intellectual interests, rather than because it might help my career"	7.9%	17.9	49.9	24.3	100.0%
"Graduate school was really a waste of time"	1.2%	2.3	27.1	69.4	100.0%
"I entered graduate school with a fairly clear idea of my vocational goal."	44.9%	39.5	12.8	2.8	100.0%
"Graduate study helped me avoid being stuck at a low level in my field."	45.0%	34.1	15.9	5.0	100.0%

▷ Among the three-quarters who pursued graduate education, three
times as many took it for career advancement as for purely
intellectual interests. Majors in science and mathematics
rated graduate study the most useful in their careers.

4

CAREER STATUS of LIBERAL ARTS ALUMNI

Psychologists tell us that one of the most basic questions we ask new acquaintances is, "What kind of work do you do?" As evidence, observe the conversation of two men who meet in a purely social setting. Just as quickly as possible, within the easy context of normal conversation, they will seek to determine the occupation of the person to whom they are talking. This process recognizes that work determines the actual way of life, the level of living, and the areas of knowledge which may characterize the man. Certainly, the life of a man and his family will differ sharply depending upon whether he elects to be a doctor, minister, elementary school teacher, salesman, military serviceman, or scientist.

Work and related travel occupy approximately 40 percent of the waking hours of the typical man. More importantly, work often provides the most creative outlet for a man's talents. Industrialization may have reduced the opportunity for many to be creative, but for professional and managerial workers, the industrial revolution has tended to increase the complexity of problems faced in their work and heightened their challenge. Work provides a standard of achievement by which man's activities may be measured. For many men. their most intellectual challenges are associated with their jobs. Noting how much better many men handle finances related to their job than their own affairs suggests that work receives their most objective insights.

In the Calvinist viewpoint, man works his way toward eternal life through prudence and diligence. Indeed, today work still is expected of man. The strangest person in many communities is the middle-aged man who has no job. Almost by nature, man accepts the role of work in life. Children at play often slip naturally into occupational roles.

To be self-sustaining, society requires work from its citizens. To the individual, work — the status from his job and his associations in it — constitute a major portion of his social life. Many men, quite literally, spend more time with their secretaries than with their wives. A man's involvement with his work can be intense, to the point where many do more than required to maintain their positions.

Historically, America's earliest liberal arts graduates pursued careers in the ministry, law and medicine. Over the years, it has been assumed that career patterns of liberal arts alumni have changed radically. Yet there is little empirical evidence available to describe or even to substantiate those changes.

This chapter presents the career status of liberal arts alumni fifteen years, ten years, and five years after graduation at the time the survey was completed. We shall examine their employers, their occupations, and their earnings.

Portrait of the Classes

Important in studying the histories of the three classes is an appreciation of their college era and the world into which they graduated. Thus we will attempt to describe the cultural and economic environment of each of the three classes.

The Class of 1948 was distinguished by the variety of its academic tenure. Few who graduated in 1948 began as freshmen in September, 1944. Most started between 1938 and 1943. The lives of most of the members of the class were influenced by a call to military service or, in fact, equally affected because they were not chosen. Some members of the class began their college life as participants in Navy or Marine V-12 units in whose life Typhoid Injection Day was as dreaded as Final Examination Week. Their college life was restricted, even the Yale Daily News reported that it had joined

Lucky Strike Green as a wartime casualty. Newly-arrived service trainees at Yale heard President Seymour say: "In the opinion of your military superiors you will profit most by participation — even though it be a limited one — in the life of a great university." [1]

From a restricted life, the campuses turned quickly into an open and crowded world with the sudden end of World War II. The 18 or 19 year old male became as much of a curiosity as the balding, married 30 year old. While most of the class had just returned from military service, the culture of the times made talk of it taboo. The only permissable discussions were of the boredom of military life, the ineptness of superior officers, and the occasional enlightening escapade. The newly-created veterans spent a great deal of time discussing the intricacies of the G. I. Bill of Rights regulations, abuses in the allotment allowed for books (one cult devoted its unused allowance to cornering the market on volumes with attractive bindings), and how friends on the unemployment rolls (the "52-20" club) were passing their time.

Veterans' villages appeared on a temporary basis, although many of these same structures were still to be in use two decades later. The crowded conditions on the campus forced colleges and universities to pay more attention to the teaching process than they ever have done since. Yet, on many campuses the life was distinctly different from what it was before the war. At Harvard, a group of students complained that less "than six months after the war with Germany had ended, it had become apparent to Harvard students and faculty alike that tutorial instruction, long a Harvard tradition, was being curtailed or abandoned in many departments of the College." [2]

While not impressed with the students' creative scholarship or their thirst for the purely academic side of college, faculty members agreed that students of this era were serious and purposeful.

As graduation lists were drawn up, it became obvious that the Class of 1948, absorbing as it did members from many entering groups, was often the largest class ever graduated. Despite its past contribution to society, members of the class found relatively few employers interested in hiring them. Those recruiters who visited the campuses were not very interested in liberal arts graduates. An insurance company representative commented years later that when he went to the University of Illinois in the spring of 1948, half of his potential insurance salesmen were engineers for whom society had no ready need.

Many employers were still hoarding profits anticipating a recession or, at least, a break in price levels. Federal agencies were more concerned with assimilating bumper wartime staffs than adding new graduates. Only school systems were eager employers — without much financial inducement. Unused G. I. Bill benefits permitted many members of the Class of 1948 to go on for advanced training and thus await a more favorable employment climate. As they found positions, members of the Class of 1948 began at salaries of $200 to $230 a month.

When the Class of 1953 entered college in the fall of 1949, its members may have been awed by the record campus enrollments. The older World War II veterans still constituted the bulk of the upper classes.

At the end of its freshman years, the class watched the Korean War begin. The war was waged furiously during their sophomore year, reached an impasse during their junior year, and ended in a draw as they achieved senior status.

Employment prospects were good, but in the face of pressure from their draft boards, seniors spent much of their time with recruiters from the military services. Those who were able to accept employment readily found jobs at starting salaries of over $325.

The history of the Class of 1958 leads to the conclusion that it was one of the most analyzed groups in history. Literature is replete with commentary, much of it from faculty members. A group of English professors labelled their students "The Careful Young men." Karl Shapiro of the University of Nebraska used the term the "Brain-Washed Generation" and said, "I am sorry for the intellectually godless. For them the mysteries are dead. I pity them; they will have no memories." [3]

With the exception of a slight recession in 1957, a favorable employment climate existed during their college years. The 1956 Annual Report for the Carnegie Corporation noted that: "Never in the history of America have so many people spent so much money in search of talent. The identification of gifted youngsters and the effective nurture of their abilities are problems of renewed interest to educators. Shortages in professional and scientific fields have become a national preoccupation." [4]

Sputnik was launched in the fall of 1957 and its shock waves generated increased federal support for technical education. Despite national concern over the threat of Atomic Missile War, most graduates of 1958 were able to satisfy their military service obligation in six months. Employer preference for technical graduates heightened. Liberal arts seniors began at $375 a month, while their engineering classmates started their first jobs at between $480 and $500.

What Do They Do?

As anticipated, literally hundreds of different occupations were reported by the 11,000 liberal arts alumni. To reduce these to manageable proportions, the following occupation index was utilized:

> Lawyer
> Clergyman
> Elementary or Secondary school teacher or administrator
> College teacher or administrator
> Salesman (including real estate agent)
> Social service worker (psychologist, social worker, etc.)
> Medical worker (physician, surgeon, dentist, veterinarian, chiropracter)
> Scientist or mathematician (biologist, chemist, engineer, mathematician, physicist, geologist, etc.)
> Fiscal, office, or management worker (accountant, banking employee, manager, office worker, claims adjuster, business trainee, etc.)
> Creative worker (architect, editor, artist, public relations worker, creative artist, communications worker)
> Other (actuary, buyer, farmer, government officer not otherwise classified, health worker, naturalist, technician, union official, market researcher, contractor, librarian, athlete, pilot, craftsman, service worker, laborer, etc.) [5]
> No answer (no information, not employed, in graduate school, etc.)

Liberal arts graduates were asked to indicate their first and their current occupations. (TABLE 30) The largest group of alumni are currently employed in fiscal, office, and management occupations. Approximately the same percentage are teachers at all levels. The traditional professions of the liberal arts — law, clergy, and medicine — account for 20 percent of the graduates.

Comparing the three graduating classes, several trends are discernible. Fewer of the new graduates are engaged in elementary and secondary teaching, in fiscal, office, and management fields, and in the creative occupations. At the same time, more of the recent alumni are teaching at the college level, working in social service occupations, and employed in other fields.

Who Employs Liberal Arts Graduates?

To determine the broad sectors of the economy in which liberal arts graduates make their careers, respondents were asked to classify their employers according to the following list:

> Private manufacturing or mining concern
>   (e.g., steel plant, clothing factory, oil refinery)
> Private non-manufacturing (e.g., telephone company,
>   construction company, wholesale or retail trade,
>   law office)
> Agriculture (privately owned farm)
> Elementary or secondary school
> College or university
> United States Military Service
> Federal government (excluding teaching)
> Research organization or institute
> Hospital, church, clinic, or welfare organization
> Other

The results show that liberal arts alumni are almost evenly distributed between the private and public sectors of the economy. (TABLE 31) Private manufacturing, private, non-manufacturing (including self-employed professionals), and private agriculture account for 48 percent of their total employment. Liberal arts employment in the public sector is most frequently in educational institutions, followed by government, welfare or service organizations (hospitals, churches, clinics, welfare groups), military service, and research organizations.

Despite the fact that state and local governments across the nation employ half again as many people as do federal agencies, more liberal arts alumni are associated with the federal government. The low percentage of college graduates in local government has, in fact, become a cause of national concern.

While many alumni have remained in the same categories since graduation, some shifts between first and current employers may be noted in Table 31. Three times as many graduates began their careers in the military service as are now affiliated with them. Hospitals, churches, and clinics show some decline between first and current employers. Private enterprise and higher education were the chief beneficiaries of shifts between initial and present employment. This analysis is complicated by the relatively high percentage (seven percent) of alumni for whom no information on current employers was available.

Employer shifts by year of graduation are presented in Table 31. These data reflect both the employment (and military) conditions existing when the alumni finished college and the actual trends in their careers. Thus, a high percentage of the 1953 and 1958 classes went directly from the campus to military — eight percent of the most recent class is still in military service. Contrasting the three benchmark groups, one notices a slight trend away from the private sector with corresponding gains scattered among various employers in the public sector.

Liberal arts graduates tend to work for a large organization, two-thirds of alumni reporting they are affiliated with organizations having over 100 employees. (TABLE 32)   Relatively few (nine percent) are employed by organizations having under four employees. Older graduates are more likely to be with small organizations, reflecting their higher rate of self-employment or work in professional practice. Almost a quarter of the more recent graduates work for organizations with over 10,000 employees.

Type of employer is related to the size of the employing organization. (TABLE 32)   Large organizations are characteristic of private manufacturing, research organizations, and colleges and universities, and, of course, federal and local governments and the U.S. military services. Thus, almost half of the graduates who work for private manufacturing concerns report their organizations employ 10,000 or more. Alumni employed in agriculture, hospitals, churches, and clinics, and private non-manufacturing concerns tend to work for smaller organizations.

Scientists and mathematicians are the most likely to work for very large organizations. (TABLE 32)   Nearly half of the lawyers and a majority of the clergymen report they work with 10 or fewer people.

Relatively few liberal arts graduates supervise significant numbers of either sub-professional or professional and managerial employees. (TABLE 33)   Thirty-six percent supervise no sub-professional employees, and 42 percent no managerial or professional persons. Obviously, older alumni are much more likely to have supervisory responsibilities. As might be expected, higher numbers of subordinates were reported within the military services than in other types of employment. Surprisingly high were the large numbers of persons supervised by graduates employed by elementary and secondary schools. Data in this table should be regarded with caution because of the large percentage of graduates who failed to answer the inquiry about number of employees supervised.

One out of every seven respondents is currently self-employed. (TABLE 34) Self-employment is much more typical of the older graduates. Twice as many alumni are self-employed on their current position as on their first job. Totals for those who were ever self-employed are only slightly higher than those for graduates currently working for themselves, suggesting that relatively few graduates have left self-employment. The alumni total of 14 percent self-employed compares favorably with the national average of 13 percent for all workers.

The occupations of liberal arts graduates are difficult to compare with results from other alumni studies because of different time periods and survey techniques. Many of the national figures developed by the U. S. Bureau of Labor Statistics use definitions too broad to be compared with our figures. For example, among persons reported working as chemists in one set of BLS statistics, only 69 percent were college graduates. [6]

One roughly comparable study that was made by the Bureau of Social Science Research (TABLE 35) is presented in Table 37. In contrast to the cross-sectional group, liberal arts alumni are found more frequently in science and mathematics, in sales and in creative fields, and less often in elementary and secondary teaching, in fiscal, office, and management positions, and, of course, in engineering. Since this BSSR study questioned alumni only two years after graduation, it must be assumed that many students were still completing advanced education. Accurate comparisons were thus not possible regarding law, college teaching, and medical fields.

How does type of employer distinguish liberal arts alumni from graduates from other fields of study? Some indication is provided in Table 35 which compares the results from our liberal arts study with a nationwide study of male graduates from all fields, analyzed two years after graduation, and with a general survey of engineering alumni from all graduating classes who are still employed. This comparison shows that liberal arts alumni are less heavily represented in private manufacturing concerns than are either of the other two groups. Yet, when private non-manufacturing concerns are included, the liberal arts graduates do not differ especially from the cross-section of all male graduates. The engineering alumni are the least heavily represented in all types of educational employment. Liberal arts alumni, on the other hand, are the most likely to be employed in colleges and universities, while they are less likely than the cross-section sample to be employed in elementary or secondary schools.

Looking at the distribution of occupations by type of employer (TABLE 36) it is noted that over three-fourths of the lawyers are employed by private businesses (non-manufacturing) — this category includes those self-employed and members of private law firms. Most of the remaining lawyers (13 percent) work for a federal, state, or local government. Clergymen, salesmen, and teachers at all levels are employed within anticipated employer categories. Social service workers, fiscal, office, and management workers, and scientists and mathematicians are spread over the widest range of employers. More medical workers are in private practice than are employed by hospitals and clinics.

Alumni Earnings

As Becker has pointed out, it is impossible to relate income directly to differences in education received.[7] No study is likely to compensate entirely for such key variables as native intelligence, aptitude for work, cultural background, and family-encouraged motivation. Becker estimates that college graduates receive a return of from 10 to 12 percent per annum on their investment in a college education, but this finding is biased, of course, by the effect of general ability on earnings.[8]

The ideal research design, and it was seriously considered, would stratify each alumnus first by years since graduation and then by both advanced education and specific occupation. Comparisons of earnings of high school teachers with master's degrees five years after completing their undergraduate work or lawyers who completed the bachelor's degree requirements fifteen years earlier would be more meaningful. Such stratification, however, simply was not practical.

Even salary figures themselves may be misleading. For example, the $7,000 per year earned by a clergyman does not reflect his car allowance, the donated manse, and possible additional income from performing special services. Equally distorted may be the use of the raw salary of $50,000 for the business executive who has to live in an expensive neighborhood, belong to appropriate clubs and entertain freely at them, contribute to civic and political activities, and yet pay a third or more of his income in taxes. Furthermore, job pressure or lack of tenure affect the worth of any position. In speaking to his faculty colleagues, Horn said:

> The time is coming when a teacher cannot command the salary of a Madison Avenue advertising executive for an academic year and at the same time be guaranteed the security that no one in any other line of work enjoys. [9]

A common and hard-to-answer question comes from college seniors who ask about the merits of paying to acquire a master's degree in business administration or beginning their careers immediately. In exploring the effect of the M.B.A. on earnings and job satisfaction, holders of M.B.A. degrees report higher than average salaries. Top students among undergraduates were four times as likely to be in the $21,000 plus bracket as all others, including the many with advanced degrees in other fields.

A final consideration is non-salary income from job-related sources (bonuses, consulting fees, etc.) which may influence choice of occupation and may not be indicated on straight salary surveys. Because of such considerations, straight salary figures must be used with some allowance for "windage."

In studying the salaries of liberal arts alumni, it is obvious that earnings are closely related to year of graduation. (TABLE 38) Whereas only 16 percent of the five-year graduates earned $10,000 or more, comparable figures for the ten-year and fifteen-year graduates were 43 percent and 61 percent.

By type of employer, the highest earnings are received by graduates employed in private non-manufacturing, followed by those in private manufacturing and research organizations and institutes. (TABLE 39)   Agriculture shows the largest percentages in both the lowest and highest salary brackets, in part the result of the small size of the agriculture sample. The lowest salaries are listed by employees of elementary and secondary schools and of hospitals, churches and clinics.

For the clearest picture of salary distinctions by type of employer it is necessary to look at data based on alumni 15 years after college. Here, little bias exists because of short-term military service or of longer periods in graduate or professional study. Excluding agriculture, the highest earnings are reported by those employed in private manufacturing and non-manufacturing and in research organizations and institutes. (TABLE 40)   The lowest salaries are earned by graduates working for elementary and secondary schools and for hospitals, churches and clinics.

Earnings by occupations show that medical workers, salesmen, lawyers, and fiscal, office, and management workers are the most likely to be in the top earnings brackets. (TABLE 39)   In the lowest brackets are the clergy and elementary and secondary teachers. Interestingly enough, many medical workers also are in the lowest salary classification, probably reflecting the very low incomes of those still in internship and residency.

When we compare the salaries of alumni five and fifteen years after college, we find that medical workers display low salaries five years after graduation, as do lawyers. For medical workers in the 15-year group, however, half report incomes of $21,000 a year or more. Clergymen report the lowest salaries of all occupations at both stages of their careers. Despite the publicized earnings of scientists and mathematicians they earn less 15 years after college than do salesmen, fiscal, office, and management workers, and even creative workers.

Income seems closely related to amount of supervision assumed on the job. While some alumni with high incomes supervise few employees, there is a definite tendency for those with large numbers of subordinates to appear in the highest earnings brackets. Overall, a third of the graduates supervise no one, another third supervise from one to three employees, and the final third supervise four or more employees. This final third reports the highest average income. The tendency would be even more pronounced if self-employed professionals (doctors, lawyers, etc.) with high incomes and few subordinates were eliminated from the analysis. Again, as with earlier tables dealing with number of employees supervised, the large percentage of respondents not answering must be noted.

How do salaries of liberal arts alumni compare with earnings of their classmates in specialized and technical fields? Using somewhat comparable figures, liberal arts alumni may be contrasted with engineers for similar periods since graduation.[10]   (TABLE 41)

These figures, and those from related studies,[11] give rise to a "Tortoise and Hare" theory about liberal arts alumni: They start out at lower salaries than those of graduates from other fields, but in 10 or 15 years they catch up.

FOOTNOTES

1. *Decade of Decision: Yale Class of Nineteen Forty-Six, 1946–1956.* New Haven, Conn. Yale Class of 1946, 1956, p. 10.

2. *Harvard Education 1948: The Student's View.* Cambridge, Mass., Harvard University Student Council, 1949, p. 7.

3. "The Careful Young Men." *Nation,* Vol. 84, March 9, 1957, p. 208.

4. *1956 Annual Report: Carnegie Corporation of New York: The Search for Talent,* p. 11.

5. When used in tables, "Other occupations" refers only to the composite of remaining fields as shown in the occupational index.

6. Wolfe, Dael, *America's Resources of Specialized Talent.* New York, Harper and Brothers, 1954, p. 81.

7. Becker, Gary S., *Human Capital.* New York, National Bureau of Economic Research, 1964, p. 79.

8. *Ibid.,* p. 154.

9. Horn, Francis H., "Forces Shaping the College of Arts and Science," *Liberal Education,* Vol. 50, No. 1, March, 1964, p. 10.

FOOTNOTES - Continued

10. As the questionnaire asked general salary ranges only, all salaries between $1 and $4,000 were estimated to be $3,000 and over all $25,000 were estimated to be $30,000. Within the other ranges, salaries were assumed to be at the midpoint.

11. See the following unpublished studies: Kelly, Walter K., *Follow-up Survey of Graduates of 1946, 1951, 1956*, New York University Placement Service, 1957; *Two Years After the College Degree, op.cit.; 1948 Survey of Notre Dame Alumni*, Alumni Association of Notre Dame, South Bend, Indiana.

TABLE 30

First and Current Types of Occupations

	All Graduates		15 Years		10 Years		5 Years	
	First Job	Current Job	First Job	Current Job	First Job	Current Job	First Job	Current Job
Lawyer	5.0%	6.8%	5.3%	6.4%	4.8%	7.9%	4.9%	6.1%
Clergyman	4.0	3.9	4.0	4.1	4.7	4.3	3.2	3.2
El-Sec. T.	7.1	11.8	8.6	11.6	5.9	11.1	6.9	12.7
College T.	8.6	5.3	10.0	7.2	6.6	5.4	9.1	3.2
Salesman	8.8	9.6	10.8	10.0	7.3	10.2	8.4	8.8
Social Ser.	4.4	4.0	4.3	3.9	3.4	4.0	5.4	4.3
Medical	8.4	8.5	7.4	7.7	9.4	9.7	8.4	8.1
Sci-Math.	12.9	11.9	14.3	11.7	12.3	12.2	12.1	11.9
Fis-Off-Mgt.	17.1	16.9	19.9	19.0	15.7	16.5	15.7	15.4
Creative	4.0	3.9	4.5	4.6	3.7	4.3	3.8	3.0
Other	17.9	9.5	9.7	8.5	25.4	8.8	18.4	11.3
No answer	1.8	7.9	1.2	5.3	0.8	5.6	3.7	12.0
Total	100.0%	100.0%	100.0%	100.0%	100.0%	100.0%	100.0%	100.0%

TABLE 31

First and Current Types of Employers of Liberal Arts Graduates

	First Employer				Current Employer			
		Years Since Graduation				Years Since Graduation		
		15	10	5		15	10	5
Private Manufacturing	16.8%	20.3%	17.1%	13.3%	17.9%	19.6%	19.0%	15.2%
Private Non-Manufacturing	25.6	30.9	21.6	24.4	29.7	33.2	31.3	24.7
Agriculture	0.3	0.4	0.3	0.2	0.3	0.4	0.4	0.2
Elem-Second. Schools	10.7	12.4	8.6	11.1	10.3	10.1	10.2	10.5
Colleges-Universities	6.9	8.2	5.6	6.9	8.8	10.2	8.8	7.6
U.S. Military Service	14.2	3.6	23.9	14.8	4.5	1.8	3.6	7.9
Federal Government	5.2	5.9	4.4	5.4	5.5	5.4	5.2	5.9
State-Local Govt.	4.6	4.9	3.8	5.2	4.1	3.8	4.0	4.5
Research Organiz.	2.5	2.3	2.0	3.0	2.6	2.3	2.7	2.9
Hospital-Church-Clinic	11.3	10.2	12.1	11.6	8.8	7.9	9.3	9.1
Other	0.2	0.2	0.1	0.4	0.3	0.3	0.2	0.2
No Answer	1.7	0.7	0.5	3.7	7.2	5.0	5.3	11.3
Total	100.0%	100.0%	100.0%	100.0%	100.0%	100.0%	100.0%	100.0%

Δ Alumni in the sample are fairly evenly distributed between the private and public sectors of the economy.

More of the liberal arts alumni are employed with the federal government than with state and local government, although state and local governments employ half again as many people as do the federal agencies.

TABLE 32

Size of Employing Organization

Approximately how many other people work for the total organization by which you are employed?

Type of Employer	Under 4	4-10	11-40	41-100	101-1,000	1,000-3,000	3,001-10,000	Over 10,000	No Answer	Total
All Graduates	9.1%	6.7	7.6	6.8	23.2	10.1	11.1	21.0	4.4	100.0%
Private Manufactur.	1.0%	1.3	3.5	4.1	16.7	11.2	18.0	43.8	0.4	100.0%
Private Non-Manufact.	20.1%	14.6	12.8	7.4	16.1	7.8	8.7	9.1	3.4	100.0%
Agriculture	43.3%	18.9	16.2	8.1	2.7	5.4	2.7	--	2.7	100.0%
Elem-Second. Schools	0.4%	1.2	10.0	16.3	45.7	9.1	7.8	8.8	0.7	100.0%
Colleges-Universities	0.3%	0.6	3.5	9.9	46.4	19.3	13.5	4.4	2.1	100.0%
U.S. Military Service	--	0.6	0.2	1.0	1.2	1.2	1.2	92.2	2.4	100.0%
Fed. Govt.	0.3%	1.0	2.3	1.5	16.0	15.0	17.7	44.7	1.5	100.0%
State-Local Govt.	1.3%	4.5	7.8	6.5	37.4	10.9	14.3	16.7	0.6	100.0%
Research Organiz.	4.2%	4.2	4.2	3.9	22.8	20.4	20.4	18.6	1.3	100.0%
Hospital-Church Clin.	20.0%	12.4	7.7	5.2	25.8	10.2	6.6	8.4	3.7	100.0%

TABLE 32 - Continued

	Under 4	4-10	11-40	41-100	101-1,000	1,000-3,000	3,001-10,000	Over 10,000	No Answer	Total
All Graduates	9.1%	6.7	7.6	6.8	23.2	10.1	11.1	21.0	4.4	100.0%
Type of Occupation										
Lawyer	27.3%	20.4	15.7	7.4	10.3	3.8	4.2	8.0	2.9	100.0%
Clergyman	38.9%	18.1	2.9	2.4	10.7	2.9	7.8	13.3	3.0	100.0%
Elem-Second.Schools	0.4%	1.4	9.3	15.7	44.8	9.4	8.3	9.2	1.5	100.0%
College Teacher	0.4%	0.2	3.5	12.3	53.4	15.8	9.5	3.3	1.6	100.0%
Salesman	8.9%	8.2	9.9	6.5	19.1	10.4	16.0	20.0	1.0	100.0%
Social Serv. Worker	2.1%	6.6	11.2	5.5	34.4	10.9	11.2	17.8	0.3	100.0%
Medical Worker	27.5%	10.8	3.9	1.9	14.6	8.9	5.1	19.0	8.3	100.0%
Scientist-Math.	1.5%	1.7	2.6	3.2	17.5	16.0	19.3	37.3	0.9	100.0%
Fiscal-Office-Mgmt.	4.5%	7.3	10.4	7.6	21.6	12.2	13.1	23.1	0.2	100.0%
Creative	7.9%	7.0	8.6	9.3	29.8	12.6	11.0	11.0	2.8	100.0%
Other	4.1%	4.0	4.6	3.3	13.0	7.7	10.9	51.0	1.4	100.0%

△ Liberal arts graduates are affiliated with large organizations.
Two-thirds work for organizations with over 100 employees.
A fourth are employed in organizations of over 10,000.

TABLE 33

Type and Number of Employees Supervised

How many employees do you directly supervise?

| | Clerical, Laboratory and Sub-Professional | | | | | | | Professional and Managerial | | | | | | |
	None	1-3	4-10	11-20	Over 20	No A.	Total	None	1-3	4-10	11-20	Over 20	No A.	Total
All Graduates	35.5%	30.4	12.9	3.4	5.8	12.0	100.0%	42.4%	15.4	9.7	2.9	4.4	25.2	100.0%
Years Since Graduation														
Fifteen	25.0%	34.1	16.9	4.4	8.2	11.4	100.0%	31.6%	18.5	13.2	4.6	7.1	25.0	100.0%
Ten	34.6%	33.3	12.9	3.0	4.6	11.6	100.0%	42.8%	17.0	10.0	2.2	3.7	24.3	100.0%
Five	46.4%	23.9	9.2	2.8	4.7	13.0	100.0%	52.4%	10.8	5.7	1.9	2.6	26.6	100.0%
Type of Employer														
Priv. Manuf.	35.0%	29.6	13.2	4.3	7.5	10.4	100.0%	41.8%	16.6	11.4	3.0	4.4	22.8	100.0%
Priv. Non-Mf.	25.6%	39.3	15.3	3.9	5.9	10.0	100.0%	37.0%	18.6	9.5	2.3	3.0	29.6	100.0%
Agriculture	27.0%	29.7	13.5	2.7	13.5	13.6	100.0%	29.7%	16.2	8.1	2.7	2.7	40.6	100.0%
El-Sec. Sch.	64.0%	9.5	7.0	1.6	2.8	15.1	100.0%	61.1%	5.0	5.9	5.6	9.7	12.7	100.0%
Coll-Univ.	43.0%	32.1	11.5	2.5	3.2	7.7	100.0%	52.1%	13.3	7.3	2.1	3.0	22.2	100.0%
U.S. Mil.	20.0%	23.1	18.8	5.4	19.4	13.3	100.0%	27.5%	18.6	16.7	5.0	12.8	19.4	100.0%
Federal Government	40.3%	34.0	12.7	4.0	2.5	6.5	100.0%	47.2%	15.0	10.3	3.3	3.5	20.7	100.0%
St-Loc. Govt.	33.2%	36.3	14.7	3.1	4.2	8.5	100.0%	39.2%	19.5	14.9	2.0	3.6	20.8	100.0%
Research Org.	34.4%	39.6	13.3	3.2	5.3	4.2	100.0%	47.0%	14.4	10.9	2.8	2.8	22.1	100.0%
Hosp-Ch-Clin.	34.1%	32.2	13.3	3.4	6.1	10.9	100.0%	39.0%	19.5	10.4	2.4	2.9	25.8	100.0%

TABLE 33 - Continued

| | Clerical, laboratory and sub-professional | | | | | | | Professional and Managerial | | | | | | |
	None	1-3	4-10	11-20	Over 20	No A.	Total	None	1-3	4-10	11-20	Over 20	No A	Total
All Graduates	35.5%	30.4	12.9	3.4	5.8	12.0	100.0%	42.4%	15.4	9.7	2.9	4.4	25.2	100.0%
Type of Occupation														
Lawyer	17.7%	65.6	8.8	1.6	0.5	5.8	100.0%	40.1%	19.0	4.8	0.7	0.8	34.6	100.0%
Clergyman	40.4%	39.2	9.5	2.1	1.7	7.1	100.0%	48.2%	16.2	4.0	0.7	1.4	29.5	100.0%
Elem-Second. Teach.	61.6%	10.6	7.6	1.8	3.0	15.4	100.0%	60.1%	5.6	6.1	5.1	9.0	14.1	100.0%
College Teacher	45.7%	31.0	9.3	2.1	3.9	8.0	100.0%	54.3%	12.3	7.0	3.2	4.0	19.2	100.0%
Salesman	48.9%	25.9	10.2	2.1	2.1	10.8	100.0%	53.9%	12.9	7.6	1.7	2.5	21.4	100.0%
Social Serv. Worker	33.3%	40.1	13.4	2.7	2.3	8.2	100.0%	40.8%	21.6	15.3	2.1	2.7	17.5	100.0%
Medical Worker	19.4%	41.7	18.2	4.9	6.7	9.1	100.0%	29.7%	21.8	9.2	2.1	2.3	34.9	100.0%
Scientist-Math.	35.7%	37.3	14.2	2.5	3.4	6.9	100.0%	44.5%	18.7	9.4	2.2	2.0	23.2	100.0%
Fis-Off-Mgt.	20.4%	26.9	20.2	7.7	13.9	10.9	100.0%	28.7%	19.5	14.8	4.3	7.1	25.6	100.0%
Creative Worker	36.6%	31.5	11.7	3.0	3.7	13.5	100.0%	43.1%	15.6	12.8	2.8	3.0	22.7	100.0%
Other	34.3%	24.9	14.3	3.4	11.7	11.4	100.0%	38.7%	15.4	14.7	3.9	7.5	19.8	100.0%

△ Despite association with large institutions, our respondents tend to supervise relatively few employees.

TABLE 34

Extent of Self-Employment

		Years Since Graduation		
	All Graduates	15	10	5
First Job				
Self-Employed	5.8%	8.6%	4.8%	4.1%
Not Self-Employed	92.8	91.1	94.8	92.3
No Answer	1.4	0.3	0.4	3.6
Total	100.0%	100.0%	100.0%	100.0%
Current Job				
Self-Employed	13.8%	20.1%	14.4%	7.1%
Not Self-Employed	79.2	75.2	80.4	81.9
No Answer	7.0	4.7	5.2	11.0
Total	100.0%	100.0%	100.0%	100.0%
Ever Self-Employed				
Self-Employed	14.6%	22.0%	15.6%	6.6%
Not Self-Employed	84.0	77.7	84.0	90.0
No Answer	1.4	0.3	0.4	3.4
Total	100.0%	100.0%	100.0%	100.0%

▷ One out of seven is self-employed, a rate comparable to the national rate.

TABLE 35

Employers of Liberal Arts Graduates, Graduates from All Fields and Engineering Graduates

Type of Employer	Male Liberal Arts Graduates	Male Graduates from All Fields	Engineering Graduates (largely Male)
Private Manufactur.	19.3%	26.1%	64.2%
Private Non-Manufact.	32.0	24.2	12.1
Agriculture	0.3	0.4	--
Elem-Second. Schools	11.1	20.8	--
Colleges-Universities	9.5	7.2	2.7
U.S. Military Service	4.9	--	--
Federal Government	5.9	6.0	11.1
State-Local Govt.	4.4	5.0	5.8
Research Organiz.	2.8	--	4.1
Hospital-Church Clin.	9.5	4.6	--
Other	0.3	5.7	--
Total	100.0%	100.0%	100.0%

SOURCES OF DATA

Liberal Arts

> Source of data is this study. The percentage of non-respondents has been eliminated to conform with the handling of data in the other two studies.

All Fields

> Based on 1958 graduates studies in 1960 from *Two Years After the College Degree*, Bureau of Social Science Research, Washington, D.C. Prepared for the NSF. Washington, D.C., U.S. Government Printing Office, 1963, p. 51.

Engineers

> From a survey of 23,618 engineering graduates from all classes, from *Professional Income of Engineers, 1964*. New York, Engineers Joint Council, 1964, p. 12.

TABLE 36

Occupational Distribution of Alumni by Type of Employer

Type of Occupation	Pvt. Man.	Pvt. Non-Man.	Agricul-ture	El-Sec. School	Coll.& Univ.	U.S. Mil.	Fed. Govt.	St & L Govt	Res. Org.	Hosp. Church	N.A.	Total
All Graduates	17.9%	29.7	0.3	10.3	8.8	4.5	5.5	4.1	2.6	8.8	7.5	100.0%
Lawyer	3.9%	78.5	--	--	0.4	2.6	6.8	6.6	--	0.3	0.9	100.0%
Clergyman	--	0.2	--	0.2	0.7	1.7	--	0.2	--	96.7	0.3	100.0%
Elem-Second. Teach	0.6%	1.0	--	81.7	9.9	0.8	1.1	1.5	0.3	2.9	0.2	100.0%
College Teacher	--	--	--	--	99.8	--	--	--	0.2	--	--	100.0%
Salesman	41.3%	56.7	0.1	--	--	--	0.1	0.3	0.5	0.3	0.7	100.0%
Social Serv. Worker	2.7%	6.4	--	3.4	13.4	1.1	13.0	28.7	6.4	24.2	0.7	100.0%
Medical Worker	0.8%	43.4	--	--	3.7	14.8	3.0	2.3	0.7	30.3	1.0	100.0%
Scientist-Math.	49.4%	9.6	0.1	0.1	7.9	1.1	12.6	5.0	13.2	1.0	0.0	100.0%
Fiscal-Office-Mgmt.	28.7%	55.2	0.3	1.9	1.1	0.2	4.7	2.9	1.7	2.7	0.6	100.0%
Creative Worker	18.7%	67.1	--	0.2	3.3	0.5	3.3	0.5	1.9	3.3	1.2	100.0%
Other	19.1%	14.9	2.8	0.7	2.1	27.4	17.3	10.5	2.7	2.3	0.2	100.0%

──────────── **TABLE 37** ────────────

Occupations of Liberal Arts Graduates and Graduates from all Fields

Occupation	Male Liberal Arts Graduates (5 years after graduation only)	Male Graduates from All Fields (2 years after graduation only)
Lawyer	6.1%	--
Clergyman	3.2	2.1%
Elem-Second. Teach.	12.7	21.4
College Teacher	3.2	3.1
Salesman	8.8	8.0
Social Serv. Worker	4.3	2.3
Medical Worker	8.1	3.5
Scientist-Math.	11.9	5.4
Fiscal-Office-Mgmt.	15.4	23.6
Creative Worker	3.0	1.3
Engineers	--	19.1
Other and no answer	23.3	10.2
Totals	100.0%	100.0%

SOURCES OF DATA

Liberal arts: This study, by classes.
All fields: *Two Years After the College Degree, op. cit.,* p. 46-47.

──────────── **TABLE 38** ────────────

Current Annual Salary Levels by Years Since Graduation

What is your current annual salary in your present position?

Annual Salary	All Graduates	Years Since Graduation		
		15	10	5
Under $4000	2.9%	1.4%	1.7%	5.4%
4000-5999	8.1	3.7	6.3	13.9
6000-7999	20.4	10.6	19.0	30.9
8000-9999	19.2	15.4	22.4	19.9
10,000-11,999	13.8	16.3	16.3	8.9
12,000-14,999	11.1	16.5	12.6	4.3
15,000-17,999	5.6	10.0	5.9	1.2
18,000-20,999	3.6	6.7	3.6	0.6
21,000-24,999	1.2	2.7	0.9	0.0
25,000 and over	4.1	8.5	3.4	0.7
No answer	10.0	8.2	7.9	14.2
Total	100.0%	100.0%	100.0%	100.0%

─────────────────────────── **TABLE 39** ───────────────────────────

Current Annual Salaries by Employer and Occupation

What is your current annual salary in your present position?

	Under $6000	$6000- 9000	$10,000- 14,999	$15,000- 20,999	$21,000 & over	No Answer	Total
All Graduates	11.0%	39.6	24.9	9.2	5.3	10.0	100.0%
Type of Employer							
Private Manufactur.	2.7%	36.6	39.8	13.6	5.6	1.7	100.0%
Private Non-Manufact.	6.1%	33.5	26.5	16.8	11.7	5.4	100.0%
Agriculture	27.0%	27.0	10.8	10.8	16.2	8.2	100.0%
Elem-Second. Schools	21.7%	64.0	11.0	0.5	0.5	2.3	100.0%
Colleges-Universities	13.3%	54.4	24.8	3.9	0.7	2.9	100.0%
U.S. Military Service	6.0%	56.8	32.2	1.5	0.4	3.1	100.0%
Federal Government	5.5%	48.9	38.2	5.8	0.2	1.4	100.0%
State Local Govt.	5.5%	48.9	38.2	5.8	0.2	1.4	100.0%
Research Organiz.	6.3%	31.6	42.1	14.0	3.9	2.1	100.0%
Hospital-Church Clin.	43.0%	35.0	9.8	3.7	4.6	3.9	100.0%
Type of Occupation							
Lawyer	5.1%	30.2	31.0	18.0	9.2	6.5	100.0%
Clergyman	47.8%	45.4	4.0	0.2	--	2.6	100.0%
Elem-Second. Teach.	22.1%	62.2	11.8	0.7	0.5	2.7	100.0%
College Teacher	10.2%	56.8	25.9	3.7	0.7	2.7	100.0%
Salesman	3.4%	38.3	32.1	14.0	9.1	3.1	100.0%
Social Serv. Worker	9.8%	57.6	25.7	4.3	1.4	1.2	100.0%
Medical Worker	21.2%	17.8	15.0	19.2	20.7	6.1	100.0%
Scientist-Math.	4.2%	39.3	43.8	10.0	1.3	1.4	100.0%
Fiscal-Office-Mgmt.	7.7%	41.7	27.1	12.8	7.8	2.9	100.0%
Creative Worker	11.2%	36.6	31.5	11.4	5.1	4.2	100.0%
Other	7.0%	48.0	33.3	7.2	2.2	2.3	100.0%

▷ Salary is influenced sharply by occupation.

Highest incomes are reported by medical workers, lawyers, salesmen, and fiscal, office, and management workers.

In the low salary brackets are clergymen, elementary and secondary teachers, and medical workers still in internships and residencies.

Despite the recent public attention given them, scientists and mathematicians are not among the highest-paid graduates.

Salaries are somewhat related to number of employees supervised and directly related to the length of time since graduation.

TABLE 40

Current Annual Salary by Type of Employer
(15-year Graduates Only)

What is your current annual salary in your present position?

	Under $6000	$6000- 9999	$10,000- 14,999	$15,000- 20,999	$21,000 & over	No Answer	Total
Fifteen-year Graduates	5.1%	26.0	32.8	16.7	11.2	8.2	100.0%
Type of Employer							
Private Manufactur.	0.9%	18.7	41.9	25.1	12.0	1.4	100.0%
Private Non-Manufact.	2.7%	16.6	28.5	24.6	20.9	6.7	100.0%
Agriculture	13.3%	26.6	20.0	6.7	26.7	6.7	100.0%
Elem-Second. Schools	11.5%	55.7	28.6	1.1	0.6	2.5	100.0%
Colleges-Univ.	4.2%	44.2	40.3	7.9	1.7	1.7	100.0%
U.S. Mil.	4.8%	16.1	67.7	9.7	--	1.7	100.0%
Federal Government	1.1%	24.7	57.9	14.2	0.5	1.6	100.0%
State-Local Govt.	1.1%	24.7	57.9	14.2	0.5	1.6	100.0%
Research Organiz.	2.5%	8.8	40.0	35.0	11.3	2.4	100.0%
Hospital-Church Clin.	23.6%	38.9	15.7	5.4	11.4	5.0	100.0%

TABLE 41

Comparative Salaries for Liberal Arts and Engineering Graduates

Years Since Graduation	Liberal Arts Grads	Graduates Currently Employed in Engineering
Five	$8,000	$9,500
Ten	$10,870	$11,425
Fifteen	$13,050	$12,800

SOURCES OF DATA

Liberal Arts
> Source of data is this study, by classes. Years since graduation computed from 1963.

Engineering
> *Professional Income of Engineers, 1964.* New York, Engineers Joint Council, 1964, p. 13. Years since graduation computed from 1964.

5

CAREER PATTERNS of LIBERAL ARTS ALUMNI

Many students enroll in college to advance their own career prospects and this may be more significant than generally recognized. One of the rare studies of student concerns was made during the time when some of our graduates were in college. To learn how best to respond to student needs, the University of Wyoming asked its freshmen to rank the problems about which they were the most concerned. Instead of listing things which colleges were best prepared to handle (such as how to study, problems in group living, dating, and heterosexual relationships), the students indicated quite a different set of concerns. Their three most important problems were: (1) securing a post-college job, (2) securing practical experience in vocations, and (3) securing information about employment outlook and financial returns in various occupations. [1]

To learn about the careers of our sample of liberal arts graduates, this chapter examines their selection of occupational goals, job changes, the extent of unemployment during their careers, influence of military service, and their geographical mobility. Their evaluation of vocational guidance and job placement assistance also is reported.

Selection of Career Goals

Despite the fact that the survey was conducted five years after the youngest graduates completed college, 13 percent of the respondents report that they have not selected a career goal, 80 percent have a goal and are working toward it, nearly five percent have a goal but are not yet working toward it, and the remaining two percent did not answer.

Interestingly enough, older alumni are somewhat less likely to have a goal than the more recent graduates (15 percent lack a goal) — a result which perhaps reflects the uncertainty accompanying greater knowledge and longer opportunity for frustration or disillusionment about initial choices of careers.

Graduates with high academic records are somewhat more likely to have a career objective. By occupation, the clearest sense of career direction is shown by medical workers, college and university professors and lawyers. The greatest uncertainty is displayed by fiscal, office, and management workers, salesmen, and scientists and mathematicians.

While not shown, 18 percent of the alumni with only a bachelor's degree have not yet selected a career goal, contrasted to six percent of those with a doctor's degree. No particular distinctions are found by undergraduate major or by type of employer.

Sixteen percent of the respondents had chosen a career goal before entering college and an additional 23 percent made such a choice during their undergraduate years. (TABLE 42) More than half of the graduates, therefore, finished college before selecting their current career objective. Responses from older alumni show that career objectives are still being developed, or perhaps changed from earlier and unsatisfactory choices, long after college. Among those who finished undergraduate studies fifteen years prior to the survey, 13 percent report they selected a career goal over six years after leaving school.

How did the alumni feel about not selecting a permanent career goal until after college? Some were concerned, as indicated in these comments:

> Select a career as early as possible in your undergraduate work and explore all possibilities in promoting that career.   *University of Southern California*

> My main problem stems from failure to accept my own advice and to work on career choice and preparation while in college.   *Bowdoin College*

Typical of the majority, who deferred career choice until after graduation, were these comments:

> I would advise today's students to avoid making a fixed decision on careers until they have been out of college for a year or two. Many occupations which they never considered will be open to them.
>
> *Tulane University*

> I erred in making an unwise career choice and wasted my college years too narrowly preparing for them.
>
> *Tufts University*

> I am sorry that I did not understand or appreciate the real values of a liberal education. I was too concerned with preparing myself for a career. This was done later in professional school.
>
> *University of Michigan*

Of those alumni who went on to graduate or professional school, 81 percent had a "fairly clear idea" of their vocational goal before they began graduate training. (TABLE 43)   Science and mathematics majors and students with high academic records were slightly more likely to have a clear idea of their vocational goal.

Vocational Guidance and Placement Assistance

One goal of this survey was to document the role of college counseling and placement services. During service as Director of Placement at the University of California at Berkeley, the author became impressed with the resources for vocational assistance on the campus of today. How are these services rated by alumni?

The respondents indicate that they made rather limited use of college assistance in the area of vocational guidance. (TABLE 44)   The resource most often used and found to be helpful was the faculty, but even here less than half the graduates had actually sought and obtained advice from faculty members. Only one in four alumni had been aided by individual guidance counseling. Only one in six had been helped in career selection by a college placement service. (Some placement services, it should be noted, make no pretense of offering vocational guidance but limit their function strictly to job placement.) Except for faculty members, the most helpful source of advice about vocation was the non-professional assistance available from one's own family. [2]

Despite the rapid development and improvement of college placement offices since the end of World War II, relatively few of the liberal arts alumni credit them with much placement assistance. (TABLE 45) Direct personal application was the most common method of obtaining positions. For all but the first job, college placement offices were listed as less helpful than personal and professional contacts and private employment agencies. As the number of job changes rose, direct contact by the prospective new employee became an increasingly important factor. State employment offices were, consistently, the least useful of all the options provided.

In defense of the college placement office, it should be noted that the high percentage of alumni who went on for graduate study may not have registered for any assistance. Also, many who obtained their first job through "direct personal application" may have first learned of the opportunity from one of those crowded placement office bulletin boards, or those who said the "employer contacted me directly" may have been referring to contact within the formal campus interview program. Finally, the alumni were speaking of placement offices fifteen to five years earlier and improvements in the field have been obvious.

Despite these potential explanations, the lack of credit given to vocational guidance and placement services is cause for concern particularly since it was given by general education graduates who have a special need for career assistance.

The respondents volunteered many comments about how the college could have helped them more with career assistance. The following are illustrative:

> A better job of career counseling could be done by the liberal arts college. I wasted some time which might have been spent in more constructive pursuits.
> *Colgate University*

> Better vocational counseling during college would have raised me to an equivalent economic level five years ago. *Brooklyn College*

> My college guidance and placement assistance was not strong enough so that I could find a worthwhile job. *Duke University*

We need better placement at both undergraduate and
graduate levels. We need to expand the placement
staffs so that the office can actively search out employers instead of the current "wait and see" attitude toward job development.

University of California, Los Angeles

One of the two general questions in the survey questionnaire
which invited general comment was about career selection. It asked:
"What advice would you give today's liberal arts students about selecting their careers?" The following comments illustrate the wide
range of differing viewpoints:

Make it a point to get to know the college professors
in your field and benefit from their occupational and
education experience and knowledge. Also, talk with
prospective employers before going to find out what
qualities they are seeking in employees.

Montana State University

Think of a dozen jobs you might like and go watch
people performing them. Ask them questions about
their work.   *University of Arkansas*

Try to imagine what a typical day in 1975 will be
like for you.   *St. Anselm's College*

Plan a career area instead of a specific career.

Concordia College

Find the field which has the fewest graduates and
become the best in that small area.

University of Minnesota

Be happy with a compromise career. Intellectual
pursuits do not bring financial rewards per se.
Financial obligations, such as marriage, often do
not permit self-dedication to the world of truth and
beauty.   *University of Dayton*

Obtain summer work in your field of interest and not
in resorts or national parks.   *Ohio State University*

Don't always consider money first, 30 to 50 years
in a job is a long time to hate it. *Colgate University*

> I grew up in the Depression. After World War II, I
> wanted to earn dollars, lots of them. I did: and it
> was and is awful. *Stanford University*

> Forget what everyone else is doing and follow your
> own preferences. *University of California*

> Aim for the stars, but don't cry if you hit the moon.
> *Fordham University*

Alternative Job Opportunities

The alumni were asked to report on the number of actual job offers when they accepted their first and their current positions. For many, such as the person who entered a family business, one offer was ample. Yet, in view of the extensive interviewing which characterizes most searches for employment, the fact that two-thirds of the alumni had only one or two offers when they accepted their first position may be cause for concern. (TABLE 46)

Twice as many science and mathematics as social science and humanities graduates had five or more offers when the first job was accepted. More offers were reported when the current position was accepted. The distinction between the first and present job might be greater except for the fact that for many their current job is their first job and that many people accept a position during their career as a result of a single job offer. While there were few distinctions by years since graduation, academic record and quality of college, significant distinctions existed by highest degree held, and that is shown.

Frequent statements report difficulties obtaining the first position after college. Two comments are typical:

> One employer commented to me, "You have a fine
> background but what are you going to do with it and
> how does it apply to your possible employment with
> us?" *New York University*

> Although I graduated near the top of a class of 1,700,
> not one firm contacted me about employment while
> mediocre engineers received at least a dozen offers.
> *University of Southern California*

Job Changes During Career

The number of job changes during the liberal arts graduates' careers varies markedly by occupational fields and tends to concentrate in the early years after graduation. (TABLE 47) Five years after receiving their undergraduate degrees, 56 percent of the alumni had changed employers at least once. Fifteen years after graduation, 76 percent had changed initial employers.

The most mobile of all occupations is college teaching; less than two percent are still with their first employer, and two-thirds have worked for three or more organizations. This reflects the fact that many college teachers begin their careers while completing graduate study, advancements often result from job changes, and little stigma is attached to switching employers. Creative workers are also highly mobile. Among the least mobile are medical workers, scientists and mathematicians, clergymen, lawyers, and elementary and secondary school teachers.

A study also was made of the number of different job titles held by the graduates during their careers: 52.7 percent of all graduates held one job title, 30 percent had held two, 11.6 percent had held three, and 4.3 percent had held four or more titles. It is interesting to note that the older alumni, ten and fifteen years after graduation, were nearly equal in the number of titles held with the ten-year group having a slight edge, 48 percent had had only one title as compared to 49 percent of the fifteen-year group. This suggests that most changes in function occur within the first ten years after graduation.

As an illustration, only one job title might be held by the salesman who remained in that role despite several changes of employers. The graduate who advanced from salesman to purchasing agent to vice-president for international operations would have held three job titles, even though he remained with the same employing organization. More than half of all the graduates have remained in the same job title throughout their careers. The respondents indicate that their chief motivation for changing positions is a desire for better opportunities for advancement rather than a wish to earn more money. While 12 percent say their last jobs were terminated because the employer had to cut back staff or to close the business, only 1.3 percent report being actually "fired" for unsuitability.

Little information details why persons left jobs. An often-cited study which stated that 90 percent of all people who lost positions did so because of personality factors, for example, actually was based upon a limited survey made several decades ago by a Connecticut high school teacher.

A third of the alumni have never left a job and a sixth left because of actions taken by their employer. Among the remaining, 26 percent left their last position to obtain a better opportunity or because of dislike for their job assignment. Ten percent desired more money, four percent had specific geographical desires, two percent did not like those with whom they worked, and eight percent left for military service, personal reasons, or to enter full-time study.

Alumni made several pertinent comments regarding job-changing:

> I would advise a young graduate to change jobs frequently (every two or three years) in the early stages of his career. Broad experience is essential to success and this can not be achieved by staying with the same firm indefinitely.   *Union College*

> Be willing to change jobs to find what you like and where you fit. Be careful about taking a job "just for now." Plan and stick to it.   *Stanford University*

> The liberal arts graduate should not begin his first job with the intention of remaining with the particular employer or that particular career.   *Rutgers University*

Unemployment Since Graduation

More than two-thirds of the 11,000 liberal arts alumni report no experience with unemployment since graduation. (TABLE 48)   Eighteen percent have been out of work for three or more months and 10 percent for five or more months.   For some, these may have been periods of anticipating military service or waiting for graduate study to begin.   The most likely to report periods of unemployment are those with the poorest academic records and those who majored in the humanities.

Military Service

Military service has had a pronounced effect upon the lives of alumni for the past several decades. Three-fourths of the graduates have served in the armed forces, ranging from 88 percent of the 1948 graduates to 62 percent of the 1958 graduates. (TABLE 49) Most of them, particularly those who graduated in 1953 and 1958, were in the Army.

The timing of military service in the lives of graduates varied widely by year of graduation. Most of the 1948 alumni finished military duty before graduation from college, whereas more than half of the 1953 and 1958 alumni did their military service after college: 78.6 percent of the 1948 graduates performed their military duties before finishing college whereas 68.6 percent of the 1953 class completed their military requirements after graduation; a slightly smaller percentage of the 1958 class (53.4 percent) did military duty after college. Fourteen percent of the 1948 class were in military service both before and after college.

Of those alumni who had served on active duty, 42 percent were privates or corporals (or comparable ranks), 22 percent were higher non-commissioned officers, and 36 percent were commissioned officers.

Community Size and Geographical Location

The liberal arts alumni obviously are affected by the urbanization of the nation. Almost 85 percent of our graduates now live in cities, or suburbs of cities, of 10,000 or more. (TABLE 50) A comparison of present communities with those of the respondents' high school days shows a definite migration to the cities and to the suburbs of large metropolitan areas. The number who live in communities of less than 10,000 or in rural areas has declined by half.

The graduates were asked to report the geographic regions where they were born, where they graduated from high school, where they lived immediately after college, and where they currently live.

The distribution of alumni by region remains fairly constant for the various stages of life, although balancing shifts in and out may have occurred. (TABLE 51) Two noticeable shifts are a decline in the portion living in the Great Lakes and Plains regions and a proportionate increase in residents of the Far West. Twice as many graduates now live in the Far West as were born there.

Alumni had two general reactions to geographical location. First, they commented on the difficulty encountered in finding suitable employment in some of the states. Many, very naturally, wanted to work near where they attended college. This comment is typical:

> Upon graduation in 1958, I had great difficulty finding any job. This seemed to be due to the economic slump and to the remoteness of my school. I wasted one and a half years looking for work in my state. I should have moved immediately to a large metropolitan area. *Montana State College*

Others felt that in the Northeast, liberal education was the most highly regarded.

> Liberal arts education is still the most desirable in the Northeastern part of the country. *Boston College*

Most of the graduates (85 percent) live in cities — or suburbs of cities — of 10,000 or more, and they have tended to migrate to large metropolitan areas since their high school days. Geographically, there has been some movement away from the Great Lakes and Plains regions and to the Far West.

FOOTNOTES

1. Hendrix, O.R., "Student Problems," *Student Personnel Administration Newsletter,* Vol. 3, No. 4., March, 1950, New York, Teachers College, Columbia University.

2. Similar results were reported in a National Opinion Research Center study of 1961 college seniors. The most helpful sources of career advice were parents (60 percent were aided by them) and faculty members (57 percent). See Davis, James A., *Under-graduate Career Decisions.* Chicago, Ill., Aldine, 1965, p. 200.

──────────────── TABLE 42 ────────────────

Point in Life When Career Goal was Selected

If you have selected an occupational goal or career objective,
when did you make this selection?

		Years Since Graduation		
	All Graduates	15	10	5
Before entering college	15.8%	14.6%	16.5%	16.1%
During first three years of college	14.4	12.7	14.1	16.4
During senior year	8.7	8.7	7.0	10.3
During graduate school	9.3	7.9	9.6	10.3
During first three years after leaving school	19.2	14.5	17.9	24.9
Before four and six years after leaving school	10.3	9.6	12.7	8.7
Over six years after leaving school	7.0	13.4	7.4	0.3
No answer or other*	15.3	18.6	14.8	13.0
Total	100.0%	100.0%	100.0%	100.0%

* Some respondents specified "during military service" but did not indicate
years before or after college.

▷ More than half the graduates completed college before determining
upon a career objective.

──────────────── TABLE 43 ────────────────

Clarity of Career Goals Among Graduate Students

Agreement or disagreement with the statement, "I entered
graduate school with a fairly clear idea of my vocational goal."

	Strongly Agree	Agree	Disagree	Disagree	No Opinion	Total
All Graduates	43.2%	38.1	12.3	2.8	3.6	100.0%
Type of Major						
Science-Mathematics	48.2%	37.2	9.6	1.9	3.1	100.0%
Social Sciences	40.2%	37.7	14.5	3.4	4.2	100.0%
Humanities	40.5%	40.4	12.8	2.8	3.5	100.0%
Academic Record						
High	45.6%	37.8	11.8	2.3	2.5	100.0%
Average	42.5%	39.0	12.5	2.5	3.5	100.0%
Low	41.9%	39.2	12.1	2.5	4.3	100.0%

TABLE 44

Sources of Assistance in Career Selection

While you were in college, did you make use of the following sources of career assistance and how helpful was each in aiding you to select an occupation?

	Didn't use	Used, of no value	Used, somewhat helpful	Used, very helpful	No answer	Total
Vocational guidance tests	53.7%	18.7	21.3	3.5	2.8	100.0%
Individual vocaional counseling	62.0%	13.9	16.7	4.1	3.3	100.0%
Occupational reading materials	50.2%	13.3	27.3	5.2	4.0	100.0%
Advice from family	39.2%	19.0	29.5	9.3	3.0	100.0%
Advice from potential employers	59.0%	8.1	20.4	8.6	3.9	100.0%
Advice from faculty members	36.9%	13.1	32.6	14.1	3.3	100.0%
Part-time and summer jobs	54.1%	12.8	17.3	11.7	4.1	100.0%
College placement services	63.5%	16.2	11.3	4.7	4.3	100.0%

▷ Graduates made little use of their schools' formal vocational guidance services.

More useful help in selecting career objectives came from their own families and from faculty members.

—————————————— TABLE 45 ——————————————

Sources of Assistance in Job Placement

Which was the single most helpful source responsible for your obtaining each of the jobs you have held?

	First Job	Second Job	Third Job	Fourth Job	Fifth Job
College placement office	12.5%	5.4%	3.6%	3.4%	3.6%
Faculty adviser or professor	8.4	4.9	4.1	2.6	2.7
Direct personal application	36.9	36.8	36.7	36.1	34.0
Private employment agencies	4.2	5.6	5.7	5.5	4.6
State employment services	1.4	1.4	1.7	1.8	2.2
Family contacts	9.0	6.4	4.3	2.9	2.4
Personal friends	8.4	12.0	12.0	13.2	11.5
Want ads	2.4	4.3	4.6	4.9	5.3
Professional societies or contacts	4.3	6.3	7.6	8.8	9.3
New employer contacted me directly	6.3	12.3	16.2	17.2	19.5
Other	6.2	4.6	3.5	3.6	4.9
Total	100.0%	100.0%	100.0%	100.0%	100.0%
Number of Cases	(10,381)	(7164)	(4185)	(2207)	(1065)

▷ College placement services were reportedly of some help in finding graduates' first jobs, although direct personal application was much more successful in obtaining both the first and all subsequent jobs.

─── **TABLE 46** ───

Number of Job Offers for Current Position

*Approximately how many solid job opportunities did you have
at the time you accepted your current job?*

	One	Two	Three or four	Five or more	No answer	Total
All Graduates	37.3%	19.0	23.2	11.3	9.2	100.0%
Years Since Graduation						
Fifteen	38.7%	19.5	22.9	10.7	8.2	100.0%
Ten	37.5%	18.7	25.2	11.2	7.4	100.0%
Five	35.8%	18.8	21.7	11.9	11.8	100.0%
Type of Major						
Science and Math.	34.4%	17.5	21.7	14.6	11.8	100.0%
Social Sciences	38.6%	19.6	24.2	9.5	8.1	100.0%
Humanities	39.3%	19.9	23.4	10.0	7.4	100.0%

▷ More than half of the alumni had only one or two solid job alternatives
when they accepted their current jobs.

─── **TABLE 47** ───

Number of Different Employers

	One	Two	Three	Four	Five	Six or Seven	Eight or nine	No Answer	Total
All Graduates	29.3%	28.4	19.8	11.5	5.2	3.3	0.8	1.7	100.0%
Years Since Graduation									
Fifteen	23.1%	23.4	21.4	15.6	8.2	6.0	1.4	0.9	100.0%
Ten	24.0%	28.3	23.3	14.1	5.7	3.4	0.6	0.6	100.0%
Five	40.4%	33.2	14.9	5.0	1.8	0.7	0.3	3.7	100.0%
Current Occupation									
Lawyer	31.0%	29.2	21.9	9.7	4.2	2.8	0.1	1.1	100.0%
Clergyman	35.2%	27.3	20.4	10.2	3.6	2.8	0.2	0.3	100.0%
El-Sec. T.	33.9%	27.0	18.7	11.9	5.0	2.7	0.4	0.4	100.0%
College T.	2.1%	31.5	31.0	19.3	8.4	6.5	1.2	-	100.0%
Salesman	22.1%	31.0	22.6	13.5	5.4	4.1	1.2	0.1	100.0%
Social Ser.	19.6%	27.8	22.3	15.7	9.8	3.6	0.7	0.5	100.0%
Medical	36.3%	31.0	14.8	11.0	4.1	1.7	0.2	0.9	100.0%
Sci-Math.	36.4%	27.9	19.3	9.0	4.6	2.3	0.5	-	100.0%
Fis-Off-Mgt	28.0%	30.6	19.8	12.1	5.8	3.0	0.7	-	100.0%
Creative	18.7%	22.4	21.9	15.2	9.3	10.5	1.9	0.1	100.0%
Other	37.3%	28.6	18.8	8.5	3.0	2.9	0.9	-	100.0%

▷ Once they had begun their careers, liberal arts alumni were mobile.
Less than 30 percent were still with their original employer;
over 20 percent had worked for four or more employers.

─────────────── TABLE 48 ───────────────

Extent of Unemployment Since Graduation

*Since receiving your bachelor's degree, approximately how
long have you been unemployed or between jobs?*

	None	One month	Two months	Three or four months	Five to Eleven months	Twelve months and more	No Answer	Total
All Graduates	66.1%	6.3	6.4	8.2	6.7	2.8	3.5	100.0%
Years Since Graduation								
Fifteen	68.2%	5.6	5.7	8.0	7.6	3.1	1.8	100.0%
Ten	66.3%	6.8	6.6	8.6	6.1	2.9	2.7	100.0%
Five	63.9%	6.5	6.8	7.9	6.3	2.4	6.2	100.0%
Academic Record								
High	75.0%	5.1	3.9	4.6	4.1	2.1	5.2	100.0%
Average	67.0%	6.4	6.3	7.8	6.5	2.4	3.6	100.0%
Low	62.7%	6.7	7.7	9.7	7.4	2.8	3.0	100.0%
Type of Major								
Science-Math.	70.8%	5.5	6.1	6.4	5.1	1.8	4.3	100.0%
Soc. Sci.	65.1%	7.0	6.9	8.6	7.0	2.5	2.9	100.0%
Humanities	60.5%	6.2	5.6	10.0	8.7	5.0	4.0	100.0%

▷ Relatively few liberal arts graduates had much experience with unemployment. Humanities majors and alumni who had poorer
academic records are the most likely to report periods of
unemployment.

─────────────── TABLE 49 ───────────────

Extent of Military Service

	Yes	No	No Answer	Total
All Graduates	74.1%	25.3	0.6	100.0%
Years Since Graduation				
Fifteen	88.1%	11.5	0.4	100.0%
Ten	73.5%	26.0	0.5	100.0%
Five	61.5%	37.9	0.6	100.0%

▷ Three-fourths of the graduates have served with the armed forces.

———————————— TABLE 50 ————————————

Type of Community During High School and Now

Which of the following best describes (a) the community in which you grew up when you went to high school and (b) the community in which you now live?

	Community During High School				Community Now			
	Years Since Graduation				Years Since Graduation			
	15	10	5	All Grads	15	10	5	All Grads
Suburb of city of over 1,000,000	14.5%	18.4%	19.0%	17.3%	26.4%	26.6%	23.9%	25.6%
Suburb of city of less than 1,000,000	4.1	4.6	5.5	4.7	8.0	7.3	6.9	7.4
City of 500,000 and over	15.0	15.2	14.7	14.9	10.4	12.9	17.2	13.5
City of 100,000 to 499,000	11.2	12.2	11.1	11.5	13.2	12.8	13.6	13.2
City of 10,000 to 99,999	23.4	23.8	23.1	23.4	24.5	23.8	27.9	24.1
City of less than 10,000	19.1	16.1	16.4	17.2	11.5	10.9	8.9	10.4
Farm or open country	11.7	9.1	9.5	10.1	4.2	4.4	4.2	4.2
No Answer	1.0	0.6	0.7	0.9	1.8	1.3	1.4	1.6
Total	100.0%	100.0%	100.0%	100.0%	100.0%	100.0%	100.0%	100.0%

▷ Most of the graduates live in cities or suburbs of cities of 10,000 or more. They have tended to migrate to large metropolitan areas since their high school days.

Geographically, there has been a movement away from the Great Lakes and Plains regions and to the Far West.

———————————— TABLE 51 ————————————

Geographical Locations During Various Stages of Life

Indicate where . . .	you were born"	you graduated from high school"	you lived immediately after college"	you live now"
New England	8.4%	9.3%	8.5%	7.6%
Mideast	26.9	26.5	24.7	25.1
Great Lakes	22.7	22.5	19.9	19.0
Plains	12.4	10.9	8.4	8.3
Southeast	10.2	10.6	11.7	11.3
Southwest	4.5	4.5	6.0	6.0
Rocky Mountains	3.3	3.4	3.4	3.2
Far West	8.5	10.9	13.9	16.9
Outside U.S.	2.9	0.9	2.9	2.3
No Answer	0.2	0.5	0.6	0.3
Total	100.0%	100.0%	100.0%	100.0%

6

FACTORS INFLUENCING The CAREERS of GRADUATES

The careers of liberal arts graduates may be influenced by many factors, including family background, type of high school and college attended, college academic record, major field of study, graduate training, self-support during college, extra-curricular activities as a student, willingness to sacrifice for the job, and minority group status. This chapter explores each of these factors.

Before exploring these, it is important to repeat the obvious. Unlike many things which depend on a single element, it is impossible to relate career progress to a controlled item or items. Consider, for example, the importance to a career of a personal friend in a strategic position, a chance encounter with a top executive, or the role of an unexpected resignation of a superior. They may contribute more to personal career progress than possession of a Phi Beta Kappa key, evenings spent completing correspondence courses, or maneuvers in office politics.

The importance of personal contact can not be overemphasized. Few obtain jobs or promotions solely on the basis of connections. However, when faced with manpower needs resulting from attrition, new functions, or growth of an organization, top executives usually begin their review of candidates by recalling those whom they know personally.

Despite the role of luck and personal contact, relying upon them is the least effective way to insure career progress. Rather, alumni must exert themselves to prepare for and advance in their careers, while hoping they will receive their share of good fortune.

Family Background

Analysis of the educational backgrounds of the parents of liberal arts alumni shows that 26 percent of the fathers and 16 percent of the mothers are college graduates. (TABLE 52)   The percentages are somewhat higher for the parents of the more recent alumni. Fathers tend to have both less and more education than mothers; more of the fathers than mothers terminated their education before highschool, and more fathers than mothers received college postgraduate degrees.

The quality of the college attended by the liberal arts graduates is related to the educational level of the parents. Sons of parents who did not attend high school are the most likely to have attended a low-quality college. The percentages of sons attending high-quality institutions climbs steadily as the educational level of the parents rises.

What are the relations between fathers' occupations and those of liberal arts alumni? Chapman observed in the late 1930's, "A generation ago, the selection of an occupation was simple enough — 75 percent of the young men followed the occupation of their fathers. Today not more than 25 percent do so." [1]   (TABLE 53)

A comparison of the occupations of our respondents and their fathers bears out Chapman's thesis. The occupational fields for fathers and sons are not directly comparable. Obviously college training shifts the laboring, clerical, and skilled trades towards the professional and managerial ranks. Some patterns do emerge.

Occupation of Son	*Occupation of Father*	*All Graduates*
Salesman	10.7% Salesman	6.8% Salesman
Lawyer	29.2% Professional	10.8% Professional
Medical	27.4% "	18.8% "
Management	21.0% Proprietors	16.6% Proprietors

Fathers in professional occupations are the most likely to have sons who are lawyers or medical workers (11.4 percent) and among the least likely to have sons who are salesmen or fiscal, office, or management workers. Fathers who are business officials or salesmen are much more likely to have sons who are salesmen (23 percent, 25 percent and 19 percent). The sons of laborers, farm owners or managers, service workers and skilled workers are the most likely to become elementary and secondary school teachers (21 percent, 20

percent, 17 percent and 16 percent). Fathers who are farm owners
or managers are considerably more likely than any other group to
have sons who are clergymen.

High School Background

Eighty percent of the liberal arts alumni attended a public high
school, eight percent a parochial school and twelve percent a private
preparatory school. Over the period covered by the survey, public
high school enrollment declined slightly.

Sixty percent of all parochial school graduates attended Catholic
colleges. The remaining 40 percent were equally distributed between
private and public institutions. Almost two-thirds of the private and
preparatory school students went on to private colleges and univer-
sitites. Public high school graduates were much more likely to attend public colleges than were the private or parochial school students, and were the least likely to attend Catholic colleges. Parochial school graduates were the most likely to attend Catholic colleges, while private or preparatory school graduates were the most
likely to attend high-quality colleges. The college academic per-
formances of the three types of high school graduates were almost
identical: 10 percent of each group made "high" records. However,
as academic standards vary considerably between high-quality and
low-quality colleges, actual academic achievement may not have
been comparable.

College Academic Background

College background has a definite effect upon level of responsibility, earnings, occupation and employer.

Graduates with the best academic records are far more likely
to work for colleges and universities than are those with poor records
— the figures are 25 percent as contrasted to two percent. (TABLE 54)
On the other hand, almost twice as many students with poor academic
records, as contrasted to those with high records, enter private
business (manufacturing and non-manufacturing). Yet alumni of
high-quality colleges are significantly more likely to enter private
non-manufacturing firms. Roughly comparable proportions from
each quality grouping are employed in private manufacturing. Only

slightly greater percentages of alumni from high-quality institutions than from medium or low-quality institutions work for colleges and universities. Graduates of low-quality institutions are the most likely to find employment with elementary and secondary schools and with hospitals, churches, and clinics. Trends by year of graduation show that older alumni are somewhat more likely to be engaged in private business (particularly non-manufacturing). As might be expected, 1958 graduates were the most likely to be in the military service.

Before noting the effect of college major upon type of employer, it might be well to review the basic philosophy of liberal education and careers. Unlike technical or professional majors, liberal arts graduates are not prepared for a specific field. There should be little concern over the fact that history majors do not become archivists, sociology majors social workers, or English majors journalists. Far from it, the great virtue of a liberal arts background is its employment flexibility.

Liberal arts graduates typically enter a wide range of employment fields. Some patterns, however, may be noted in the relationships between various majors and employers. (TABLE 56) Humanities majors (particularly in foreign language and fine arts) are the most likely to enter teaching at all levels. More than a quarter of all science and mathematics majors (including 39 percent of chemistry majors and 33 percent of all other physical sciences majors) enter private manufacturing. Economics majors are much more likely to work for business (both manufacturing and non-manufacturing) than is true of any other major. A third of all majors in philosophy and religion are employed by hospitals, churches and clinics — or at least the "churches" segment.

Then exploring the relationship between college background and current occupation, responses indicated that graduates of high-quality colleges are three times as likely to become lawyers as are graduates of low-quality institutions. Graduates of the better schools are also more likely than those from poorer schools to become salesmen, fiscal, office and management workers, and medical workers. A slightly higher proportion of graduates from "average" schools than from high-quality schools enter medical work, however. Alumni of low-quality colleges are much more likely than those from the best schools to become clergymen or elementary and secondary school teachers.

No strong patterns appear to result from the type of college attended. Graduates of Catholic colleges are slightly more likely to become elementary and secondary school teachers, salesmen, or fiscal, office, and management workers; whereas graduates of private colleges are slightly more likely to become lawyers or clergymen. Public college alumni lead slightly in the proportions becoming medical workers and scientists and mathematicians.

A comparison of college majors and current occupations of the graduates is presented in Table 55 and shows some expected patterns. Science and mathematics majors are by far the most likely to become scientists and mathematicians — this occupational field is selected by 46 percent of all chemistry majors, 58 percent of all other physical science majors, and 31 percent of all mathematics majors.

Biological science majors, however, are the most likely to enter the medical field. Nearly one-fifth of the mathematics majors become elementary and secondary school teachers, but those humanities majors who took philosophy or religion as their area of concentration are more likely to become clergymen. Significant proportions of English majors and fine arts majors enter creative fields. The two majors which appear to lead to the most diverse occupational patterns are English and social sciences other than economics. It is interesting to note that at least a few graduates from each major field are represented in every occupational group.

The relationship between college major and current salary is presented in Table 56. Generally speaking, majors in biology, economics and chemistry report the highest salaries: Nearly one-fourth of the biology majors, for example, report annual earnings of $15,000 or more. In contrast, only four percent of the fine arts majors report comparable earnings.

In exploring the relations between various academic background factors and the graduates' current income in greater detail, data for the 1948 graduates only have been used. (TABLE 57) These data cover persons in mid-career, with graduate school, military service and early job changes for career exploration largely behind them. As Table 57 shows, science and mathematics majors are more likely to receive high incomes, overall, than are social sciences majors or humanities majors. A third of the science and mathematics majors earn $15,000 or more, in contrast to 27 percent of the social sciences and 19 percent of the humanities majors.

Alumni with the highest academic records are more likely to be earning $15,000 or more than are those with average or poor records. Quality of the college attended also affects income: 38 percent of those from highest-ranking schools earn $15,000 or more, as compared with 18 percent from low-quality colleges. The highest incomes are reported by holders of professional degrees, half receive $15,000 or more. While graduates who hold doctorates are concentrated in the $10,000 to $15,000 income bracket (47 percent), they fall substantially behind professional degree holders in top income brackets.

A further analysis was made of the income and occupational patterns of the fifteen-year graduates in terms of another classification of the colleges and universities attended.

Graduates of Ivy League colleges are the most likely of all these groups to reach the top income brackets: 20 percent earn $21,000 or more, compared to 16 percent from the "best public universities," 14 percent from the "average universities," eight percent from the "weak universities," and only four percent from the "weak liberal arts colleges." Occupationally, alumni from the "best Catholic universities" and the Ivy League colleges are the most likely to become lawyers. Alumni from the "weak liberal arts colleges" are by far the most likely to become clergymen, while none of our sample from the "best public universities" entered the clergy. Graduates of the "weak liberal arts colleges" and the "weak universities" are also the most likely to become elementary and secondary school teachers. Relatively similar proportions of all college groupings, however, enter college teaching.

Graduates who report they worked much harder than their classmates in college are no more likely to earn higher salaries. (TABLE 58) Yet, the hardest workers as students are more likely to earn master's and doctor's degrees.

Self-Support During College

There is a myth that the self-supporting student in college is more likely to earn high salaries in later life. Actually, there is only a slight correlation between self-sufficiency as an undergraduate and current income. Forty-two percent of those who did not support themselves at all in college are now earning $10,000 or more, compared with 39 percent of those who provided at least three-quarters of their own support.

Self-support in college is more closely related to current occupation. Of those alumni who are now clergymen, 43 percent earned half or more of their college expenses. Forty percent of the scientists and mathematicians and 36 percent of the elementary and secondary school teachers provided half or more of their own support in college. Only 23 percent of the lawyers and 21 percent of those in medical fields earned half or more of their college expenses.

As is the case with self-support and income, there is only a slight correlation between the holding of scholarships and current income: those who did not report a scholarship are slightly more likely to be in the higher income brackets than those with scholarships. Of the 29.2 percent who held a scholarship, 12 percent were earning under $6,000 and only three percent were earning over $25,000; of the 70.8 percent who did not hold scholarships, 10 percent were earning under $6,000 and nearly five percent were earning over $25,000.

Scholarship holding is, however, related to the earning of advanced degrees. Those with scholarships are more likely to have received doctorates as are those without scholarships. While not shown, scholarship holding varies by current occupation. More than 40 percent of the college teachers and clergymen and a third of the medical workers were scholarship holders in college, while only a fifth of the salesmen and the fiscal, office, and management workers had scholarships.

Extra-Curricular Activities

How do athletes, student government office holders, and campus editors fare after college? Did they receive temporary recreation and diversion or did long-range career implications result from their participation? The debate over extra-curricular life has always been keen.

Student participation in extra-curricular activities appears to have little relation to current income. Of the 9.4 percent who held student government office, 9.9 percent were earning less than $6,000 and 5. 7 percent were earning over $25,000 compared to the 90 percent who did not hold office who were represented in the under $6,000 bracket by 11 percent and in the over $25,000 by four percent; participation in college publication activities showed less than a percentage point of difference between income brackets of those who held office and those who did not.

Some patterns are evident when participation in different types of activities is compared with highest degree earned. Those alumni who held a major student government post are more likely to have master's or professional degrees than those who did not. More ex-college editors hold master's or professional degrees than those who did not participate in college publications. Only slight differences exist at the level of the doctorate. While not shown, lawyers are much more likely than other occupational groups to have been student government leaders, and creative workers to have been student editors.

Salesmen and elementary and secondary school teachers report the greatest participation in varsity athletics, while creative workers and social service workers were the least athletically inclined.

Employers seeking to recruit college graduates may be interested in the differing career patterns by type of college experience. Among alumni fifteen years after graduation, top students report higher salaries than those who had strong extra-curricular records. College teachers are the most likely to have combined leadership on the campus with a strong academic record. Scientists and mathematicians were the least involved in extra-curricular activities and among the most likely to have earned top grades.

Sacrifices for the Job

Graduating into what caustic writers labelled "The Age of Security" college seniors of the 1940's and 1950's were accused of searching for the adult version of the security blanket instead of opportunity and challenge. The lives of the alumni show this accusation had little basis in fact. Nearly half frequently take work home or are at the office after normal working hours and on weekends. (TABLE 59) Another quarter say they do "a fair amount" of such extra work, and only eight percent report no such instances.

Occupational and employer distinctions are much more significant than year of graduation. Graduates with educational institutions
at all levels and hospitals, churches, and clinics are the most likely
to work longer hours, and those employed by government are the
least likely. Three-quarters of the clergymen and the college teachers
report heavy amounts of extra work, in contrast to less than a third
of the social service workers and the scientists and mathematicians.

A third of the graduates say they "definitely" would move to
another state to further their careers, and another third say they
"probably" would make such a move. (TABLE 60)   Not surprisingly,
the younger alumni and those in the lower income brackets indicate
the greatest willingness to move in order to obtain a promotion or a
better job. College teachers, clergymen, and scientists and mathematicians are the most willing to change job locales, while lawyers
and medical workers are the least willing.

A quarter of all the graduates report they held two income-
producing jobs at the same time during the previous 12 months.
Half of all those employed by elementary and secondary schools and
a third of those employed by colleges and universities and by state
and local governments held second jobs. The least likely to hold a
second job were affiliated with military services (11 percent) or
private manufacturing concerns (13 percent).

Minority Group Status

Race is assuredly a factor influencing vocational patterns. Some
minority group alumni were drawn in our sample and, although their
numbers are small, their responses provide some tentative conclusions. One immediate conclusion, of course, is that relatively few
minority group members attended our sample colleges and universities. Among our alumni 98.4 percent were white, 0.8 percent
Negro, 0.5 percent Oriental and 0.3 percent other or no answer.

Half of all the Negro alumni included attended low-quality colleges, in contrast to 33 percent of the White alumni and 24 percent
of the Oriental alumni.   (TABLE 61)

Negro graduates are the most likely to hold master's degrees,
Orientals to hold professional degrees and Whites to hold doctor's
degrees. More than a third of all Oriental graduates are medical
workers, compared with 10 percent of the White and seven percent
of the Negro alumni. Negroes are disproportionately represented

in elementary and secondary school teaching and social service work: 42 percent in contrast to 19 percent of the white and 15 percent of the Oriental graduates. Negroes and Orientals are much less likely than whites to enter the private business fields of sales and fiscal, office, and management. Interestingly, slightly more Negro than white respondents become college teachers.

Despite current attention to problems of race, relatively few comments dealt with this topic:

> Being a minority group member, an Oriental, has not posed any problems.   *University of California*

> As a Negro, my abilities are more noticeable because there are so few Negro professionals in the Puget Sound area. This has enabled me to have access to better career opportunities than I might have had otherwise. On the other hand, my clientele is largely Negro which places a definite ceiling on potential income.   *University of California*

FOOTNOTE

1. Chapman, Paul W., *Occupational Guidance.* Atlanta, Ga., T.E. Smith and Co., 1937, p. 33.

——————————————— TABLE 52 ———————————————

Parents' Education

Please check highest educational attainment of your parents.

Father's Education

	Eighth Grade or less	Some High School	High School Graduate	Some College	College Graduate	Post- Graduate Degree	No Answer	Total
All Graduates	28.6%	14.2	16.4	14.2	12.0	14.1	0.5	100.0%
Years Since Graduation								
Fifteen	32.9%	14.0	15.3	14.5	10.4	11.9	1.0	100.0%
Ten	29.1%	14.4	16.3	13.1	12.3	14.2	0.6	100.0%
Five	23.9%	14.2	17.4	14.9	13.1	16.1	0.4	100.0%

Quality of College

	Eighth Grade or less	Some High School	High School Graduate	Some College	College Graduate	Post- Graduate Degree
High	12.1%	15.2%	20.5%	21.8%	35.1%	33.9%
Medium	42.4	45.6	48.1	49.5	45.3	44.3
Low	45.5	39.2	31.4	28.7	19.6	21.8
100.0%=	(3108)	(1543)	(1778)	(1540)	(1301)	(1534)

Mother's Education

	Eighth Grade or less	Some High School	High School Graduate	Some College	College Graduate	Post- Graduate Degree	No Answer	Total
All Graduates	21.2%	15.1	29.2	17.5	13.5	**2.9**	0.6	100.0%
Years Since Graduation								
Fifteen	26.5%	15.8	27.2	15.6	11.7	2.2	1.0	100.0%
Ten	22.2%	14.2	28.0	18.2	14.0	2.8	0.6	100.0%
Five	15.1%	15.2	32.2	18.6	14.8	3.6	0.5	100.0%

Quality of College

	Eighth Grade or less	Some High School	High School Graduate	Some College	College Graduate	Post- Graduate Degree
High	12.3%	14.0%	22.7%	23.5%	33.2%	37.6%
Medium	40.1	45.6	46.8	49.0	46.6	43.4
Low	47.6	40.4	30.5	27.5	20.2	19.0
100.0%=	(2303)	(1638)	(3170)	(1899)	(1469)	(316)

▷ A quarter of the graduates' fathers and 16 percent of the mothers are college graduates.

The level of the parents' education is clearly related to the quality of the college attended by the sons.

TABLE 53

Comparison of Father's and Son's Occupations

Current Occupations of Alumni	Professional	Proprietor	Business Official	Salesman	Clerical Worker	Farm owner or manager	Technician	Skilled Worker	Service Worker	Laborer
Lawyer	11.4%	8.9%	6.3%	7.4%	6.1%	3.2%	5.3%	4.7%	6.0%	4.3%
Clergyman	4.2	2.9	3.0	2.7	3.8	10.8	6.1	4.2	4.4	5.8
Elem- Second. Teach.	11.3	10.9	7.9	11.6	11.9	19.7	11.5	16.0	17.4	21.2
College Teacher	6.1	4.3	4.7	4.7	6.6	5.6	7.6	6.1	6.0	7.1
Salesman	7.2	12.7	15.9	15.9	8.6	5.0	7.6	7.5	7.3	7.3
Social Serv. Worker	4.2	3.8	3.4	5.1	5.3	2.2	6.9	4.8	6.0	6.8
Medical	13.3	11.0	7.3	9.1	6.1	9.9	9.2	6.4	7.0	7.3
Sci-Math.	13.0	9.9	10.7	10.1	17.0	14.2	16.8	17.7	14.3	11.4
Fis-Off-Mgt.	13.0	23.0	25.3	18.9	17.7	11.8	12.9	16.2	14.3	15.7
Creative	5.1	4.0	4.7	5.0	3.8	2.9	4.6	3.6	3.6	2.5
Student	1.3	0.6	0.9	1.1	0.5	1.5	0.0	1.2	0.8	0.8
Other	9.9	8.0	9.9	8.4	12.6	13.2	11.5	11.6	12.9	9.8
100% =	(1897)	(1680)	(1624)	(704)	(395)	(585)	(131)	(1514)	(385)	(396)

Δ There is no such clear pattern governing relations between fathers' and sons' occupations.

The data make evident the effect of college education in shifting the sons' occupations toward the professional and managerial ranks and in dispersing their occupations over a wide range of fields.

TABLE 54

Influence of College Background on Current Employment

	Priv. Manuf.	Priv. Non-Mf.	Agri-culture	El-Sec. Sch.	Coll-Univ.	U.S. Mil.	Fed. Govt.	St-L. Govt.	Res. Org.	Hosp-Ch-Clin	Other & No Answer	Total
All Graduates	17.9%	29.7	0.4	10.3	8.8	4.5	5.5	4.1	2.6	8.8	7.4	100.0%
Years Since Graduation												
Fifteen	19.6%	33.2	0.4	10.1	10.2	1.8	5.4	3.8	2.3	7.9	5.3	100.0%
Ten	19.0%	31.3	0.4	10.2	8.8	3.6	5.2	4.0	2.7	9.3	5.5	100.0%
Five	15.2%	24.7	0.2	10.5	7.6	7.9	5.9	4.5	2.9	9.1	11.5	100.0%
Academic Record												
High	11.5%	18.9	0.1	5.7	25.2	4.1	7.0	1.7	3.9	11.9	10.0	100.0%
Average	16.5%	26.9	0.3	10.9	10.0	4.7	6.0	3.9	3.0	10.2	7.6	100.0%
Low	22.7%	43.0	0.3	6.9	2.4	2.1	3.4	2.3	2.3	9.1	5.5	100.0%
Quality of College												
High	17.8%	37.3	0.5	5.8	10.8	3.5	4.9	3.2	2.9	5.6	7.7	100.0%
Medium	19.0%	30.1	0.3	7.4	8.4	5.4	6.4	4.7	2.8	8.5	7.0	100.0%
Low	16.5%	24.2	0.3	16.9	8.2	3.7	4.8	4.0	2.2	11.1	8.1	100.0%

TABLE 54 - Continued

Influence of College Background on Current Employment: College Major

	Priv. Manuf.	Priv. Non-Mf.	Agri-culture	El-Sec. Sch.	Coll-Univ.	U.S. Mil.	Fed. Govt.	St&L. Govt.	Res. Org.	Hosp-Ch-Clin.	Other & No Answer	Total
All Graduates	17.9%	29.7	0.4	10.3	8.8	4.5	5.5	4.1	2.6	8.8	7.4	100.0%
College Major												
Chemistry	39.1%	15.3	0.3	3.9	10.1	3.4	5.0	1.1	7.1	6.8	7.9	100.0%
Phys. Sci.	33.3%	11.9	0.1	4.2	10.6	3.6	13.0	4.2	9.9	0.8	8.4	100.0%
Bio. Sci	10.2%	29.6	0.4	7.2	8.2	9.6	4.7	4.1	1.9	15.2	8.9	100.0%
Math	26.0%	17.6	0.4	17.3	12.6	6.1	5.7	2.3	5.9	1.1	5.0	100.0%
Economics	26.8%	47.4	0.5	4.5	2.8	2.4	4.6	2.7	0.9	2.6	4.8	100.0%
Soc. Sci.	11.8%	31.4	0.4	13.1	8.5	4.5	6.2	6.6	1.4	9.1	7.0	100.0%
English	12.4%	35.2	0.2	13.0	11.2	2.7	2.9	2.8	1.4	9.4	8.8	100.0%
Foreign L.	12.0%	20.7	--	17.8	16.8	3.9	5.8	3.9	0.5	6.7	11.9	100.0%
Phil-Rel.	7.9%	19.2	0.3	8.6	10.1	1.2	3.2	1.5	1.5	35.9	10.6	100.0%
Arts	9.9%	22.5	--	28.8	15.3	3.2	1.8	3.2	0.9	5.4	9.0	100.0%

Δ College major shows some relation to both income and vocational choice. Graduates who majored in science and mathematics tend to receive the highest incomes, humanities majors the lowest. Biological science majors tend to enter medical fields; majors in the physical sciences to become scientists and mathematicians and to enter private manufacturing.

TABLE 55

Current Occupation by College Major

Current Occupation	All Graduates	Chemistry	Other Phy. Sci.	Biol. Sci.	Sci. Math	Econ.	Other Soc. Sci.	English	Languages	Phil-Rel.	Fine Arts
Lawyer	6.8%	0.7%	0.4%	1.3%	1.3%	9.3%	12.2%	7.2%	2.4%	5.4%	1.4%
Clergyman	3.9	0.8	0.3	0.2	0.4	0.8	5.1	5.7	3.4	31.0	1.8
Elem-Second. Teach.	11.8	5.9	6.0	8.2	19.0	4.8	14.1	15.9	24.0	12.0	32.4
College Teacher	5.3	4.2	3.6	4.3	7.7	1.9	5.2	8.6	10.6	7.1	11.3
Salesman	9.6	4.6	4.3	5.3	6.1	20.4	10.4	10.6	7.7	5.4	4.1
Social Serv. Worker	4.0	0.3	0.1	0.6	0.5	2.2	9.4	2.1	2.4	2.7	2.3
Medical Worker	8.5	16.1	0.3	44.3	0.9	0.4	2.3	2.0	2.9	1.7	0.9
Scientist-Math.	11.9	46.3	58.3	11.9	31.3	2.5	1.5	0.9	3.4	2.0	1.8
Fiscal-Office-Mgmt.	16.9	6.8	6.9	6.1	10.3	40.2	18.4	15.5	18.3	14.7	7.2
Creative Worker	3.9	0.6	0.6	1.0	1.1	2.1	3.1	15.5	3.4	1.7	20.7
Other	9.5	5.9	10.1	7.8	16.4	10.4	11.0	7.5	9.1	4.9	7.2
No Answer	7.9	8.8	9.1	9.0	5.0	5.0	7.3	8.5	12.4	11.4	8.9
Total	100.0%	100.0%	100.0%	100.0%	100.0%	100.0%	100.0%	100.0%	100.0%	100.0%	100.0%

△Humanities majors are the most likely to become teachers.

Sixty percent of all economics majors enter private business.

The majors leading to the most diverse occupational patterns are English and the general social sciences.

TABLE 56

Current Earnings by College Major: Total Sample

What is your current annual salary in your present position?

	Under $4,000	$4,000-7,999	$8,000-11,999	$12,000-14,999	$15,000-17,999	$18,000-24,999	$25,000 or more	No Answer	Total
All Graduates	2.9%	28.4	33.0	11.1	5.6	4.8	4.1	10.1	100.0%
College Major									
All Sci.-Math.	3.1%	19.9	37.1	14.2	6.6	5.1	4.2	9.8	100.0%
Chemistry	3.9%	14.6	38.2	16.4	7.1	5.1	4.3	10.4	100.0%
Other Phy. Sci.	1.4%	19.8	42.2	15.7	7.1	2.9	1.2	9.7	100.0%
Biol. Sci.	5.5%	22.3	26.7	8.7	6.2	8.6	9.3	12.7	100.0%
Math.-Stat.	1.6%	23.0	41.3	15.8	6.1	3.9	2.0	6.3	100.0%
All Soc. Sci.	1.4%	27.9	34.3	12.1	5.9	5.3	4.6	8.5	100.0%
Economics	0.9%	22.5	35.0	14.2	6.9	7.2	6.1	7.2	100.0%
Soc. Sci.	2.0%	33.3	33.6	10.0	4.9	3.5	3.0	9.7	100.0%
Humanities	5.0%	41.9	26.8	5.6	3.5	2.5	2.0	12.7	100.0%
English	3.1%	34.9	29.1	8.9	5.3	4.2	3.4	11.1	100.0%
For. Lang.	5.3%	41.8	27.4	3.4	2.9	1.9	2.4	14.9	100.0%
Phil.-Rel.	8.6%	44.7	19.9	4.4	3.4	3.2	1.2	14.6	100.0%
Fine Arts	3.2%	45.9	30.6	5.9	2.3	0.9	0.9	10.3	100.0%

―――――――――――――――――― **TABLE 57** ――――――――――――――――――

Current Income: 15-year Graduates Only

	Under $6000	6000- 9999	10,000- 14,999	15,000- 20,999	21,000 and over	No Answer	Total
All Graduates	5.1%	26.0	32.8	16.8	11.2	8.1	100.0%
Type of Major							
Science-Math.	3.7%	19.9	34.5	19.5	14.5	7.9	100.0%
Social Sciences	4.6%	27.4	33.0	16.3	10.7	8.0	100.0%
Humanities	9.3%	33.7	28.8	12.8	5.9	9.5	100.0%
Academic Record							
High	6.1%	20.5	30.9	20.9	12.6	9.0	100.0%
Average	4.4%	26.0	32.4	17.5	11.4	8.3	100.0%
Low	5.8%	32.8	31.8	13.8	8.9	6.9	100.0%
Amount of Graduate Training							
None	4.1%	25.7	34.4	18.6	10.7	6.5	100.0%
Some, but no advanced degree	7.0%	27.1	35.8	13.8	7.7	8.6	100.0%
Master's	5.5%	37.3	36.9	8.9	4.0	7.4	100.0%
Professional	7.2%	14.1	16.8	23.3	25.3	13.3	100.0%
Doctor's	1.4%	22.6	47.3	19.6	4.6	4.5	100.0%
Quality of College							
High	3.3%	17.9	33.3	22.6	15.0	7.9	100.0%
Medium	4.0%	24.2	33.3	18.0	12.9	7.6	100.0%
Low	7.7%	33.3	31.7	11.5	6.6	9.2	100.0%

TABLE 58 ---

How Hard Alumni Worked in College

*Compared to other students in your class in college, how
hard would you say you worked on your studies?*

	Consid-erably harder	Some-what harder	About the same	Some-what less	Consid-erably less	No Answer	Total
All Graduates	9.8%	32.8	35.0	16.6	5.4	0.4	100.0%

Income

Under $6000	10.9%	11.8%	11.2%	10.1%	7.6%		
$6000-9999	36.8	38.6	41.5	39.7	36.8		
$10,000-14,999	23.7	23.9	25.2	26.1	25.8		
$15,000-20,999	9.9	9.9	8.3	9.2	11.7		
$21,000-24,999	1.5	1.4	1.0	1.2	0.7		
$25,000 and over	4.7	4.0	3.9	4.2	5.3		
No answer	12.5	10.4	8.9	9.5	12.1		
100.0% =	(1067)	(3568)	(3806)	(1810)	(590)		

Highest Degree Earned

Bachelor's	35.1%	42.2%	54.3%	54.4%	55.9%		
Master's	25.7	23.5	20.3	19.4	17.5		
Professional	23.5	23.6	19.0	20.1	21.7		
Doctorate	14.1	9.2	4.8	4.3	4.2		
No answer	1.6	1.5	1.6	1.8	0.7		
100.0% =	(1067)	(3568)	(3806)	(1810)	(590)		

─────────────────────── **TABLE 59** ───────────────────────

How Hard Alumni Work Now

Do you frequently take work home or come into your office
after working hours or on weekends?

	Quite a lot	A Fair Amount	A Little	None	No Answer	Total
All Graduates	45.8%	24.3	20.3	7.5	2.1	100.0%

Years Since Graduation

▷ Nearly half the graduates take work home frequently or work after hours or weekends at the office.

	Quite a lot	A Fair Amount	A Little	None	No Answer	Total
Fifteen	46.3%	26.0	20.9	5.7	1.1	100.0%
Ten	46.6%	24.5	20.9	6.9	1.1	100.0%
Five	44.4%	22.4	18.9	9.6	4.7	100.0%

Income

	Quite a lot	A Fair Amount	A Little	None	No Answer	Total
Under $6000	59.5%	16.0	12.7	10.6	1.2	100.0%
6000-9999	41.6%	25.8	23.4	9.2	-	100.0%
10,000-14,999	43.1%	27.7	23.7	5.2	0.3	100.0%
15,000-20,999	55.5%	25.3	15.6	3.5	0.1	100.0%
21,000 and over	56.0%	24.5	15.7	3.8	-	100.0%

Employer

▷ Extra work is more typical of those in the higher income brackets.

	Quite a lot	A Fair Amount	A Little	None	No Answer	Total
Private Manufactur.	34.8%	28.5	27.0	9.5	0.2	100.0%
Private Non-Manufact.	43.5%	26.1	22.5	7.4	0.5	100.0%
Agriculture	54.1%	21.6	13.5	10.8	-	100.0%
Elem-Second. Schools	60.3%	23.3	14.3	2.0	0.1	100.0%
Colleges-Universities	73.0%	17.5	7.6	1.5	0.4	100.0%
U.S. Military Serv.	37.6%	26.5	22.7	11.2	2.0	100.0%
Federal Government	24.5%	27.0	29.3	18.7	0.5	100.0%
State-Local Govt.	22.9%	27.2	33.4	16.3	0.2	100.0%
Research Organiz.	30.5%	28.8	32.6	7.4	0.7	100.0%
Hospital-Church Clin.	64.5%	20.7	10.8	3.0	1.0	100.0%

Occupation

	Quite a lot	A Fair Amount	A Little	None	No Answer	Total
Lawyer	53.2%	26.9	15.8	3.7	0.4	100.0%
Clergyman	77.7%	15.2	4.5	1.9	0.7	100.0%
Elem-Second. Teach.	63.2%	21.3	12.9	2.3	0.3	100.0%
College Teacher	76.5%	16.6	6.1	0.4	0.4	100.0%
Salesman	48.1%	25.6	21.3	4.8	0.2	100.0%
Social Serv. Worker	31.0%	27.6	29.6	11.6	0.2	100.0%
Medical Worker	53.4%	24.1	15.1	6.4	1.0	100.0%
Scientist-Math.	29.2%	29.9	31.4	9.5	-	100.0%
Fiscal-Office-Mgmt.	33.3%	27.1	28.5	11.0	0.1	100.0%
Creative Worker	42.0%	23.8	21.5	11.4	1.3	100.0%
Other	31.9%	27.3	25.5	14.4	0.9	100.0%

———————————————— TABLE 60 ————————————————

Willingness of Alumni to Relocate for a New Job

Would you be willing to move to another state to accept a promotion or a better job?

	Definitely Yes	Probably Yes	Probably No	Definitely No	No Answer	Total
All Graduates	32.3%	34.1	22.5	9.0	2.1	100.0%
Years Since Graduation						
Fifteen	27.7%	33.8	26.0	11.5	1.0	100.0%
Ten	32.0%	34.2	23.3	9.2	1.3	100.0%
Five	37.0%	34.2	18.3	6.5	4.0	100.0%
Employer						
Private Manufactur.	42.8%	35.6	16.5	4.8	0.3	100.0%
Private Non-Manufact.	24.3%	30.5	29.8	15.0	0.4	100.0%
Agriculture	18.9%	24.3	29.7	27.1	-	100.0%
Ele-Second. Schools	25.7%	37.7	27.7	8.8	0.1	100.0%
Colleges-Universities	44.5%	35.7	14.4	4.6	0.8	100.0%
U.S. Military Service	55.6%	27.7	7.9	5.2	3.6	100.0%
Federal Government	34.8%	39.0	20.3	5.2	0.7	100.0%
State-Local Govt.	22.9%	37.0	31.9	8.0	0.2	100.0%
Research Organiz.	31.2%	40.4	21.8	6.3	0.3	100.0%
Hospital-Church Clin.	27.2%	41.6	22.2	6.9	2.1	100.0%
Income						
Under $6000	31.4%	36.7	20.7	10.0	1.2	100.0%
6000-9999	34.9%	36.9	21.7	6.2	0.3	100.0%
10,000-14,999	35.0%	34.9	22.2	7.5	0.4	100.0%
15,000-20,999	25.5%	29.4	29.7	14.9	0.5	100.0%
21,000 and over	22.8%	25.4	30.6	20.8	0.4	100.0%
Occupation						
Lawyer	17.2%	29.9	36.3	16.4	0.2	100.0%
Clergyman	26.1%	50.4	17.6	3.8	2.1	100.0%
Elem-Second. Teach.	28.5%	36.4	26.5	8.2	0.4	100.0%
College Teacher	42.6%	38.9	13.8	4.0	0.7	100.0%
Salesman	37.0%	32.2	20.6	9.8	0.4	100.0%
Social Serv. Worker	33.7%	33.9	24.8	7.3	0.3	100.0%
Medical Worker	23.4%	26.2	30.1	18.4	1.9	100.0%
Scientist-Math.	36.4%	39.8	19.2	4.6	-	100.0%
Fiscal-Office-Mgmt.	34.2%	34.1	22.5	8.9	0.3	100.0%
Creative Worker	30.8%	30.8	29.6	8.2	0.6	100.0%
Other	41.0%	34.2	16.0	7.3	1.5	100.0%

▷ A third of the graduates would be willing to move to another state to better their careers. Younger graduates in the lower income brackets are the most willing to move.

─────── **TABLE 61** ───────

Effect of Race on College Education and Occupation

	White	Negro	Oriental	Other	No Answer	Total
All Graduates	98.4%	0.8%	0.5%	0.1%	0.2%	100.0%

Quality of College

	White	Negro	Oriental
High	21.3%	13.3%	27.3%
Medium	45.4	36.1	49.1
Low	33.4	50.6	23.6
100.0% =	(10,698)	(83)	(55)

Academic Record

	White	Negro	Oriental
High	10.2%	4.8%	8.9%
Average	56.2	48.4	62.2
Low	33.6	46.8	28.9
100.0% =	(8361)	(62)	(45)

Highest Degree Held

	White	Negro	Oriental
Bachelor's	48.6%	49.4%	45.5%
Master's	21.5	33.7	20.0
Professional	21.5	13.3	29.1
Doctorate	7.1	1.2	3.6
No answer	1.3	2.4	1.8
100.0% =	(10,698)	(83)	(55)

Occupation

	White	Negro	Oriental
Lawyer	8.2%	2.7%	7.7%
Clergy	4.6	5.5	-
Elem-Second. Teach.	14.1	21.9	7.7
College Teacher	6.3	6.8	2.6
Salesman	11.6	5.5	-
Social Serv. Worker	4.7	21.9	7.7
Medical Worker	10.1	6.9	35.9
Scientist-Math.	14.1	16.4	25.6
Fiscal-Office-Mgmt.	20.4	11.0	12.8
Creative Worker	4.8	-	-
Student	1.1	1.4	-
100% =	(8957)	(73)	(39)

▷ Minority group status affects the quality of college attended,
academic performance and occupational choice.
Negroes are the most likely to hold master's degrees
and to become elementary and secondary school
teachers and social service workers.
Oriental alumni are the most likely to hold professional
degrees and to enter medical fields.
White graduates are the most likely to hold doctor's
degrees and are dispersed throughout the widest
variety of occupational fields.

7

HOW LIBERAL ARTS GRADUATES
APPRAISE THEIR CAREERS

The alumni commented freely on their jobs, their current career progress, to an extent revealing a deep personal interest in the outcomes of a liberal education. In addition to evaluating their jobs, their employers, and their salaries, the graduates appraised those with whom they worked as subordinates, colleagues, and superiors. Most important were their judgments of liberal education as preparation for a career.

Satisfaction with Jobs

Liberal arts graduates are highly satisfied with the work they are doing (TABLE 62) : 69 percent like their jobs very much and 22 percent fairly much. Older alumni are the most satisfied, possibly reflecting both greater tolerance toward job limitations and a seniority status which provides more challenging job assignments.

In contrast to the theory that money is often a substitute for satisfying work, income is related to job satisfaction. Those earning over $15,000 a year are the most pleased with their work. The greatest satisfaction is reported by clergymen, medical workers, and university professors and the least by fiscal, office, and management workers, salesmen, scientists and mathematicians, and social service workers.

Only one of ten alumni desires to be in an occupation other than his current choice. (TABLE 63) This is especially true of alumni in lower income brackets and those who graduated most recently. Those occupational groups least desirous of changing occupations are medical workers, college teachers, lawyers, and clergymen. When year of graduation is considered, there is a suggestion that certain occupations may become more satisfying over time: older alumni are more satisfied than younger graduates with careers in social science work, creative fields, and fiscal, office, and management occupations.

Few alumni definitely plan to change occupations (TABLE 64), and the likelihood of change is related to time elapsed since graduation. Twenty percent of the younger alumni will or may change in contrast to 12 percent of the older graduates. Clergymen, medical workers, and lawyers least anticipate making a change. The most inclined to change occupations are currently in social service fields, sales and fiscal, office, and management. Graduates in the lower income brackets report the greatest likelihood of an occupational change.

It is interesting to note what fields graduates now prefer. When they express a desire to change to another occupation, liberal arts alumni now would prefer teaching, medical fields, law, and creative occupations. (TABLE 65)

Without discounting alumni preferences for various occupations, it should be recognized that until someone has actually worked in a field his ratings may have a romantic, rather than a realistic, basis. Consider, for example, the harassed business executive who returns for the 15th anniversary of his college graduation. Classmates and former professors have never been friendlier or more interesting. The campus has never looked more attractive and the freshly mown lawns, the peaceful Georgian architecture, and the quietness in the college library stir a desire for college teaching.

This is just as realistic as the view, perhaps that fall, when a college professor calls on one of his former classmates, now a business executive. After a week of tedious clerical work in connection with registration of entering freshmen, the professor is impressed by the power, people, and problems faced by the executive. In contrast to the vagueness of college teaching, the businessman has a numerical standard by which his achievements may be measured. He works with a team, rather than by himself. Besides, after those repetitive faculty receptions, the stack of unpaid bills, and the quiet shabbiness of the college town, the professor is awed by the variety, wealth, and excitement of metropolitan living.

Making use of a scale originally developed at Cornell, the questionnaire probed the relative importance of eight occupational characteristics and the extent to which current jobs met these traits. The alumni indicated that most important were the opportunities to use special abilities, to be creative and original, to help others and to enjoy a stable future. (TABLE 66) Less important were social status and prestige and the chance to earn a great deal of money. While current jobs fell somewhat short of alumni ideals, they were rated highest in those traits which alumni held most important, with one exception — the opportunity to be creative and original.

Almost every graduate took advantage of this survey to comment on his career. Some of the more typical are as follows:

> I found it very difficult to appreciate that hard work is the only way to achieve success. *University of Michigan*

> It is still difficult for me to accept the fact that all types of work are 95 percent routine and five percent variety. *Columbia University*

> In the cruel world of politics (in a university, government, or industry), you must learn to develop your own rules of competitive activity or conformity. *Fordham University*

> Many of my friends are over-concerned with retirement and fringe benefits and they miss the excitement of living. *Columbia University*

> The real helping hand is at the end of your own arm. *University of Redlands*

> Colleges should give some thought to preparation for self-employment, rather than mass producing trainees for big business. *Stanford University*

Satisfaction with Employers

A fairly high level of satisfaction was expressed toward the graduates' present employers. Only 11 percent definitely wish they were working for another employer, while 18 percent are not sure.

A change of employer in the next three years is definitely planned by 11 percent of the graduates and is a possibility for another 20 percent. In contrast to the oldest graduates, alumni of five years earlier are almost twice as likely to plan a definite switch.

Not surprisingly, low income is closely related to desires and plans for changing employers. Military servicemen, state and local government employees are the least satisfied with their employers. The most pleased are those affiliated with agricultural enterprises, hospitals, churches, and clinics, private non-manufacturing organizations, colleges and universities, and elementary and secondary schools. Yet, when asked if they expect to change employers in the next three years, college and university employees and those working for hospitals, churches and clinics are more likely to plan a change than all other groups except military servicemen. While 12 percent of those working for a private manufacturing concern say they would like to change, only six percent plan to do so.

Alumni who expressed a desire to change employers were asked what type of employer they would now prefer, and they indicate a strong preference for colleges and universities. (TABLE 67) The federal government also proved a popular choice. The big shift would be away from elementary or secondary schools, military services and state and local government.

Attitudes toward employer promotion policies are shown much more diverse. (TABLE 68) Two-thirds of the graduates are at least fairly satisfied with their employer's policy for promotion, while one-third dislike it either slightly or greatly. There are no significant differences among the three graduating classes. By type of employer, those who most approve of their employers' promotion policies are in private non-manufacturing, in hospitals, churches, and clinics, in research organizations and institutes, and in the federal government. (Those in agriculture are disregarded in this and several subsequent tables because of the very small number of alumni involved.) Among the least satisfied are military servicemen and employees of state and local governments.

Do persons who change jobs learn from their experience and become more satisfied with their jobs and their employers? What is the relationship between job changes and earnings? Actually, alumni who changed jobs frequently show no increase in job satisfaction. In fact, among graduates who worked for seven or eight different employers, a relatively high percentage "dislike greatly" their work.

Those with fewer job changes are more satisfied with their occupations. Men who changed jobs frequently are more likely to desire still another change. Total earnings do not seem to be influenced by number of job changes. While there is a slight tendency for those who changed jobs the most to report lower salaries, this may represent the high proportion of elementary and secondary school teachers among the mobile group.

Satisfaction with Fellow Workers

The alumni were asked how they liked their supervisors, their colleagues, and their subordinates. Here they reserved the greatest criticism for those above them. (Since substantial but varying numbers of alumni had no job associates of one kind or another, these three tables are based only upon those alumni who responded with answers other than "not applicable.")

Only 11 percent of the respondents dislike their supervisors, and only two percent dislike them "greatly." (TABLE 69)   Those affiliated with colleges or universities and with hospitals, churches, and clinics express the greatest satisfaction with their supervisors, while those employed by elementary and secondary schools or in the military services are the least satisfied. There are only slight variations by year of graduation.

Almost all alumni (97 percent) like the colleagues with whom they work. (TABLE 70)   Differences by year of graduation and by type of employer are slight.

Satisfaction with subordinates is even greater (98 percent), (TABLE 71)   The slight differences showed alumni who were employed by a military service or by a state or local government tend to be the least satisfied with their subordinates and those with an educational or research institute the most satisfied.

In reminiscing about their careers, numerous alumni pointed out the role of people and personal contact.

> The major problems encountered in the business world deal with human nature, human error, and human understanding.   *St. Louis University*

> As a military officer, I am aware that people are the most important component of the Defense Department.

If we could contract for qualified, enthusiastic, and well-trained people with the same vigor with which we obligate defense hardware, we could provide twice the defense at the same price. Why have a million dollar computer run by a $10,000 a year man when you could do the same job or better with a half-million dollar machine and a $20,000 a year man.

University of Minnesota

Your employer eventually will judge you more on how much work you can get others to do rather than how much you can do yourself.   *Duke University*

Satisfaction with Income

Two-thirds of the alumni are generally satisfied with their income. (TABLE 72) Not surprisingly, satisfaction with income is most pronounced among older alumni who tend to earn the most money.

When graduates with the longest career experience (fifteen years after finishing their baccalaureate) are studied, medical workers report the most satisfaction with their incomes and teachers at all levels, the least. (TABLE 72) Despite their relatively low salary levels, fewer clergymen dislike their income "greatly" than do any other occupational groups. Graduates working for research organizations and for private non-manufacturing are the most likely to be very satisfied with their incomes. Despite traditional reports to the contrary, federal government employees are less dissatisfied with their salaries than the average for all graduates. Satisfaction with income, not unexpectedly, rises with income.

Satisfaction with Career Progress

Fortunately for the egos of the men involved, and interesting from a research point of view, the majority of the graduates rate their careers as more successful than those of their classmates. Two-thirds say their careers have "definitely" or "probably" been more successful, and less than one-third say their careers have probably or definitely not been as successful. (TABLE 73) Appraisals of success rise with income. By occupation, medical workers, lawyers, and college professors feel they have been relatively the most successful; the least relative success is reported by elementary and secondary school teachers and clergymen. Surprisingly enough, time since graduation has little effect on satisfaction with career progress.

Despite this general satisfaction, a number of individual comments indicate considerable concern about careers:

> At age 40, I am not afraid to admit that I am not completely satisfied with what I am doing and would make a complete change if I had the opportunity.
> *Boston College*

> I have worked like a dog trying to make a career with no success. I have taught math in high school, farmed and ranched on a rather large scale, and operated an insurance agency. I have worked very hard and long for practically nothing. I don't really blame anybody but myself. *Colorado State University*

Satisfaction with career progress is influenced by future expectations as well as by past accomplishments. Two-thirds of the alumni expect a promotion in the next three years (TABLE 74), ranging from 74 percent of the youngest graduates to 58 percent of the oldest class. Federal employees anticipate the most promotions (89 percent), and elementary and secondary school employees the least (53 percent). Again, agricultural workers are disregarded here because of the small numbers involved. By occupation, college professors, social service workers, and scientists and mathematicians expect the most promotions, and clergymen and elementary and secondary teachers and medical workers, the least.

Satisfaction with Undergraduate Education

In Chapter Three, alumni evaluated their liberal arts education as preparation for life. Now they were asked how well liberal education had prepared them for careers — careers, it should be emphasized, which may pit them against specialists and technicians in competing for hiring and promotion.

While some graduates are dissatisfied with liberal education as preparation for vocational life, almost three times as many are pleased. (TABLE 75) Differences in satisfaction by year of graduation are very slight. Science and mathematics majors are somewhat more satisfied with their liberal arts training than are humanities alumni, with social science graduates the least satisfied.

Satisfaction with undergraduate training is closely related to academic record; the best students are much more satisfied than are lower-ranking undergraduates. Men from Catholic institutions are somewhat more satisfied with their educational preparation than are those from public or private colleges. Alumni from the smaller colleges are more satisfied with their educational background than are those from medium or large-sized institutions.

To obtain the most meaningful assessment of liberal education in terms of current occupation, the graduates who had been in the work force the longest time were studied. Among these graduates, medical workers and clergymen are found to be most pleased with liberal education as vocational preparation, followed by college teachers. (TABLE 75) Salesmen and fiscal, office, and management workers are the least satisfied. While not shown, current income shows very little relation to satisfaction with undergraduate preparation.

Alumni had many comments to make regarding the adequacy of liberal arts education for a life of work. The more negative included:

> I would advise today's students not to waste time on liberal arts. Today's world is a very hard one and one must have a skill to obtain a job.
> *New York University*

> Everyone needs two educations — one with which to earn a living and the other to make life rich and full.
> *University of Southern California*

> Liberal arts gives an invaluable appreciation of our culture, but is very poor background for making a living.
> *Washington University*

> Liberal arts contributes to fascinating undergraduate discussions. But what is the graduate to do when he has to support a family? Perhaps he can become a school teacher, as I did. But then he can't afford the very things he has learned to appreciate.
> *Arizona State University*

Equally strong, and much more numerous, comments defend the vocational results of a liberal education.

> College didn't fit me for any certain career, but it taught me how to learn.
> *Fresno State College*

Stick to your educational goals and avoid treating college as a trade school.   *Oberlin College*

Most of the fields I have worked in are not covered by specific college courses.   *Colorado State University*

The world is changing too fast to tie yourself to a career. The best a person can do is to select the broadest possible field. The one in which I am now working didn't exist 30 years ago and was only added to the curriculum at my Alma Mater five or six years ago. The solution is to prepare for a career by learning as much as you can about as many things as you can encompass.   *Wayne State University*

The alumni were asked to comment on the extent to which their current job used certain skills usually provided by a liberal education. (TABLE 76)   While less than 10 percent say they now use a foreign language, almost all utilized both writing (76 percent) and creative thinking (84 percent). Foreign language is most used by clergymen and college professors. Writing is particularly important to those working as lawyers, clergymen, social service workers, and creative workers. While most graduates agree their job requires creative thinking, this is particularly true of lawyers, clergymen, and those in creative fields.

Comments from individual alumni stress the importance they place upon the ability to communicate, both orally and in writing.

I have observed that time and time again those who are able to express themselves clearly and simply — in either the spoken or written word — move ahead most rapidly.   *Hamline University*

Although I am a successful salesman, my inability to speak to a large group of people has been my worst career difficulty.   *University of Dayton*

One of my key problems as a chemist has been to summarize in a clear, concise form the most pertinent information needed for the reader or audience.   *Wayne State University*

> The ability to communicate is the single most important asset an individual can have. *Rutgers University*

Satisfaction with Graduate Education

Graduate education is rated as important in their careers by 85 percent of the alumni. (TABLE 77)   The greatest utility is assigned by those who earned the highest degrees: 99. 6 percent of those with a doctorate feel graduate training is useful or at least desirable in their work.   Even among those with only a bachelor's degree, over two-thirds rate advanced education as at least desirable.

In the tables, the variable amount of graduate training is given in addition to the highest degrees earned to indicate how many took advanced study whether or not they received an advanced degree.

While 92 percent of the science and mathematics majors feel graduate training is essential or desirable, less interest is shown by those who studied social sciences (81 percent) or humanities (80 percent). Those who earned the best grades as undergraduates have the highest respect for graduate training.

Significant distinctions are shown by occupations. Men employed in what are essentially business operations (sales and fiscal, office, and management), or in creative fields are the least likely to feel that advanced education is important. As anticipated, professionals in fields which require specific advanced education (law, college teaching and medicine) show the strongest appreciation for such training.

Another question asked alumni with graduate training whether they thought such training has helped them to avoid being stranded at a low level in their field. (TABLE 78)   More than two-thirds of the respondents agree that this has been the case.   Again, science and mathematics majors and those who held the highest degrees are the most likely to credit graduate training with helping them in career advancement. By occupation, medical workers and college professors agree most strongly that graduate training has been helpful to their careers, while salesmen and fiscal, office, and management workers are the most likely to question its value to them.

———————————— **TABLE 62** ————————————

Satisfaction with Work

How much do you like the kind of work you are doing?

	Very Much	Fairly Much	Dislike Slightly	Dislike Greatly	Not Applicable or No Answer	Total
All Graduates	69.3%	22.2	4.4	1.1	3.0	100.0%
Years Since Graduation						
Fifteen	73.3%	21.4	3.2	0.7	1.4	100.0%
Ten	71.2%	21.8	4.4	0.8	1.8	100.0%
Five	63.7%	23.2	5.5	1.8	5.8	100.0%
Current Income						
Under $6,000	70.6%	21.5	4.3	1.9	1.7	100.0%
6000-9999	66.7%	25.7	5.9	1.2	0.5	100.0%
10,000-14,999	73.7%	22.4	3.0	0.7	0.2	100.0%
15,000-20,999	80.1%	16.4	2.9	0.4	0.2	100.0%
21,000 and over	81.4%	16.3	1.6	0.5	0.2	100.0%
Occupation						
Lawyer	73.8%	22.2	2.6	0.5	0.9	100.0%
Clergyman	81.5%	16.2	1.7	0.2	0.4	100.0%
Elem-Second. Teach.	74.9%	21.0	2.9	0.7	0.5	100.0%
College Teacher	81.8%	15.4	1.9	0.4	0.5	100.0%
Salesman	68.8%	23.7	5.6	1.1	0.8	100.0%
Social Serv. Worker	71.1%	21.2	5.9	1.4	0.4	100.0%
Medical Worker	83.1%	12.0	2.5	0.3	2.1	100.0%
Scientist-Math.	63.2%	29.3	5.6	1.5	0.4	100.0%
Fiscal-Office-Mgmt.	65.7%	26.4	6.1	1.5	0.3	100.0%
Creative Worker	70.9%	23.5	3.7	1.4	0.5	100.0%
Other	64.5%	25.8	6.5	1.9	1.3	100.0%

▷ Most of the graduates express general satisfaction with their jobs.

There is a high correlation between job satisfaction and income.

─────────────────────── TABLE 63 ───────────────────────

Desire to be in Another Occupation

Do you wish you were in an occupation other than your present one?

	Years Since Graduation		
Percent saying "Yes"	15	10	5
All Graduates	10.0	9.4	11.2
Current Income			
Under $6,000	13.0	10.6	11.1
6000-9999	13.3	11.2	12.3
10,000-14,999	10.2	8.0	7.8
15,000-20,999	6.8	6.0	5.7
21,000 and over	3.9	7.0	6.3
Occupation			
Lawyer	5.7	3.5	3.5
Clergyman	1.4	3.2	3.4
Elem-Second. Teach.	9.5	8.4	10.2
College Teacher	2.3	5.1	2.5
Salesman	15.0	12.7	14.2
Social Serv. Worker	11.0	14.0	16.4
Medical Worker	3.3	2.8	1.7
Scientist-Math.	10.9	14.5	10.9
Fiscal-Office-Mgmt.	12.5	11.7	18.1
Creative Worker	11.0	10.9	16.4
Other	16.3	11.4	17.9

▷ Only one out of ten graduates definitely wishes he were in another
occupation or working for another employer.

——————— **TABLE 64** ———————

Whether Alumni Plan to Change Occupations

In the next three years, do you think you will change to another occupation?

Percent saying "definitely yes" or "probably yes"	15-years out		10-years out		5-years out	
	Def.	Prob.	Def.	Prob.	Def.	Prob.
All Graduates	3.5	8.1	4.2	8.7	8.9	11.7
Occupation						
Lawyer	0.9	2.2	11.1	4.9	3.5	4.0
Clergyman	2.7	3.4	1.3	7.6	1.7	5.1
Elem. - Second. Teacher	3.2	8.3	2.7	8.9	6.2	10.6
College Teacher	2.3	4.7	0.5	5.6	10.9	5.0
Salesman	3.4	8.8	3.2	11.9	9.9	12.3
Social Service Worker	2.2	13.9	7.0	11.9	11.3	14.5
Medical Worker	1.5	1.5	3.1	2.3	6.7	1.3
Scientist-Mathematician	3.4	7.2	4.3	9.7	7.1	13.2
Fiscal-Office-Mgmt.	3.6	10.8	5.2	10.2	10.2	19.0
Creative	1.2	8.6	3.2	12.2	10.9	20.9
Other	7.0	12.3	5.1	10.1	10.7	15.5
Income						
Under $6,000	6.0	7.1	4.2	15.0	11.9	9.5
6000-9999	3.9	10.8	4.2	9.7	7.9	13.3
10,000-14,999	3.5	8.6	2.6	8.5	5.2	9.1
15,000-20,999	1.7	5.2	2.6	3.3	5.7	5.7
21,000 and over	1.4	3.5	2.7	5.5	-	8.3

▷ Alumni gave a variety of reasons for changing jobs; the most common involved professional or personal advancement.

TABLE 65

Occupations Alumni Wish They Had Entered
(Those who desire a change)

Do you wish you were in an occupation other than your present one?
Which one?

	Percent Actually Employed in the Field (Total Sample)*	Percent Who Would Like to Change to the Field **
Teacher and Educational Administrator (all levels)	17.1%	20.4%
Medical Worker	8.5	11.7
Creative Worker	3.9	10.6
Other	9.5	10.6
Lawyer	6.8	10.2
Fiscal-Office-Mgmt.	16.9	8.1
Scientist-Math.	11.9	7.0
Social Serv. Worker	4.0	5.2
Salesman	9.6	4.5
Clergyman	3.9	1.6
No Answer	7.9	10.1
Total	100.0%	100.0%

*The percentages of the total sample actually employed in each field are shown for purposes of comparison.

**This column is based upon responses by the 1,087 graduates who expressed a wish to change occupations and specified a choice.

▷ Twenty percent of the younger alumni and 12 percent of the older
alumni say they may change their occupational field.
They would now elect law, college teaching, medical work,
or creative fields.
They tend to reject sales, science and mathematics careers,
and fiscal, office, and management work.

—————————————————— **TABLE 66** ——————————————————

Important Job Traits and Whether Current Job Satisfies Them

Below are some of the characteristics often associated with occupations and professions. Please indicate . . .

How important each characteristic is to you.

	Very	Some	Little	None	No Answer	Total
Opportunity to use my special abilities	77.4%	19.1	1.5	0.4	1.6	100.0%
Chance to earn a great deal of money	21.5%	52.1	19.8	5.0	1.6	100.0%
Permit me to be creative and original	57.4%	34.4	5.8	0.8	1.6	100.0%
Give me social status and prestige .	14.8%	53.3	24.5	5.7	1.7	100.0%
Enable me to look forward to a stable future	47.0%	41.6	8.1	1.6	1.7	100.0%
Leave me relatively free of supervision	44.2%	39.9	10.3	3.8	1.8	100.0%
Give me a chance to exercise leadership	53.7%	35.1	8.0	1.5	1.7	100.0%

The extent to which your current job has each characteristic.

	To a High Degree	Moderately	Slightly	Not at All	No Answer	Total
Opportunity to use my special abilities	55.4%	30.9	8.1	1.7	3.9	100.0%
Chance to earn a great deal of money	13.8%	35.1	24.7	22.4	4.0	100.0%
Permit me to be creative and original	38.6%	38.3	15.7	3.5	3.9	100.0%
Give me social status and prestige.	19.6%	49.3	21.3	5.7	4.1	100.0%
Enable me to look foward to a stable future	44.9%	37.3	10.0	3.8	4.0	100.0%
Leave me relatively free of supervision	44.0%	35.8	10.8	5.4	4.0	100.0%
Give me a chance to exercise leadership	37.6%	36.9	16.4	5.2	3.9	100.0%
Give me an opportunity to help others	50.2%	28.1	14.0	3.7	4.0	100.0%

▷ In evaluating job characteristics, graduates show a strong desire for positions where they can use their special abilities, be creative, help others and enjoy a stable future.

Less important are social status and the chance to earn a great deal of money.

──────────────── **TABLE 67** ────────────────

Employers Alumni Now Prefer
(Those who desire a different type of employer)

Do you wish you were working for an employer other than your
present one? What type of employer?

	Percent Actually Working for This Type of Employer (Total Sample)[*]	Percent Who Would Like to Work for This Type of Employer[**]
College or university	8.8%	35.1%
Private non-manufacturing	29.7	22.1
Private manufacturing	17.9	12.1
Hospital, Church, or Clinic	8.8	8.9
Federal government	5.5	8.7
Elem-Second. Schools	10.3	6.2
Research Organization	2.6	5.7
U.S. Military Service	4.5	0.5
State-Local Govt.	4.1	0.5
Agriculture	0.3	0.2
No Answer	7.5	--
Total	100.0%	100.0%

[*]The percentages of the total sample actually working for each type of employer are shown for purposes of comparison.

[**]This column is based upon responses from the 437 graduates who expressed a wish to change employers, and who specified what type of employer they would prefer.

──

▷ The most desirable new employer is a college or university for those expressing a desire to change employers.

Federal government jobs and jobs with research organizations and institutes were also popular with graduates.

TABLE 68

Satisfaction with Employer's Promotion Policy
(Those who responded "not applicable" omitted)

How much do you like your employer's promotion policy?

	Very Much	Fairly Much	Dislike Slightly	Dislike Greatly	No Answer	Total	N
All Graduates	24.5%	36.8	21.1	10.2	7.4	100.0%	(8302)
Years Since Graduation							
Fifteen	24.9%	36.7	20.9	9.3	8.2	100.0%	(2667)
Ten	25.3%	37.5	21.4	10.4	5.4	100.0%	(2776)
Five	23.4%	36.3	21.1	10.9	8.3	100.0%	(2858)
Current Employer							
Private Manufactur.	26.5%	38.4	23.9	9.4	1.8	100.0%	(1799)
Private Non-Manufact.	30.7%	32.2	17.5	8.4	11.2	100.0%	(2131)
Agricultural	35.7%	21.4	7.1	--	35.8	100.0%	(14)
Elem-Second. Schools	17.3%	41.2	25.5	13.3	2.7	100.0%	(873)
Colleges-Universities	21.7%	43.0	24.1	8.4	2.8	100.0%	(833)
U.S. Military	20.2%	32.5	25.2	18.4	3.7	100.0%	(440)
Federal Government	25.5%	44.0	20.6	9.0	0.9	100.0%	(568)
State-Local Govt.	18.5%	35.6	26.4	18.5	1.0	100.0%	(379)
Research Organiz.	25.9%	44.0	21.0	7.4	1.7	100.0%	(243)
Hospital-Church Clin.	26.7%	38.7	18.2	7.2	9.2	100.0%	(499)

———————————————— **TABLE 69** ————————————————

Satisfaction with Supervisors on Job
(Those who responded "not applicable" omitted)

How much do you like the supervisors for whom you work?

	Very Much	Fairly Much	Dislike Slightly	Dislike Greatly	Total	N
All Graduates	49.9%	38.9	8.8	2.4	100.0%	(8,806)
Years Since Graduation						
Fifteen	50.6%	38.8	7.9	2.7	100.0%	(2,760)
Ten	48.8%	40.1	9.2	1.9	100.0%	(2,972)
Five	48.6%	40.0	9.1	2.3	100.0%	(3,164)
Employer						
Private Manufactur.	47.2%	39.9	10.8	2.1	100.0%	(1,817)
Private Non-Manufact.	53.4%	36.8	8.0	1.8	100.0%	(2,094)
Agriculture	66.7%	22.2	11.1	--	100.0%	(9)
Elem-Second. Schools	45.1%	41.8	10.6	2.5	100.0%	(1,089)
Colleges-Universities	53.6%	37.9	6.0	2.5	100.0%	(899)
U.S. Military Service	36.9%	50.9	8.2	4.0	100.0%	(451)
Federal Government	45.9%	43.4	7.9	2.8	100.0%	(587)
State-Local Govt.	47.2%	41.5	8.6	2.7	100.0%	(417)
Research Organiz.	52.5%	36.1	8.8	2.6	100.0%	(272)
Hospital-Church Clin.	57.9%	34.7	5.8	1.6	100.0%	(722)

▷ Strong satisfaction is reported with supervisors, colleagues, and
subordinates on the job.

TABLE 70

Satisfaction with Colleagues on the Job
(Those who responded "not applicable" omitted)

How much do you like the colleagues who work with you?

	Very Much	Fairly Much	Dislike Slightly	Dislike Greatly	Total	N
All Graduates	54.2%	42.7	2.9	0.2	100.0%	(10,083)
Years Since Graduation						
Fifteen	55.5%	41.9	2.4	0.2	100.0%	(3,293)
Ten	54.0%	43.0	2.8	0.2	100.0%	(3,417)
Five	53.8%	42.5	3.5	0.2	100.0%	(3,373)
Employer						
Private Manufactur.	51.6%	45.5	2.5	0.4	100.0%	(1,898)
Private Non-Manufact.	55.8%	41.1	3.0	0.1	100.0%	(2,921)
Agriculture	59.3%	37.0	3.7	--	100.0%	(27)
Elem-Second. Schools	52.0%	44.5	3.3	0.2	100.0%	(1,100)
Colleges-Universities	55.3%	42.6	2.0	0.1	100.0%	(942)
U.S. Military Service	53.5%	43.9	2.6	--	100.0%	(476)
Federal Government	51.7%	45.5	2.8	--	100.0%	(596)
State-Local Govt.	51.7%	45.2	2.9	0.2	100.0%	(441)
Research Organiz.	51.5%	43.8	4.3	0.4	100.0%	(278)
Hospital-Church-Clin.	61.8%	35.2	2.7	0.3	100.0%	(879)

———— TABLE 71 ————

Satisfaction with Subordinates on the Job
(Those who responded "not applicable" omitted)

How much do you like the people who work for you?

	Very Much	Fairly Much	Dislike Slightly	Dislike Greatly	Total	N
All Graduates	51.1%	46.6	2.1	0.2	100.0%	(7997)
Years Since Graduation						
Fifteen	53.7%	44.8	1.4	0.1	100.0%	(2929)
Ten	51.9%	46.2	1.7	0.2	100.0%	(2735)
Five	46.9%	49.4	3.2	0.5	100.0%	(2333)
Employer						
Private Manufactur.	48.6%	49.8	1.5	0.1	100.0%	(1530)
Private Non-Manufact.	50.0%	48.0	1.9	0.1	100.0%	(2621)
Agriculture	44.4%	51.9	--	3.7	100.0%	(27)
Elem-Second. Schools	57.8%	40.3	1.7	0.2	100.0%	(588)
Colleges-Universities	56.7%	41.1	1.9	0.3	100.0%	(633)
U.S. Military Service	41.8%	54.9	3.2	0.1	100.0%	(436)
Federal Government	46.0%	51.4	2.6	0.0	100.0%	(469)
State-Local Govt.	47.5%	48.5	3.1	0.9	100.0%	(356)
Research Organiz.	54.6%	43.6	1.8	--	100.0%	(218)
Hospital-Church Clin.	59.8%	38.1	1.7	0.4	100.0%	(742)

─────────── **TABLE 72** ───────────

Satisfaction with Income

How much do you like your income from your job?

	Very Much	Fairly Much	Dislike Slightly	Dislike Greatly	No Answer	Total
All Graduates	23.5%	42.5	19.8	8.6	5.6	100.0%
Years Since Graduation						
Fifteen	28.6%	44.7	17.5	5.7	3.5	100.0%
Ten	24.1%	43.6	20.5	7.5	4.3	100.0%
Five	17.9%	39.3	21.2	12.3	9.3	100.0%

▷ Satisfaction with income is generally high.

Occupation						
Lawyer	35.5%	42.7	12.3	6.2	3.3	100.0%
Clergyman	26.7%	39.7	22.6	2.1	8.9	100.0%
Elem-Second. Teach.	15.6%	48.1	23.9	9.5	2.9	100.0%
College Teacher	21.4%	42.0	26.5	7.8	2.3	100.0%
Salesman	27.4%	46.3	17.8	6.2	2.3	100.0%
Social Serv. Worker	27.7%	51.1	13.9	5.1	2.2	100.0%
Medical Worker	57.1%	29.3	5.6	2.6	5.4	100.0%
Scientist-Math.	27.0%	52.5	14.9	4.3	1.3	100.0%
Fiscal-Office-Mgmt.	31.3%	45.4	16.5	4.8	2.0	100.0%
Creative Worker	21.5%	44.2	25.8	6.1	2.4	100.0%
Other	25.6%	49.2	18.3	3.7	3.2	100.0%

Employer						
Private Manufactur.	27.4%	48.4	19.0	4.2	1.0	100.0%
Private Non-Manufact.	31.7%	42.1	17.5	5.8	2.9	100.0%
Agriculture	21.6%	48.7	16.2	2.7	10.8	100.0%
Elem-Second. Schools	10.4%	40.5	29.3	17.9	1.9	100.0%
Colleges-Universities	15.7%	44.3	25.8	10.4	3.8	100.0%
U.S. Military Service	19.6%	48.6	21.3	6.4	4.1	100.0%
Federal Government	26.0%	54.2	15.2	3.2	1.4	100.0%
State-Local Govt.	16.3%	45.4	24.3	13.1	0.9	100.0%
Research Organiz.	33.3%	47.4	13.0	4.2	2.1	100.0%
Hospital-Church Clin.	20.6%	34.2	20.7	15.7	8.8	100.0%

▷ The least satisfied with their income are elementary and secondary teachers and college teachers.

Income						
Under $6,000	8.2%	21.9	24.6	33.3	12.0	100.0%
6000,9999	13.8%	48.0	27.9	8.9	1.4	100.0%
10,000-14,999	31.6%	50.8	14.0	2.5	1.1	100.0%
15,000-20,999	46.2%	45.4	5.6	1.2	1.6	100.0%
$21,000 and over	68.3%	27.0	2.3	0.5	1.9	100.0%

-- TABLE 73 --

Self-Appraisal of Career Success

Contrasted with your college classmates, would you say that
your career had been more successful?

	Definitely Yes	Probably Yes	Probably No	Definitely No	No Answer	Total
All Graduates	13.2%	53.2	28.1	2.2	3.3	100.0%
Years Since Graduation						
Fifteen	12.9%	53.4	29.4	2.1	2.2	100.0%
Ten	13.4%	53.3	28.6	2.3	2.4	100.0%
Five	13.4%	52.8	26.5	2.1	5.2	100.0%
Current Income						
Under $6000	13.5%	42.1	35.7	5.7	3.0	100.0%
6000-9999	7.5%	51.3	37.2	2.3	1.7	100.0%
10,000-14,999	12.9%	62.7	22.7	.5	1.2	100.0%
15,000-20,999	26.3%	65.0	7.7	--	1.0	100.0%
21,000 and over	37.8%	56.7	4.2	.2	1.1	100.0%
Occupation						
Lawyer	18.3%	64.1	15.6	1.0	1.0	100.0%
Clergyman	8.1%	49.4	37.8	1.4	3.3	100.0%
Elem-Second. Teach.	8.8%	48.8	38.6	1.5	2.3	100.0%
College Teacher	16.3%	60.3	18.0	1.8	3.6	100.0%
Salesman	13.9%	51.6	31.1	2.0	1.4	100.0%
Social Serv. Worker	10.7%	55.1	30.1	1.8	2.3	100.0%
Medical Worker	28.4%	59.1	10.2	0.2	2.1	100.0%
Scientist-Math.	9.2%	56.4	31.4	1.5	1.5	100.0%
Fiscal-Office-Mgmt.	12.4%	51.6	32.1	2.3	1.6	100.0%
Creative Worker	14.0%	49.4	31.2	2.8	2.6	100.0%
Other	8.3%	56.2	30.7	3.8	1.0	100.0%

▷ Two-thirds of the alumni say their own careers are either definitely
or probably more successful than those of their classmates.

────────── **TABLE 74** ──────────

Expectation of Promotion

In the next three years, do you expect to receive a promotion?

	Definitely Yes	Probably Yes	Probably No	Definitely No	No Answer	Total
All Graduates	30.8%	36.5	19.2	9.1	4.4	100.0%
Years Since Graduation						
Fifteen	19.1%	38.7	25.3	12.8	4.1	100.0%
Ten	30.5%	39.3	18.4	8.4	3.4	100.0%
Five	42.2%	31.8	14.1	6.3	5.6	100.0%
Employer						
Private Manufactur.	34.9%	44.9	15.9	3.1	1.2	100.0%
Private Non-Manufact.	27.9%	32.3	18.0	16.5	5.3	100.0%
Agriculture	13.5%	21.6	35.1	24.3	5.5	100.0%
Elem-Second, Schools	15.3%	37.7	38.3	7.3	1.4	100.0%
Colleges-Universities	37.6%	42.8	16.4	2.6	0.6	100.0%
U.S. Military Service	32.9%	30.8	19.0	15.3	2.0	100.0%
Federal Government	47.3%	41.8	9.5	1.4	--	100.0%
State-Local Govt.	31.2%	40.1	21.8	5.8	1.1	100.0%
Research Organiz.	33.0%	45.3	17.9	2.8	1.0	100.0%
Hospital-Church Clin.	31.6%	32.7	22.6	9.5	3.6	100.0%
Occupation						
Lawyer	30.9%	30.2	16.5	14.5	7.9	100.0%
Clergyman	13.1%	43.2	30.4	10.0	3.3	100.0%
Elem-Second. Teach.	18.9%	37.6	35.1	6.8	1.6	100.0%
College Teacher	34.3%	44.5	17.9	3.0	0.3	100.0%
Salesman	30.9%	39.5	19.0	7.2	3.4	100.0%
Social Serv. Worker	39.9%	41.5	14.1	4.1	0.4	100.0%
Medical Worker	33.3%	17.5	12.5	30.7	6.0	100.0%
Scientist-Math.	33.4%	45.7	17.4	2.9	0.6	100.0%
Fiscal-Office, Mgmt.	33.7%	38.9	17.7	7.8	1.9	100.0%
Creative Worker	30.5%	42.4	17.7	6.3	3.1	100.0%
Other	36.4%	36.9	17.9	7.5	1.3	100.0%

——————————————— TABLE 75 ———————————————

Appraisal of Liberal Education as Preparation for Vocational Life

*To what extent do you agree or disagree with the following
statement about your undergraduate training: I received good
preparation for my vocational life?*

	Strongly Agree	Agree	Disagree	Strongly Disagree	No Answer	Total
All Graduates	16.8%	55.9	21.6	4.9	0.8	100.0%

Years Since Graduation   ▷ Most alumni feel their liberal arts background has provided good preparation for vocational life.

	Strongly Agree	Agree	Disagree	Strongly Disagree	No Answer	Total
Fifteen	16.7%	57.2	20.3	4.7	1.1	100.0%
Ten	17.2%	54.5	22.7	5.1	0.5	100.0%
Five	16.5%	55.9	21.9	4.9	0.8	100.0%

Type of Major

	Strongly Agree	Agree	Disagree	Strongly Disagree	No Answer	Total
Social Sciences	13.9%	55.7	24.4	5.2	0.8	100.0%
Humanities	19.3%	51.6	22.3	5.8	1.0	100.0%
Science and Math.	19.5%	58.6	17.4	4.0	0.5	100.0%

Academic Record

	Strongly Agree	Agree	Disagree	Strongly Disagree	No Answer	Total
High	24.1%	57.3	16.1	2.1	0.4	100.0%
Average	18.0%	56.9	19.8	4.4	0.9	100.0%
Low	12.9%	54.3	25.8	6.3	0.7	100.0%

Size of College   ▷ Graduates with high academic records and those who studied science and mathematics are the most satisfied.

	Strongly Agree	Agree	Disagree	Strongly Disagree	No Answer	Total
Small	19.1%	57.7	18.9	3.6	0.7	100.0%
Medium	16.2%	55.9	21.8	5.2	0.9	100.0%
Large	14.6%	53.4	25.0	6.2	0.8	100.0%

Occupation (15-year Graduates Only):   ▷ Alumni from smaller colleges are more satisfied than those from large institutions.

	Strongly Agree	Agree	Disagree	Strongly Disagree	No Answer	Total
Lawyer	18.4%	55.7	20.6	4.0	1.3	100.0%
Clergyman	28.1%	59.6	11.6	--	0.7	100.0%
Elem-Second. Teach.	16.3%	64.2	14.2	4.4	0.9	100.0%
College Teacher	22.2%	58.0	14.4	3.1	2.3	100.0%
Salesman	7.6%	51.1	34.8	5.4	1.1	100.0%
Social Serv. Worker	16.8%	59.9	19.0	3.7	0.6	100.0%
Medical Worker	31.1%	53.9	11.4	3.6	--	100.0%
Scientist-Math.	18.3%	63.4	14.0	4.1	0.2	100.0%
Fiscal-Office-Mgmt.	12.2%	55.5	26.0	6.1	0.2	100.0%
Creative Worker	15.3%	50.3	26.4	4.9	3.1	100.0%
Other	11.0%	59.5	22.3	6.3	0.9	100.0%

TABLE 76

Extent to Which Job Uses Liberal Education Skills

Does your position involve speaking, reading, or writing a foreign language?

	Quite a Lot	A Fair Amount	A Little	None	No Answer	Total
All Graduates	4.9%	4.3	19.4	68.6	2.8	100.0%
Occupation						
Lawyer	2.6%	2.0	16.2	77.8	1.4	100.0%
Clergyman	14.5%	10.7	36.3	37.8	0.7	100.0%
Elem-Second. Teach.	8.6%	4.1	18.4	67.9	1.0	100.0%
College Teacher	11.4%	10.0	34.3	44.0	0.3	100.0%
Salesman	2.7%	1.8	7.2	86.9	1.4	100.0%
Social Serv. Worker	3.2%	3.0	18.5	74.7	0.6	100.0%
Medical Worker	1.8%	3.6	25.0	68.2	1.4	100.0%
Scientist-Math.	2.0%	6.7	31.9	58.9	0.5	100.0%
Fiscal-Office-Mgmt.	3.2%	2.6	10.5	83.3	0.4	100.0%
Creative Worker	4.4%	3.5	21.0	69.0	2.1	100.0%
Other	4.8%	4.3	16.7	73.3	0.9	100.0%

Does your work involve much writing?

	Quite a Lot	A Fair Amount	A Little	None	No Answer	Total
All Graduates	41.0%	35.4	18.2	3.1	2.3	100.0%
Occupation						
Lawyer	79.8%	16.4	2.8	0.4	0.6	100.0%
Clergyman	60.6%	31.6	7.1	0.2	0.5	100.0%
Elem-Second. Teach.	34.5%	38.5	23.4	3.2	0.4	100.0%
College Teacher	46.1%	37.7	14.5	1.4	0.3	100.0%
Salesman	27.9%	41.2	25.9	4.4	0.6	100.0%
Social Serv. Worker	57.2%	34.6	8.0	0.2	--	100.0%
Medical Worker	29.2%	37.0	27.4	5.3	1.1	100.0%
Scientist-Math.	33.9%	47.1	17.6	1.3	0.1	100.0%
Fiscal-Office-Mgmt.	36.4%	38.7	21.7	2.9	0.3	100.0%
Creative Worker	62.2%	20.1	12.8	3.7	1.2	100.0%
Other	41.5%	32.5	18.7	6.6	0.7	100.0%

Does your work involve creative thinking?

	Quite a Lot	A Fair Amount	A Little	None	No Answer	Total
All Graduates	54.1%	30.3	10.4	2.5	2.7	100.0%
Occupation						
Lawyer	74.2%	20.3	3.8	1.0	0.7	100.0%
Clergyman	86.0%	12.1	1.2	--	0.7	100.0%
Elem-Second. Teacher	57.9%	32.5	7.6	0.9	1.1	100.0%
Colleges-Teacher	66.7%	26.3	5.8	0.5	0.7	100.0%
Salesman	51.5%	34.9	10.5	2.4	0.7	100.0%
Social Serv. Worker	61.5%	28.0	8.7	1.4	0.4	100.0%
Medical Worker	35.7%	38.1	19.5	5.1	1.6	100.0%
Scientist-Math.	58.9%	31.1	8.3	1.0	0.7	100.0%
Fiscal-Office-Mgmt.	43.1%	37.1	15.1	4.0	0.7	100.0%
Creative Worker	72.5%	19.8	6.5	0.5	0.7	100.0%
Other	45.8%	32.6	15.0	5.2	1.4	100.0%

△ There is general agreement that effective writing and creative thinking are important career assets.

Additional comments by alumni stress the importance of effective self-expression in vocational life.

———————————————————— TABLE 77 ————————————————————

Appraisal of Graduate Training as Help in Career

*Generally speaking, do you feel that advanced academic training
is important to people working in your field?*

	Yes, essential	Yes, desirable	No, only slightly helpful	No, of no use at all	No Answer	Total
All Graduates	54.8%	29.7	12.7	2.6	0.2	100.0%
Academic Record						
High	72.2%	20.1	6.1	1.5	0.1	100.0%
Average	57.7%	29.1	10.8	2.1	0.3	100.0%
Low	44.0%	35.0	17.6	3.0	0.4	100.0%
Type of Major						
Science-Math	65.4%	26.7	6.6	1.1	0.2	100.0%
Social Sci.	48.7%	32.3	15.7	2.9	0.4	100.0%
Humanities	51.2%	28.4	15.8	4.4	0.2	100.0%
Amount of Graduate Training						
None	24.3%	44.3	25.7	5.3	0.4	100.0%
Some, but no advanced degree	45.2%	36.6	13.6	4.3	0.3	100.0%
Master's Degree	68.3%	25.6	5.2	0.8	0.1	100.0%
Professional Degree	80.7%	14.1	4.3	0.7	0.2	100.0%
Doctorate	94.3%	5.3	0.1	0.1	0.2	100.0%
Occupation						
Lawyer	79.7%	11.2	7.9	1.0	0.2	100.0%
Clergymen	69.1%	27.8	2.9	--	0.2	100.0%
Elem-Second. Teacher	72.7%	23.4	3.3	0.2	0.4	100.0%
College Teacher	88.4%	10.3	1.2	--	0.1	100.0%
Salesman	16.2%	42.2	33.1	8.2	0.3	100.0%
Social Serv. Worker	76.8%	18.2	3.4	1.4	0.2	100.0%
Medical Worker	88.2%	9.4	2.3	--	0.1	100.0%
Scientist-Math.	60.1%	33.7	5.6	0.6	0.0	100.0%
Fiscal-Office-Mgmt.	23.9%	45.2	24.6	6.0	0.3	100.0%
Creative	21.5%	39.9	33.1	5.4	0.1	100.0%
Other	37.2%	45.4	15.0	2.1	0.3	100.0%

——————TABLE 78 ——————

Role of Graduate Study in Career Level
(7,434 alumni who attended graduate or professional school)

Please indicate the extent to which you agree or disagree with the following statement: Graduate study helped me avoid being stuck at a low level in my field.

	Strongly Agree	Agree	No Opinion	Disagree	Strongly Disagree	Total
All Graduates	38.4%	29.2	14.5	13.6	4.3	100.0%
Type of Major						
Science-Math	45.9%	29.4	11.8	10.2	2.7	100.0%
Social Sciences	35.1%	28.3	15.9	15.8	4.9	100.0%
Humanities	31.8%	30.9	16.3	15.3	5.7	100.0%
Amount of Graduate Training						
Some grad training but no advanced degree	17.4%	25.7	18.5	28.1	10.3	100.0%
Master's degree	34.1%	38.5	10.8	13.4	3.2	100.0%
Professional degree	48.0%	24.0	19.1	6.6	2.3	100.0%
Doctorate	70.9%	22.6	3.8	2.0	0.7	100.0%
Occupation						
Lawyer	48.1%	21.4	21.6	6.9	2.0	100.0%
Clergyman	31.7%	36.7	18.4	9.9	3.3	100.0%
Elem-Second. Teacher	33.3%	39.9	11.4	13.1	2.3	100.0%
College Teacher	55.0%	32.4	6.7	4.2	1.7	100.0%
Salesman	7.7%	20.5	20.2	35.6	16.0	100.0%
Social Serv. Worker	53.8%	28.3	6.5	9.8	1.6	100.0%
Medical Worker	59.3%	20.9	15.5	2.6	1.7	100.0%
Scientist-Math	42.8%	31.7	8.9	13.5	3.1	100.0%
Fiscal-Office-Mgmt.	16.2%	28.8	18.2	27.0	9.8	100.0%
Creative Worker	13.9%	22.4	17.2	32.6	13.9	100.0%
Other	23.2%	28.0	18.0	24.8	6.0	100.0%

▷ Graduate training is also highly valued.
　　Three-quarters of alumni who have taken graduate work say it has helped them avoid being stuck at a low level in their fields.

8

INTELLECTUAL and CULTURAL INTERESTS
of LIBERAL ARTS GRADUATES

Educators agree that college should be a prelude to a life of meaningful intellectual and cultural activity. Yet there has been little relevant data assessing the extent to which collegiate education is followed by continued study and growth.

Continued Education

Despite the lapse of time since the baccalaureate, eight percent of the graduates still are students. This ranges from 13 percent of the alumni of five years earlier, to six percent of the ten-year class, to three percent of the graduates of fifteen years earlier.

Many still plan additional study: eight percent say they may enroll as full-time students during the next three years. (TABLE 79) Four percent of the graduates of fifteen years still are considering additional full-time study. Teachers, social service workers, and medical workers are the most likely to contemplate further full-time training. The least interested are lawyers, salesmen, fiscal, office, and management workers, and creative workers.

As was shown in Chapter One (TABLE 6) , 21 percent of the alumni expect to receive an additional degree in the next few years — 10 percent of those out 15 years, 17 percent of ten years, and 35 percent of five. Many of these alumni, it should be pointed out, will receive degrees as a result of part-time study.

142

Among the comments made by graduates on the need for additional education were the following:

> Continued education is necessary to keep pace with modern technology. *Stanford University*

> Education does not stop with graduation from college. I read a number of periodicals and three or four good books each month. Education is only a ticket to a full life, not an all-expenses guided tour. *Miami University*

> The problem of constant, continuing education is one of the most difficult problems of the present and future. One must remain a perpetual student. *Stanford University*

Intellectual and Cultural Discussions

Four out of every ten alumni now are participating in literary, art, discussion, or study groups. (TABLE 80) Older graduates are somewhat more likely to be participating. Among those who majored in the humanities, 53 percent are now in discussion groups in contrast to 34 percent of former science and mathematics students. While not shown, graduates who had high academic records or who hold doctor's degrees are more likely to belong to discussion groups.

Over half of the clergymen, elementary and secondary school teachers, college professors, and social service workers belong to a formal discussion group. The least frequent participants are salesmen, fiscal, office, and management workers, and scientists and mathematicians.

Reading of Books and Periodicals

Despite the many demands on their time, alumni read fairly extensively. The next three tables indicate the extent of reading books related to work (TABLE 81), general non-fiction (TABLE 82), and fiction (TABLE 83).

In all, the typical graduate reads between 11 and 15 books a year, slightly less than half related to his work. Nearly a quarter of the alumni read more than 15 job-related books. Somewhat less reading of fiction was reported — 43 percent read five or more fiction works in the twelve-month period and 16 percent read more than 15 books of fiction. Non-fiction (other than books related to work) was the least heavily-read — only 36 percent of the graduates read five or more such books during the year and only 11 percent read more than 15 non-fiction books.

Younger alumni tend to read the most job-related books. College and university professors and clergymen do the most reading in their field and salesmen and fiscal, office, and management workers read the least. Despite wide fluctuations by occupation, every field has about 10 percent or more graduates who read more than 15 books related to their work during the year. While not shown, income level is not related to professional reading.

Graduates with high academic records are somewhat more likely to do non-vocational reading (both fiction and non-fiction). There is a somewhat stronger relationship between college major and amount of non-vocational reading, with former humanities majors reporting the most reading and science and mathematics majors the least.

Almost half the alumni read five or more periodicals related to their work during the twelve-month period preceding the survey. (TABLE 84)   Those with higher incomes tend to read more such periodicals, particularly medical workers, lawyers, and creative workers. As was true of books, younger alumni do slightly more professional reading of periodicals.

Fewer alumni read general periodicals. (TABLE 85)   Non-professional magazines are more heavily read by graduates with lower academic records and by those who hold only the bachelor's degree. Alumni who majored in science and mathematics read fewer general publications than do graduates from other major fields.

Cultural Activities

The role of liberal education in developing cultural interests is mentioned frequently. Sanford, writing in *The American College*, comments:

> There is much evidence that in the United States today the kind of culture that is acquired in a liberal arts college is highly important to success in the more prestigeful professions, not so much because the culture prepares for the work to be done as much

as because it makes possible the associations and
styles of life that go with these professions. [1]

Seldom, however, has adequate documentation illustrated the extent
to which graduates participate in cultural activities. Our survey ex-
amined the extent to which liberal arts alumni attend the theater,
musical events, or public lectures, or visit museums.   (TABLE 86)
Roughly, two out of three graduates attended the theater or a public
lecture or visited an art museum in the last year. More than a third
attended two or more operas or symphonic concerts. This data may
understate actual inclinations of alumni, who encounter a paucity
of opportunities in some areas of the country.

Attendance at theatrical productions, musical events, and art
museums tends to rise with quality of college attended. Attendance
at public lectures shows little variation by quality of college. Going
to the theater rises with higher income, while attendance at public
lectures decreases — a possible commentary on the relative levels
of the admission fees.

Public Speaking and Writing

Two-thirds of the graduates gave one or more public speeches
in the last year. (TABLE 87)   Public speaking was more common among
the older alumni. At least 60 percent of those in every occupation
gave at least one talk. Not surprisingly, clergymen and college
teachers led the list.

The most surprising statistic may be the fact that one percent
of the clergymen did not give a single public address!

Not all the articles were written by assistant and associate professors aspiring for promotion. While almost half the college teachers
published an article during the past year, authors were found in every
occupation — particularly the clergy, social service, science and
mathematics, and in creative fields. College professors wrote the
most books (eight percent wrote one in the last year), but even doctors, lawyers, and scientists became authors.

FOOTNOTE

1.   Sanford, Nevitt, editor, *The American College.* New York, John Wiley and Sons,
     1962, p. 34.

——————————— **TABLE 79** ———————————

Plans for Additional Full-Time Study

In the next three years, do you expect to enroll as a full-time student?

	Definitely Yes	Probably Yes	Probably No	Definitely No	No Answer	Total
All Graduates	3.5%	4.9	30.4	59.1	2.1	100.0%
Years Since Graduation						
Fifteen	1.2%	2.6	25.2	70.0	1.0	100.0%
Ten	2.6%	4.3	31.3	60.7	1.1	100.0%
Five	6.5%	7.6	34.5	47.1	4.3	100.0%
Academic Record						
High	5.0%	4.0	23.8	63.0	4.2	100.0%
Average	3.6%	4.6	32.0	57.8	2.0	100.0%
Low	3.1%	5.6	31.9	57.8	1.6	100.0%
Current Occupation						
Lawyer	0.4%	0.3	18.7	80.1	0.5	100.0%
Clergyman	2.9%	5.5	48.5	42.5	0.6	100.0%
Elem-Second. Teacher	4.2%	10.6	43.3	41.5	0.4	100.0%
College Teacher	4.7%	6.8	24.5	62.9	1.1	100.0%
Salesman	0.9%	1.6	26.6	70.4	0.5	100.0%
Social Serv. Worker	5.7%	8.7	34.2	51.4	--	100.0%
Medical Worker	4.7%	3.5	18.2	72.2	1.4	100.0%
Scientist-Math.	1.9%	3.5	34.1	60.1	0.4	100.0%
Fiscal-Office-Mgmt.	0.8%	2.4	31.3	65.0	0.5	100.0%
Creative Worker	0.5%	2.8	25.9	70.2	0.6	100.0%
Other	4.1%	8.6	36.0	50.9	0.4	100.0%

——————————————— **TABLE 80** ———————————————

Alumni Participation in Discussion Groups

*During the past 12 months have you participated in a literary,
art, discussion, or study group?*

	Yes	No	No Answer	Total
All Graduates	38.8%	60.3%	0.9	100%
Years Since Graduation				
Fifteen	41.0%	58.0	1.0	100%
Ten	38.9%	60.1	1.0	100%
Five	36.6%	62.6	0.8	100%
Type of Major				
Science and Math.	33.6%	65.5	0.9	100%
Social Science	36.8%	62.2	1.0	100%
Humanities	52.7%	46.5	0.8	100%
Occupation				
Lawyer	32.9%	66.3	0.8	100%
Clergyman	77.4%	22.1	0.5	100%
Elem-Second. Teach.	54.7%	44.2	1.1	100%
College Teacher	63.8%	36.1	0.1	100%
Salesman	25.6%	73.3	1.1	100%
Social Serv. Worker	50.3%	49.4	0.3	100%
Medical Worker	41.0%	58.1	0.9	100%
Scientist-Math.	26.4%	72.7	0.9	100%
Fiscal-Office-Mgmt.	27.7%	71.5	0.8	100%
Creative Worker	43.1%	56.4	0.5	100%
Other	27.2%	72.2	0.6	100%

▷ Liberal arts graduates report a fairly active intellectual and cultural life.

Four out of ten graduates participate in intellectual or cultural discussion
groups.

——————— **TABLE 81** ———————

Reading of Books Related to Work

| | Number of Books Read During the Year | | | | | | | | |
	None	1-2	3-4	5-7	8-10	11-15	Over 15	No Answer	Total
All Graduates	8.4%	21.4	20.0	12.6	9.3	4.2	23.2	0.9	100.0%

Years Since Graduation

	None	1-2	3-4	5-7	8-10	11-15	Over 15	No Answer	Total
Fifteen	8.7%	23.0	21.2	12.4	9.3	4.1	19.8	1.5	100.0%
Ten	9.1%	22.4	19.7	12.8	9.3	4.3	21.8	0.6	100.0%
Five	7.4%	18.9	19.2	12.5	9.3	4.1	27.8	0.8	100.0%

Employer

	None	1-2	3-4	5-7	8-10	11-15	Over 15	No Answer	Total
Private Manufactur.	14.0%	31.6	21.8	10.6	7.5	2.6	10.8	1.1	100.0%
Private Non-Manuf.	12.8%	26.9	20.4	11.1	6.3	2.9	18.7	0.9	100.0%
Agriculture	16.2%	21.6	16.2	8.1	10.8	-	18.9	8.2	100.0%
Elem-Second. Sch.	3.8%	18.4	24.8	17.1	13.7	4.5	16.8	0.9	100.0%
Coll-Univ.	0.7%	6.4	13.3	14.3	12.1	5.4	47.1	0.7	100.0%
U.S. Mil.	3.1%	12.4	22.1	13.8	12.8	6.0	28.9	0.9	100.0%
Federal Govt.	9.3%	26.8	21.2	12.2	8.0	4.7	17.2	0.6	100.0%
State-Local Govt.	6.9%	23.6	22.9	14.7	9.8	3.1	18.0	1.0	100.0%
Research Org.	4.2%	21.4	26.7	13.3	9.1	3.2	21.8	0.3	100.0%
Hosp-Ch-Clin.	1.8%	9.2	16.3	13.9	13.3	9.2	35.3	1.0	100.0%

Occupation

	None	1-2	3-4	5-7	8-10	11-15	Over 15	No Answer	Total
Lawyer	5.1%	18.0	20.2	11.5	7.7	2.7	34.4	0.4	100.0%
Clergyman	0.2%	3.1	8.1	14.7	15.9	14.7	42.0	1.3	100.0%
Elem-Second. Teach.	3.3%	16.6	23.5	15.4	13.8	4.6	21.9	0.9	100.0%
College Teacher	0.4%	5.4	12.8	14.5	11.6	6.8	47.8	0.7	100.0%
Salesman	16.5%	31.6	21.5	10.5	5.7	2.6	10.4	1.2	100.0%
Social Ser.	4.6%	16.0	18.5	17.8	12.8	6.2	23.7	0.4	100.0%
Medical Worker	2.8%	15.8	19.7	15.0	9.7	5.2	31.4	0.4	100.0%
Scientist-Math.	7.9%	25.2	23.5	11.1	9.9	3.3	18.4	0.7	100.0%
Fiscal-Office-Mgt.	16.7%	32.8	21.1	10.0	6.4	2.3	9.6	1.1	100.0%
Creative Worker	11.2%	26.3	19.4	12.8	5.6	2.6	21.2	0.9	100.0%
Other	10.4%	23.8	22.6	13.1	8.3	3.6	17.3	0.9	100.0%

▷ Half the alumni reported reading five or more books related to their work during the past year, and nearly a quarter said they read more than 15 such books.

TABLE 82

Reading of Non-Fiction Books

	Number of Books Read During Year								
	None	1-2	3-4	5-7	8-10	11-15	Over 15	No Answer	Total
All Graduates	11.6%	27.4	22.8	13.2	8.5	3.6	11.2	**1.7**	100.0%
Years Since Graduation									
Fifteen	10.9%	26.3	22.7	13.5	8.7	3.9	12.0	2.0	100.0%
Ten	12.2%	29.6	22.6	12.4	8.4	3.3	9.6	1.9	100.0%
Five	11.7%	26.3	23.0	13.5	8.4	3.7	12.0	1.4	100.0%
Academic Record									
High	8.6%	24.9	23.5	14.4	9.9	4.7	12.2	1.8	100.0%
Average	10.9%	27.8	23.3	13.4	8.4	3.2	11.5	1.5	100.0%
Low	15.9%	24.1	23.2	13.1	8.2	3.3	10.3	1.9	100.0%
Type of Major									
Science-Math	13.5%	31.6	22.9	12.2	7.2	3.0	8.0	1.6	100.0%
Social Sci.	11.5%	26.4	23.0	13.6	8.7	3.9	11.1	1.8	100.0%
Humanities	8.7%	22.5	21.9	13.8	10.2	4.2	17.0	1.7	100.0%

▷ Graduates who majored in the humanities and those with high academic
records are the heaviest readers of general non-fiction and fiction.

——— **TABLE 83** ———

Reading of Fiction Books

| | Number of Books Read During the Year | | | | | | | | |
	None	1-2	3-4	5-7	8-10	11-15	Over 15	No Answer	Total
All Graduates	15.0%	21.2	18.9	12.9	9.1	5.2	15.8	1.9	100.0%
Years Since Graduation									
Fifteen	14.6%	20.5	19.6	12.9	9.6	5.1	15.4	2.3	100.0%
Ten	16.5%	22.9	19.3	12.6	8.3	4.5	14.4	1.5	100.0%
Five	14.1%	20.3	17.9	13.2	9.4	6.1	17.5	1.5	100.0%
Academic Record									
High	12.9%	21.8	16.8	12.1	11.5	6.2	16.8	1.9	100.0%
Average	14.2%	21.7	19.8	12.5	9.7	5.0	15.4	1.7	100.0%
Low	18.8%	22.7	18.0	12.2	7.7	4.5	14.3	1.8	100.0%
Type of Major									
Science-Math.	17.7%	24.3	19.0	12.8	8.1	4.1	12.6	1.4	100.0%
Social Sci.	15.2%	20.2	19.7	12.9	9.5	5.5	15.0	2.0	100.0%
Humanities	10.0%	18.4	17.0	13.2	9.8	6.7	23.1	1.8	100.0%

▷ Alumni read fairly extensively, with the heaviest concentration on work-related books, followed by fiction, and then non-fiction.

──────── TABLE 84 ────────

Reading of Periodicals Related to Work

Number of Periodicals Read During Year

	None	1-2	3-4	5-7	8-10	11-15	Over 15	No Answer	Total
All Graduates	4.9%	19.0	28.8	17.2	8.5	4.1	16.6	0.9	100.0%
Years Since Graduation									
Fifteen	3.5%	17.3	29.4	20.4	9.2	3.8	15.4	1.0	100.0%
Ten	4.3%	18.5	29.0	17.1	9.1	4.3	16.8	0.9	100.0%
Five	7.0%	21.1	27.9	14.3	7.1	4.2	17.4	1.0	100.0%
Income									
Under $6000	6.0%	23.9	28.9	16.9	7.2	3.8	12.4	0.9	100.0%
6000-9999	6.4%	22.3	28.3	15.6	7.9	3.8	14.8	0.9	100.0%
10,000-14,999	2.5%	17.1	29.4	18.0	9.5	5.0	17.8	0.7	100.0%
15,000-20,999	1.6%	10.7	29.0	21.3	9.4	5.4	21.9	0.7	100.0%
$21,000 and over	1.7%	13.5	28.5	21.6	9.4	3.5	21.1	0.7	100.0%
Occupation									
Lawyer	1.8%	16.9	29.0	17.3	8.5	4.3	21.7	0.5	100.0%
Clergyman	0.7%	10.2	36.3	25.7	10.2	5.5	9.7	1.7	100.0%
Elem-Second. Teach.	4.5%	24.1	32.4	17.5	6.5	3.1	11.0	0.9	100.0%
College Teacher	2.6%	14.2	28.4	23.8	11.6	3.3	15.8	0.3	100.0%
Salesman	5.5%	21.5	30.9	13.9	7.8	4.2	15.5	0.7	100.0%
Social Serv. Worker	3.4%	19.1	31.9	14.4	9.8	4.6	15.9	0.9	100.0%
Medical Worker	0.4%	11.6	31.1	20.2	8.1	4.3	23.9	0.4	100.0%
Scientist-Math.	4.2%	16.6	26.4	18.3	9.1	4.8	19.4	1.2	100.0%
Fiscal-Office-Mgmt.	7.6%	22.8	27.7	15.2	8.3	3.9	13.5	1.0	100.0%
Creative Worker	8.9%	17.9	22.6	13.5	11.2	4.2	20.8	0.9	100.0%
Other	6.9%	21.7	25.2	14.7	8.2	4.8	17.6	0.9	100.0%

▷ Over 20 percent of all medical workers, lawyers and creative workers
read regularly more than 15 periodicals in their field.

——————————————————— TABLE 85 ———————————————————

Reading of General Periodicals

| | | | | Number of Periodicals Read During Year | | | | | |
	None	1-2	3-4	5-7	8-10	11-15	Over 15	No Answer	Total
All Graduates	5.4%	25.3	33.6	17.5	6.1	2.4	8.2	1.5	100.0%
Years Since Graduation									
Fifteen	3.9%	23.7	35.2	19.0	6.4	2.3	7.7	1.8	100.0%
Ten	5.7%	24.8	34.2	17.1	6.1	2.4	8.2	1.5	100.0%
Five	6.6%	27.3	31.4	16.4	5.9	2.5	8.7	1.2	100.0%
Academic Record									
High	5.5%	28.8	33.5	17.3	5.3	2.3	6.1	1.2	100.0%
Average	5.2%	26.0	35.1	16.8	5.9	2.3	7.1	1.6	100.0%
Low	5.4%	24.4	30.8	18.0	6.5	2.7	10.7	1.5	100.0%
Type of Major									
Science-Math	6.8%	28.1	33.1	16.7	5.1	2.2	6.6	1.4	100.0%
Social Science	5.0%	24.3	33.7	17.7	6.4	2.4	9.0	1.5	100.0%
Humanities	4.2%	23.1	34.0	18.4	7.3	2.5	9.0	1.5	100.0%
Amount of Graduate Training									
None	5.0%	23.6	32.9	17.9	6.5	2.7	9.5	1.9	100.0%
Some, but no advanced degree	5.5%	25.3	32.4	17.9	6.6	2.0	8.9	1.4	100.0%
Master's	5.5%	26.5	33.6	17.5	5.9	2.6	7.2	1.2	100.0%
Prof.	6.4%	26.8	34.5	15.6	5.6	2.2	7.6	1.3	100.0%
Doctor's	4.0%	24.5	37.9	20.4	5.2	2.0	5.3	0.7	100.0%

TABLE 86

Cultural Activities of Alumni

During the past 12 months have you . . .

	Attended two or more theatrical productions?				Attended one or more public lectures?				Attended two or more opera or symphonic concerts?				Visited an art museum?			
	Yes	No	No Ans.	Total	Yes	No	No Ans.	Total	Yes	No	No Ans.	Total	Yes	No	No Ans.	Total
All Graduates	65.5%	33.4	1.1	100.0%	68.2%	31.2	0.6	100.0%	35.7%	63.5	0.8	100.0%	60.2%	38.9	0.9	100.0%
Years Since Graduation																
Fifteen	67.6%	31.3	1.1	100.0%	71.4%	27.8	0.8	100.0%	35.7%	63.2	1.1	100.0%	62.4%	36.7	0.9	100.0%
Ten	64.6%	34.6	0.8	100.0%	66.6%	32.7	0.7	100.0%	33.5%	65.6	0.9	100.0%	58.2%	40.9	0.9	100.0%
Five	65.4%	33.9	0.7	100.0%	66.5%	32.8	0.7	100.0%	37.7%	61.7	0.6	100.0%	60.0%	39.2	0.3	100.0%
Quality of College																
High	76.7%	22.7	0.6	100.0%	69.7%	29.6	0.7	100.0%	44.3%	55.0	0.7	100.0%	68.4%	30.9	0.7	100.0%
Medium	66.6%	32.6	0.8	100.0%	67.4%	32.0	0.6	100.0%	35.9%	63.3	0.8	100.0%	60.2%	39.0	0.8	100.0%
Low	58.0%	41.0	1.0	100.0%	68.2%	31.0	0.8	100.0%	29.9%	69.2	0.9	100.0%	55.0%	44.0	1.0	100.0%
Income																
Under $6,000	63.3%	36.3	0.4	100.0%	74.4%	25.3	0.3	100.0%	41.6%	57.9	0.5	100.0%	61.4%	38.0	0.6	100.0%
6000-9999	61.1%	38.3	0.6	100.0%	67.4%	32.0	0.6	100.0%	32.8%	66.6	0.6	100.0%	58.2%	41.0	0.8	100.0%
10,000-14,999	68.9%	30.4	0.7	100.0%	66.2%	33.2	0.6	100.0%	35.2%	64.1	0.7	100.0%	60.9%	38.4	0.7	100.0%
15,000-20,999	73.4%	25.8	0.8	100.0%	68.2%	31.1	0.7	100.0%	37.3%	61.9	0.8	100.0%	62.8%	36.5	0.7	100.0%
21,000 and over	83.0%	16.4	0.6	100.0%	66.4%	32.7	0.9	100.0%	35.5%	63.3	1.2	100.0%	63.0%	36.4	0.6	100.0%

△ During the past year, 66 percent of the graduates attended two or more theatrical productions; 68 percent, one or more public lectures; 36 percent, two or more operas or symphonic concerts: 60 percent, one or more art museums.

TABLE 87

Speeches and Publications by Alumni

During the past 12 months have you . . .

	Given one or more speeches?				Published an article?				Published a book?			
	Yes	No	No Ans.	Total	Yes	No	No Ans.	Total	Yes	No	No Ans.	Total
All Graduates	67.1%	32.2	0.7	100.0%	22.1%	76.9	1.0	100.0%	1.8%	96.9	1.3	100.0%
Years Since Graduation												
Fifteen	73.7%	25.6	0.7	100.0%	26.1%	72.8	1.1	100.0%	2.8%	95.5	1.7	100.0%
Ten	68.7%	30.6	0.7	100.0%	22.8%	76.4	0.8	100.0%	1.9%	96.9	1.2	100.0%
Five	59.1%	40.3	0.6	100.0%	17.8%	81.4	0.8	100.0%	0.9%	98.1	1.0	100.0%
Occupation												
Lawyer	70.0%	29.5	0.5	100.0%	15.7%	83.8	0.5	100.0%	1.2%	97.8	1.0	100.0%
Clergyman	99.0%	1.0	-	100.0%	40.3%	58.9	0.8	100.0%	1.7%	97.4	0.9	100.0%
El-Sec. T.	69.3%	29.8	0.9	100.0%	15.7%	82.9	1.4	100.0%	2.0%	95.8	2.2	100.0%
College T.	82.3%	17.5	0.2	100.0%	46.1%	53.4	0.5	100.0%	8.2%	90.4	1.4	100.0%
Salesman	61.5%	37.9	0.6	100.0%	7.2%	91.5	1.3	100.0%	0.2%	98.5	1.3	100.0%
Social Ser.	78.1%	21.4	0.5	100.0%	33.9%	65.4	0.7	100.0%	4.3%	94.3	1.4	100.0%
Medical Worker	72.7%	26.8	0.5	100.0%	23.6%	75.7	0.7	100.0%	0.8%	98.6	0.6	100.0%
Sci-Math.	59.5%	40.3	0.2	100.0%	35.3%	64.3	0.4	100.0%	1.9%	97.2	0.9	100.0%
Fis-Off-Mgt.	60.5%	38.9	0.6	100.0%	11.5%	87.6	0.9	100.0%	0.8%	98.1	1.1	100.0%
Creative	59.7%	40.1	0.2	100.0%	40.8%	59.2	--	100.0%	4.0%	95.1	0.9	100.0%
Other	65.2%	34.4	0.4	100.0%	17.1%	82.2	0.7	100.0%	0.8%	98.1	1.1	100.0%

△ Two-thirds of the graduates gave one or more public speeches during the year, 22 percent published an article, and two percent published a book.

9

CIVIC and SOCIAL CONTRIBUTIONS
of LIBERAL ARTS GRADUATES

Too many assume that the goal of today's college graduate is to move from commencement to a split-level suburban home with space for two cars, swimming pool privileges, and the opportunity to pass from bland youth to mediocre old age. The concerns of this mythical graduate would be limited to his financial, paternal, and social needs.

In contrast, the challenge of today is highlighted by Odegard:

> The type of specialization and analysis that has been pulling man and his world apart have at the same time made them everywhere more interdependent. That each man is his brother's keeper is no longer a question but a condition. ... This lays a special obligation on the social sciences because they are by definition concerned with man and society. So-called behavioral science ... has no mandate to be indifferent to human goals or values. [1]

Community Activities

During the past year, a third of the alumni worked on community fund-raising drives, a third attended two or more meetings of the P. T. A. (it should be recalled that all our respondents are men), and a quarter led or helped lead a scout troop or youth group. (TABLE 88) Participation in all these community services rises sharply among older alumni, probably as a result of deeper community roots and the presence of school-age children in their families.

155

Graduates who majored in science and mathematics and those who had the highest academic records are the least likely to participate in these community activities, although differences are not great. Involvement in fund-raising and P. T. A. participation increases with rising income, while leadership of youth groups is highest among low-income groups, because of the fact that relatively low-paid clergymen are by far the most active youth group leaders.

Participation by occupation varies sharply depending upon the type of community activity. The three leading occupational groups taking part in the activity most oriented to the business world — fund-raising — are lawyers, fiscal, office and management workers, and salesmen. The leaders, by far, in youth group and P. T. A. participation are clergymen and elementary and secondary school teachers. The occupational groups least active in community services are medical workers, college teachers, and scientists and mathematicians.

How do gratuates feel about civic responsibilities? Most graduates (82 percent) themselves agree that liberal education should develop a sense of responsibility to participate in community and public affairs. (TABLE 89)   The strongest commitment to this purpose is reported by former social science majors and the least by those who studied science and mathematics. While not shown, older alumni and poorer students academically are more likely to feel that training for civic responsibility is important.

When asked whether their own education had developed this sense of responsibility, only 53 percent said it had (contrasted to 82 percent who felt that it should). Majors in social sciences are the most likely to rate their own education highly in this respect, while those in science and mathematics are the least.

Political Activities and Preferences

Speaking to mid-year graduates of the University of Illinois in 1957, John F. Kennedy said:

> Your campus is visited by prospective employers, ranging from corporation vice-presidents to professional football coaches. ... But in the midst of all these pleas, plans and pressures, few, I dare say, if any will be urging upon you a career in the field of

politics. Some will point out the advantages of civil
service positions. Others will talk in noble terms
of public service and statesmanship. But few will
urge you to become a politician.

How did the graduates, some of whom were actually in the group
to which Senator Kennedy spoke, respond to his concern for more
active involvement in political affairs?

First, it is clear that no one political label characterizes the
liberal arts graduates: their political beliefs span most of the political spectrum. Almost as many graduates now label themselves
Conservative Republicans (17 percent) as Liberal Democrats (20
percent). (TABLE 90) Any election limited to those included in our
sample would be close indeed. Eliminating the 12 percent who described themselves as "middle-of-the-road" or who did not respond,
we find 43 percent of the alumni aligned with the Democrats and 45
percent with the Republicans.

A definite shift in attitudes since graduation is noted, with alumni now more conservative: 52 percent of the 1948 alumni said they
were Democrats or independent and liberal while in college, in contrast to only 45 percent of the 1958 alumni.

There is a correlation between political leanings and college
background. The best students in college now are the most likely to
have liberal political beliefs. (TABLE 91) Graduates in science and
mathematics tend to have more conservative views, while humanities majors are more likely to hold liberal views. In contrast to
those who stopped with their bachelor's, alumni with doctorates are
much more liberal.

Distinctive patterns of current political thought also appear when
analyzed by career patterns of alumni. (TABLE 92) Graduates earning the least money tend to be somewhat more liberal, while the
most conservative are in the higher income brackets (the smallest
percentage of Liberal Democrats and the largest percentage of Conservative Republicans appear, however, not in the highest income
bracket but rather in the next highest).

The extent of political involvement seems equally significant.
During the past year almost half of the graduates wrote to or talked
with a public official about a current program or proposed bill, but
less than 20 percent belonged to a political club or political action
group. (TABLE 93) In the last 12 months, one out of every 20 gradu-

ates campaigned for or held a public office. In each of these political activities, participation is markedly higher among the older graduates. Participation also increases with rising income in each activity. While not shown, lawyers are clearly the most politically active occupational group, with 17 percent having either run for or held a public office during the past year.

By occupation, a scale of political beliefs might be developed as follows:

Most Liberal

College Professor
Social Service Worker
Elementary or Secondary
    School Teachers

Most Conservative

Salesman
Medical Worker
Fiscal, Office, and
    Management Worker

Slightly Left of Center

Clergyman
Creative Worker
Other

Middle of the Road

Scientist and Mathematician
Lawyer

Organizational Memberships

The survey inquired about the graduates' membership in professional associations, service clubs, veterans organizations, and labor unions. Results show that 71 percent belong to professional associations, while much smaller numbers belong to service clubs (20 percent), and veterans groups (nine percent). (TABLE 94) Five percent belong to labor unions, but because the percentages were so low, these data were not included in the table. Older alumni are consistently more likely to belong to each such organization.

Among occupational groups, lawyers were the most likely to belong to professional associations, service clubs, and veterans organizations. Professional associations are strongest (with over 90 percent of the alumni involved in them) among lawyers, college teachers, medical workers, and elementary and secondary school teachers. By contrast, less than half of the salesmen and the fiscal, office, and management workers belong to professional groups.

Service club membership characterizes salesmen, fiscal, office and management workers, lawyers and clergymen and is least typical among scientists and mathematicians, college teachers, and creative workers. Although 74 percent of the graduates were eligible, through prior military service, less than 10 percent bothered to join a veteran's group. There was a striking lack of participation by college professors (three percent) and by clergymen (five percent).

Religious Activities and Preferences

Historically, an important goal of the liberal arts college was to train the "perfect Christian gentleman." Typical was Amherst College, founded to "prepare for the gospel ministry young men in indigent circumstances but of hopeful piety and promising talent." Among its first 3,428 graduates, 1,284 were ordained clergymen and missionaries.[2]

While alumni of today feel that college should play a role in developing appropriate values for life, the schools themselves debate the use of religion and moral training in the academic and extra-class life. Often those who most support the study of religion as an academic discipline are opposed to its being used within a humanistic framework.

At the other extreme, of course, are colleges with a much different philosophy. Church-related institutions often feel that religion should permeate every facet of college life, rather than be treated as just another academic discipline. At some, higher standards of religious participation prevail than are found in most churches.

While training for the ministry now is conducted in seminaries, the alumni clearly expect a liberal education to concern itself with ethical and moral questions. Almost 90 percent of the graduates say it is "fairly important" or "very important" for a liberal education to "develop moral capacities, ethical standards and values." (TABLE 95) This objective is more important to those graduates who attended Roman Catholic institutions and to the older alumni. Slightly over two-thirds of the graduates feel their own education met this objective, ranging from 89 percent of those from Roman Catholic schools to 58 percent of graduates of public colleges and universities.

Alumni from all types of colleges agree that religion is more important to them now than when they were college seniors. (TABLE 96) The percentage who feel religion is "very important" has climbed from 32 percent when they were college seniors to 42 percent today. Alumni of Catholic institutions are far more likely to rate religion important than graduates of public or private schools. While not shown, current attitudes toward religion seem relatively unaffected by academic record and type of college major.

Aside from clergymen, elementary and secondary school teachers consider religion the most important, followed by salesmen and fiscal, office, and management workers. (TABLE 97) The least concerned about religion are social service workers and those in creative fields. Alumni who rate religion as "very important" are more likely to come from the lower income brackets.

Actual religious preferences show that 52 percent of the graduates are Protestant, 21 percent are Catholic, 10 percent Jewish, and 14 percent have no religious preference. (TABLE 98) As college seniors, Catholics accounted for 93 percent of the enrollment at Roman Catholic institutions but only 11 percent at private colleges and 14 percent at public schools. Comparisons of religious choices when in college and now show slight declines in Jewish and Roman Catholic preferences and in all Protestant affiliations except for gains in Episcopalians and Presbyterians. The main increase occurred in the categories of other religions and no religious preference. This decline in attachment to formal religious groups is somewhat curious in the light of Table 96 which showed a 10 percent increase between college days to now in graduates who rate religion as "very important."

Although 85 percent of the graduates (TABLE 98) report a religious preference, only 58 percent attended church services "on a fairly regular basis" during the past year. (TABLE 99) A quarter of the graduates served on the governing boards of religious organizations, and 29 percent worked on fund-raising for a church. As also was true of community services and political activities, older alumni play a more active role in all of these church activities. Participation is higher among graduates of lower-quality schools and among alumni of Roman Catholic schools. By occupation, the most active participants in religious activities are lawyers, elementary and secondary school teachers, salesmen, and fiscal, office, and management workers. Consistently the least active are social service workers and those in creative fields.

Alumni Activities

Almost half of the graduates attended an alumni function or visited their undergraduate campus during the past year, and nearly as many contributed financially to their undergraduate college. (TABLE 100)   Attendance at college functions is highest among most recent graduates (reversing the pattern of higher participation by older graduates in all other activities noted in this chapter). Graduates of small schools and of high-quality schools are more likely to attend college functions.

In view of the importance of outside financial support to higher education, the fact that nearly 50 percent of all graduates contributed financially to their Alma Maters is significant. Fifty-seven percent of both Catholic and private school graduates gave money to their institutions, but support from public school alumni dropped to only 33 percent. Financial support is also substantially lower among graduates of large schools (34 percent) than of small schools (54 percent.) The percentage contributing to their colleges rises with the age of the alumni (resuming the pattern cited above), and with the level of income.

FOOTNOTES

1. Odegard, Peter H., "The Social Sciences and Society," *The Educational Record,* Vol. 45, Spring, 1964, p. 197.

2. Kennedy, Gail, *Education at Amherst: The New Program.* New York, Harper and Brothers, 1955, p. 330.

TABLE 88

Community Activities of Alumni

During the past 12 months have you . . . .

	Worked on fund-raising drives for United Fund or other such charitable organization?				Led or assisted in the leadership of a scout troop or youth group?				Attended two or more meetings of the PTA?			
	Yes	No	No Answer	Total	Yes	No	No Answer	Total	Yes	No	No Answer	Total
All Graduates	35.0%	63.9	1.1	100.0%	24.9%	74.1	1.0	100.0%	34.1%	65.0	0.9	100.0%
Years Since Graduation												
Fifteen	43.1%	55.5	1.4	100.0%	32.8%	66.1	1.1	100.0%	52.6%	46.3	1.1	100.0%
Ten	35.6%	63.2	1.2	100.0%	23.8%	75.1	1.1	100.0%	33.5%	65.5	1.0	100.0%
Five	26.7%	72.5	0.8	100.0%	18.3%	80.7	1.0	100.0%	16.8%	82.2	1.0	100.0%
Type of Major												
Social Sciences	41.1%	57.7	1.2	100.0%	26.2%	72.5	1.3	100.0%	35.6%	63.3	1.1	100.0%
Humanities	32.5%	66.3	1.2	100.0%	27.3%	71.8	0.9	100.0%	33.2%	65.7	1.1	100.0%
Science & Math	27.8%	71.4	0.8	100.0%	21.6%	77.5	0.9	100.0%	32.2%	67.0	0.8	100.0%
Academic Record												
High	28.4%	69.7	1.9	100.0%	19.9%	79.3	0.8	100.0%	27.3%	71.6	1.1	100.0%
Average	33.4%	65.6	1.0	100.0%	24.3%	74.7	1.0	100.0%	33.1%	65.9	1.0	100.0%
Low	38.8%	60.1	1.1	100.0%	28.8%	69.9	1.3	100.0%	36.6%	62.5	0.9	100.0%

▷ A third of all alumni worked on community fund-raising drives, a third attended two or more P.T.A. meetings, and a quarter led or helped lead youth groups during the past year.

TABLE 88 - Continued

During the past 12 months have you . . . .

	Worked on fund-raising drives for United Fund or other such charitable organization?				Led or assisted in the leadership of a scout troop or youth group?				Attended two or more meetings of the PTA?			
	Yes	No	No Answer	Total	Yes	No	No Answer	Total	Yes	No	No Answer	Total
Current Income												
Under $6000	21.5%	77.2	1.3	100.0%	29.1%	69.9	1.0	100.0%	25.4%	73.7	0.9	100.0%
6000-9999	32.2%	67.0	0.8	100.0%	24.2%	74.8	1.0	100.0%	32.2%	67.1	0.7	100.0%
10,000-14,999	40.6%	58.5	0.9	100.0%	24.1%	75.0	0.9	100.0%	38.0%	61.0	1.0	100.0%
15,000-20,999	47.8%	51.2	1.0	100.0%	24.3%	74.9	0.8	100.0%	42.6%	56.9	0.5	100.0%
21,000 and over	51.0%	47.9	1.1	100.0%	23.7%	75.4	0.9	100.0%	46.1%	52.7	1.2	100.0%
Occupation												
Lawyer	53.0%	46.4	0.6	100.0%	20.3%	79.0	0.7	100.0%	24.6%	74.7	0.7	100.0%
Clergyman	43.9%	53.2	2.9	100.0%	84.8%	14.9	0.3	100.0%	52.5%	46.6	0.9	100.0%
Elem-Second. Teach.	30.5%	68.2	1.3	100.0%	35.1%	63.2	1.7	100.0%	67.8%	31.1	1.1	100.0%
College Teacher	24.0%	75.8	0.2	100.0%	17.5%	82.1	0.4	100.0%	31.5%	67.8	0.7	100.0%
Salesman	40.0%	58.9	1.1	100.0%	22.2%	76.4	1.4	100.0%	33.6%	65.2	1.2	100.0%
Social Serv. Worker	28.3%	70.2	1.5	100.0%	22.3%	76.3	1.4	100.0%	29.8%	69.5	0.7	100.0%
Medical Worker	28.0%	71.2	0.8	100.0%	15.9%	83.2	0.9	100.0%	24.2%	74.8	1.0	100.0%
Scientist-Math.	22.3%	77.2	0.5	100.0%	19.2%	80.4	0.4	100.0%	30.1%	69.7	0.2	100.0%
Fiscal-Office-Mgmt.	48.0%	51.1	0.9	100.0%	23.7%	75.3	1.0	100.0%	30.8%	68.0	1.2	100.0%
Creative Worker	33.6%	66.0	0.4	100.0%	19.8%	79.7	0.5	100.0%	22.8%	76.5	0.7	100.0%
Other	40.0%	58.9	1.1	100.0%	22.3%	76.8	0.9	100.0%	28.4%	70.9	0.7	100.0%

△ Community activities are important to the liberal arts graduates.

TABLE 89

Role of Liberal Education in Developing Civic Responsibility

Evaluation of statement: "Liberal arts education should . . . develop a sense of responsibility to participate in community and public affairs."

Importance in Education

	Very Important	Fairly Important	Fairly Unimportant	Not at all Important	No Answer	Total
All Graduates	35.8%	46.3	14.2	3.3	0.4	100.0%
Type of Major						
Sci-Math	27.8%	51.0	16.7	3.9	0.6	100.0%
Soc. Sci.	41.3%	43.4	12.1	2.8	0.4	100.0%
Humanities	36.2%	45.1	14.9	3.5	0.3	100.0%

Did your education provide this?

	Yes	No	No Answer	Total
All Graduates	52.5%	41.9	5.6	100.0%
Type of Major				
Sci-Math	43.0%	51.4	5.6	100.0%
Soc. Sci.	59.4%	35.1	5.5	100.0%
Humanities	51.9%	42.1	6.0	100.0%

Δ Most (82 percent) feel that liberal education should develop a sense of responsibility to participate in community and public affairs; but only 53 percent say their own education met this objective.

——————————————————TABLE 90——————————————————

Political Preferences of Alumni in College and Now

*Which of the following best represents your political leanings
(a) when you were a college senior, and (b) at the present time?*

| | All Graduates | | Years Since Graduation | | | | | |
| | | | Fifteen | | Ten | | Five | |
	College	Now	College	Now	College	Now	College	Now
Liberal Democrat	24.1%	20.3%	26.0%	21.2%	23.7%	19.0%	22.9%	20.9%
Conservative Democrat	9.7	9.1	10.5	9.5	10.0	9.1	8.6	8.6
Independent and liberal	13.9	13.5	15.0	12.2	13.1	13.5	13.7	14.7
Independent and middle-of-the-road	12.5	11.5	11.3	11.3	12.1	11.2	14.0	11.9
Independent and conservative	6.7	9.5	5.6	9.1	6.8	9.3	7.7	10.1
Liberal Republican	17.5	17.6	16.8	18.5	18.1	18.2	17.6	16.1
Conservative Republican	14.7	17.4	14.1	17.1	15.4	18.7	14.5	16.4
No Answer	0.9	1.1	0.7	1.1	0.8	1.0	1.0	1.3
Total	100.0%	100.0%	100.0%	100.0%	100.0%	100.0%	100.0%	100.0%

▷ Politically, the graduates are somewhat more conservative than when
they were in college.

TABLE 91

Current Political Preferences of Alumni

Which of the following best represents your political leanings?

	Liberal Democrat	Cons. Democrat	Indep. Liberal	Indep. & middle-of-the-road	Indep. & Cons.	Liberal Repub.	Cons. Repub.	No Answer	Total
All Graduates	20.3%	9.1	13.5	11.5	9.5	17.6	17.4	1.1	100.0%
Academic Record									
High	28.2%	7.4	16.5	11.1	8.4	14.6	13.2	0.6	100.0%
Average	21.0%	9.1	14.2	11.8	9.3	17.4	16.2	1.0	100.0%
Low	15.3%	9.9	10.9	10.9	10.3	19.1	21.9	1.7	100.0%

△ Those with high academic standing in college and those who received doctor's degrees tend to be more liberal.

	Liberal Democrat	Cons. Democrat	Indep. Liberal	Indep. & middle-of-the-road	Indep. & Cons.	Liberal Repub.	Cons. Repub.	No Answer	Total
Type of Major									
Science-Math	14.4%	9.3	12.8	13.2	11.7	16.7	20.8	1.1	100.0%
Social Sci.	22.0%	9.0	12.3	10.7	8.5	19.0	17.4	1.1	100.0%
Humanities	26.5%	8.9	17.6	10.5	8.2	15.4	11.3	1.6	100.0%

△ Majors in the humanities tend to be the most liberal; those who majored in science and mathematics tend to be the most conservative.

	Liberal Democrat	Cons. Democrat	Indep. Liberal	Indep. & middle-of-the-road	Indep. & Cons.	Liberal Repub.	Cons. Repub.	No Answer	Total
Amount of Graduate Training									
None	14.8%	9.2	9.8	12.3	10.3	19.9	22.1	1.6	100.0%
Some, but no advanced degree	20.3%	9.6	15.5	11.0	10.2	16.7	15.5	1.2	100.0%
Master's	26.2%	8.5	16.6	11.2	8.4	15.6	12.7	0.8	100.0%
Professional	18.8%	9.7	10.5	11.2	10.1	18.6	20.2	0.9	100.0%
Doctor's	32.9%	6.0	25.4	11.1	6.1	11.3	6.2	1.0	100.0%

TABLE 92

Current Political Preferences Analyzed by Income and Occupation

	Liberal Democrat	Cons. Democrat	Indep. Liberal	Indep. & middle-of-the-road	Indep.& Cons.	Liberal Repub.	Cons. Repub.	No Answer	Total
All Grads	20.3%	9.1	13.5	11.5	9.5	17.6	17.4	1.1	100.0%
Income									
Under $6000	21.1%	8.2	14.4	14.1	10.7	14.4	15.6	1.5	100.0%
6000-9999	22.3%	9.6	13.9	11.8	9.6	16.3	15.4	1.1	100.0%
10,000-14,999	18.4%	8.4	13.1	11.3	9.1	20.3	18.5	0.9	100.0%
15,000-20,999	14.4%	7.8	11.8	11.1	10.1	20.5	24.3	0.0	100.0%
21,000 and over	17.2%	10.3	8.3	8.6	10.1	24.6	20.2	0.7	100.0%
Occupation									
Lawyer	24.5%	12.7	9.3	7.2	6.9	18.5	19.8	1.1	100.0%
Clergyman	21.1%	8.8	14.7	14.7	8.6	19.2	12.4	0.5	100.0%
El-Sec. T.	28.3%	11.5	15.8	11.0	8.1	15.4	9.0	0.9	100.0%
College T.	40.3%	4.7	18.0	13.1	5.3	12.3	5.6	0.7	100.0%
Salesman	12.6%	7.7	9.2	10.1	10.6	21.5	27.0	1.3	100.0%
Social Ser.	38.7%	9.3	24.2	7.1	4.3	8.7	7.1	0.6	100.0%
Medical	11.1%	8.1	9.0	13.2	12.5	18.3	26.7	1.1	100.0%
Sci-Math.	14.2%	9.4	14.8	12.7	11.6	17.6	18.8	0.9	100.0%
Fis-Off-Mgt.	12.9%	8.8	9.1	11.9	10.8	22.5	22.7	1.3	100.0%
Creative	24.7%	5.6	23.3	11.2	7.7	15.6	10.5	1.4	100.0%
Other	21.1%	9.9	14.4	12.3	10.3	15.6	15.0	1.4	100.0%

△ In terms of occupation, college professors and social service workers are the most liberal while salesmen and office workers are the most conservative.

TABLE 93

Current Political Activities

During the past 12 months have you....

	Run for, or held a public office?				Belonged to a political club or political action group?				Written to or talked with a public official about a current program or proposed bill?			
	Yes	No	No Answer	Total	Yes	No	No Answer	Total	Yes	No	No Answer	Total
All Graduates	5.1%	93.8	1.1	100.0%	17.6%	81.4	1.0	100.0%	44.7%	54.4	0.9	100.0%
Years Since Graduation												
Fifteen	7.2%	91.3	1.5	100.0%	20.6%	78.1	1.3	100.0%	55.4%	43.7	0.9	100.0%
Ten	5.5%	93.5	1.0	100.0%	18.5%	80.7	0.8	100.0%	44.9%	54.2	0.9	100.0%
Five	2.6%	96.5	0.9	100.0%	13.9%	85.4	0.7	100.0%	34.4%	64.9	0.7	100.0%
Income												
Under $6000	3.2%	95.8	1.0	100.0%	11.6%	87.5	0.9	100.0%	37.1%	62.3	0.6	100.0%
6000-9999	4.1%	95.0	0.9	100.0%	16.1%	83.2	0.7	100.0%	42.6%	56.8	0.6	100.0%
10,000-14,999	5.2%	93.7	1.1	100.0%	17.9%	81.1	1.0	100.0%	46.1%	53.2	0.7	100.0%
15,000-20,999	9.4%	89.5	1.1	100.0%	24.6%	74.7	0.7	100.0%	55.2%	44.3	0.5	100.0%
21,000 and over	9.5%	89.0	1.5	100.0%	26.1%	72.7	1.2	100.0%	57.0%	41.7	1.3	100.0%

△ One out of 20 graduates ran for or held a public office.

△ During the past year, almost half wrote or talked with a public official about pending political matters. Less than 20 percent, however, belong to a political club or political action group.

TABLE 94

Membership in Organizations

During the past 12 months have you . . . .

	Belonged to a professional association?				Belonged to a service club (Rotary, Kiwanis, etc.)?				Belonged to a veterans' organization?			
	Yes	No	No Answer	Total	Yes	No	No Answer	Total	Yes	No	No Answer	Total
All Graduates	70.7%	28.6	0.7	100.0%	19.8%	79.2	1.0	100.0%	9.1%	89.8	1.1	100.0%
Years Since Graduation												
Fifteen	75.4%	23.9	0.7	100.0%	23.4%	75.5	1.1	100.0%	14.9%	83.9	1.2	100.0%
Ten	72.9%	26.5	0.6	100.0%	20.8%	78.3	0.9	100.0%	7.5%	91.4	1.1	100.0%
Five	64.1%	35.2	0.7	100.0%	15.5%	83.8	0.7	100.0%	5.1%	93.9	1.0	100.0%
Current Occupation												
Lawyer	94.7%	5.1	0.2	100.0%	35.3%	64.1	0.6	100.0%	14.2%	85.0	0.8	100.0%
Clergyman	83.1%	16.6	0.3	100.0%	30.6%	68.7	0.7	100.0%	4.8%	94.1	1.1	100.0%
El-Sec. T.	90.3%	8.5	1.2	100.0%	18.2%	80.4	1.4	100.0%	12.1	86.4	1.5	100.0%
College T.	93.7%	6.1	0.2	100.0%	10.7%	88.8	0.5	100.0%	3.3%	95.8	0.9	100.0%
Salesman	46.6%	52.5	0.9	100.0%	25.3%	73.9	0.8	100.0%	11.4%	87.5	1.1	100.0%
Social Ser.	82.5%	17.1	0.4	100.0%	13.7%	85.4	0.9	100.0%	5.5%	94.1	0.4	100.0%
Medical	92.5%	6.9	0.6	100.0%	21.1%	78.3	0.6	100.0%	6.1%	93.2	0.7	100.0%
Sci-Math.	76.3%	23.3	0.4	100.0%	9.6%	89.8	0.6	100.0%	6.1%	93.2	0.7	100.0%
Fis-Off-Mgt.	48.7%	50.8	0.5	100.0%	27.8%	71.3	0.9	100.0%	10.9%	87.9	1.2	100.0%
Creative	50.1%	49.7	0.2	100.0%	11.7%	87.9	0.4	100.0%	7.5%	92.1	0.4	100.0%
Other	56.9%	42.5	0.6	100.0%	16.2%	82.9	0.9	100.0%	12.0%	87.4	0.6	100.0%

△ A high proportion of all graduates belong to professional associations, including 90 percent of all lawyers, college teachers, medical workers, and elementary and secondary school teachers.

△ Smaller numbers of graduates belong to service clubs. Very small numbers belong to veterans organizations, and still less to labor unions.

TABLE 95

Role of Liberal Education in Developing Moral Values

Evaluation of statement: "Liberal arts education . . . should develop moral capacities, ethical standards and values."

	Importance in Education						Did your education provide this?			
	Very Important	Fairly Important	Fairly un-important	Not at all Important	No Answer	Total	Yes	No	No Answer	Total
All Graduates	56.8%	31.1	8.6	3.0	0.5	100.0%	68.3%	25.9	5.8	100.0%
Years Since Graduation										
Fifteen	60.3%	29.8	6.6	2.4	0.9	100.0%	67.8%	25.3	6.9	100.0%
Ten	56.5%	31.6	8.6	2.8	0.5	100.0%	68.5%	26.3	5.2	100.0%
Five	53.6%	31.8	10.4	3.8	0.4	100.0%	68.6%	26.1	5.3	100.0%
Control of College										
Catholic	76.8%	20.1	1.6	0.7	0.8	100.0%	89.4%	4.3	6.3	100.0%
Public	51.0%	33.5	10.8	4.1	0.6	100.0%	58.3%	36.0	5.7	100.0%
Private	53.6%	31.7	8.5	2.7	3.5	100.0%	70.8%	23.4	5.8	100.0%
Occupation										
Lawyer	61.2%	28.7	6.9	2.7	0.5	100.0%	69.2%	26.4	4.4	100.0%
Clergyman	66.3%	27.8	5.0	0.5	0.4	100.0%	72.9%	20.9	6.2	100.0%
El-Sec. T.	62.5%	29.1	6.3	1.8	0.3	100.0%	71.6%	21.6	6.8	100.0%
College T.	52.5%	35.0	9.1	2.8	0.6	100.0%	69.5%	23.3	7.2	100.0%
Salesman	61.6%	27.1	8.1	2.9	0.3	100.0%	69.0%	25.3	5.7	100.0%
Social Ser.	49.0%	34.9	11.6	4.3	0.2	100.0%	66.5%	29.6	3.9	100.0%
Medical	52.7%	36.1	8.7	2.2	0.3	100.0%	65.6%	29.2	5.2	100.0%
Sci-Math.	47.9%	35.4	10.9	4.8	1.0	100.0%	62.3%	32.4	5.3	100.0%
Fis-Off-Mgt	57.9%	29.7	8.2	3.3	0.9	100.0%	71.4%	23.1	5.5	100.0%
Creative	59.4%	27.5	9.3	3.5	0.3	100.0%	66.7%	27.0	6.3	100.0%
Other	55.1%	31.6	10.2	2.7	0.4	100.0%	68.3%	26.8	4.9	100.0%

△ A large majority (almost 90 percent) feel that liberal education should develop moral capacities, ethical standards and values.

△ Fewer graduates (68 percent) say their college education met this goal; a high of 89 percent among graduates of Catholic colleges in contrast to 58 percent of those from public institutions.

----------- TABLE 96 -----------

Importance of Religion During College and Now

*Which of the following best represents how important religion was
to you when you were in college and how important it is now?*

| | When a College Senior | | | | Now | | | |
| | All Grads | Type of Control | | | All Grads | Type of Control | | |
Importance		Catholic	Public	Pvt.		Catholic	Public	Private
Very important	31.8%	77.0%	21.9%	29.1%	42.3%	82.5%	34.2%	39.4%
Of some importance	34.3	18.1	36.5	36.3	32.0	12.2	34.8	34.2
Of little importance	20.3	2.8	24.8	20.9	12.7	2.7	15.0	13.3
Completely unimportant	8.9	0.7	11.3	8.9	8.7	0.9	10.8	9.0
No opinion or no answer	4.7	1.4	5.5	4.8	4.3	1.7	5.2	4.1
Total	100.0%	100.0%	100.0%	100.0%	100.0%	100.0%	100.0%	100.0%

▷ Religion has grown in importance for the graduates — from 32 percent
to 42 percent in the "very important" rating.

———————————————— TABLE 97 ————————————————

Importance of Religion Now

Which of the following represents how important religion is now?

	Very Important	Of some importance	Of little importance	Completely unimportant	No Answer or no opinion	Total
All Graduates	42.3%	32.0	12.7	8.7	4.3	100.0%
Occupation						
Lawyer	34.4%	37.6	15.6	9.6	2.8	100.0%
Clergyman	97.9%	1.7	--	--	0.4	100.0%
El-Sec. T.	51.5%	28.2	9.9	5.9	4.5	100.0%
College T.	35.7%	29.1	17.0	14.4	3.8	100.0%
Salesman	42.7%	37.4	9.8	6.2	3.9	100.0%
Social Ser.	29.6%	30.5	18.5	18.0	3.4	100.0%
Medical	36.5%	38.5	15.4	6.6	3.0	100.0%
Sci-Math.	40.5%	30.7	13.6	10.4	4.8	100.0%
Fis-Off-Mgt.	41.3%	34.6	12.8	6.9	4.4	100.0%
Creative	32.6%	31.9	14.2	14.7	6.6	100.0%
Other	39.5%	35.7	12.0	8.2	4.6	100.0%
Income						
Under $6000	50.0%	26.7	11.1	7.9	4.3	100.0%
6000-9999	44.2%	31.4	11.7	8.6	4.1	100.0%
10,000-14,999	39.0%	34.9	13.4	8.5	4.2	100.0%
15,000-20,999	37.6%	35.7	14.4	8.5	3.8	100.0%
21,000 and over	37.7%	36.8	14.3	8.7	2.5	100.0%

▷ Alumni from the lower income brackets are the most likely to rate religion
as "very important". The least concerned about religion are social
service workers and those in creative fields.

——————————————— TABLE 98 ———————————————

Religious Preferences in College and Now

What was your religious preference when you graduated from college and what is it now?

| | When a College Senior | | | | Now | | | |
| | All | Control of College | | | All | Control of College | | |
Religious Preference	Grads	Roman Catholic	Public	Private	Grads	Roman Catholic	Public	Private
Baptist	7.9%	0.3%	7.4%	10.0%	5.8%	0.1%	4.9%	7.7%
Congregational (United Church of Christ)	4.6	0.3	3.8	6.2	4.5	0.2	3.9	5.9
Episcopal	7.0	0.3	7.5	8.1	8.3	0.5	9.3	9.3
Lutheran	6.0	0.8	6.3	6.9	5.8	0.9	5.9	6.7
Methodist	11.7	0.6	14.2	12.4	10.3	0.6	12.3	11.1
Presbyterian	9.3	0.7	10.0	10.6	9.8	0.6	10.2	11.4
Other Protestant	7.9	0.7	7.7	9.6	7.5	0.9	7.4	9.0
Roman Catholic	21.3	92.9	14.0	10.9	21.0	91.1	14.2	10.7
Jewish	10.5	1.1	11.2	11.9	10.0	1.0	10.7	11.4
Other, Non-Prot.	1.2	0.5	1.5	1.1	1.7	0.6	2.1	1.7
None	12.0	1.0	15.8	11.7	14.4	2.7	18.3	14.2
No Answer	0.6	0.6	0.8	0.6	0.9	0.8	0.8	0.9
Total	100.0%	100.0%	100.0%	100.0%	100.0%	100.0%	100.0%	100.0%

▷ 52 percent are Protestants
  21 percent are Roman Catholics
  10 percent are Jewish
  14 percent have no religious preference

———————————————————— TABLE 99 ————————————————————

Current Participation in Religious Activities

During the past 12 months have you . . .

	Attended religious services on a fairly regular basis?				Served on a church or synagogue board or committee?				Worked on fund-raising for your church?			
	Yes	No	No Ans.	Total	Yes	No	No Ans.	Total	Yes	No	No Ans.	Total
All Graduates	57.6%	41.8	0.6	100.0%	25.7%	73.4	0.9	100.0%	29.9%	69.8	1.3	100.0%
Years Since Graduation												
Fifteen	63.2%	36.2	0.6	100.0%	33.5%	65.5	1.0	100.0%	39.4%	59.2	1.4	100.0%
Ten	58.3%	41.0	0.7	100.0%	27.6%	71.4	1.0	100.0%	30.1%	68.9	1.0	100.0%
Five	51.6%	48.0	0.4	100.0%	16.3%	82.9	0.8	100.0%	18.4%	80.8	0.8	100.0%
Quality of College												
High	44.5%	54.9	0.6	100.0%	18.6%	80.4	1.0	100.0%	22.4%	76.6	1.0	100.0%
Medium	52.6%	46.8	0.6	100.0%	23.3%	75.9	0.8	100.0%	26.0%	73.1	0.9	100.0%
Low	72.7%	26.8	0.5	100.0%	33.4%	65.6	1.0	100.0%	37.8%	61.0	1.2	100.0%
Control of College												
Catholic	90.8%	8.7	0.5	100.0%	21.2%	77.6	1.2	100.0%	36.7%	62.1	1.2	100.0%
Public	50.4%	48.9	0.7	100.0%	23.1%	76.0	0.9	100.0%	25.6%	73.2	1.2	100.0%
Private	55.5%	44.0	0.5	100.0%	28.5%	70.7	0.8	100.0%	30.0%	69.1	0.9	100.0%
Occupation												
Lawyer	51.4%	48.0	0.6	100.0%	28.0%	71.5	0.5	100.0%	32.3%	66.7	1.0	100.0%
Clergyman	99.5%	0.2	0.3	100.0%	94.8%	4.5	0.7	100.0%	93.4%	6.6	--	100.0%
El-Sec. T.	66.1%	33.1	0.8	100.0%	30.9%	67.7	1.4	100.0%	32.2%	66.1	1.7	100.0%
College T.	48.2%	51.3	0.5	100.0%	22.6%	76.9	0.5	100.0%	22.4%	76.7	0.9	100.0%
Salesman	62.0%	37.7	0.3	100.0%	22.2%	77.0	0.8	100.0%	32.7%	66.4	0.9	100.0%
Social Ser.	43.1%	56.9	--	100.0%	18.5%	80.6	0.9	100.0%	18.7%	80.2	1.1	100.0%
Medical	51.7%	47.7	0.6	100.0%	18.6%	80.5	0.9	100.0%	20.5%	78.3	1.2	100.0%
Sci-Math.	57.6%	42.2	0.2	100.0%	22.2%	77.4	0.4	100.0%	24.8%	74.7	0.5	100.0%
Fis-Off-Mgt.	59.5%	40.0	0.5	100.0%	25.6%	73.7	0.7	100.0%	30.9%	68.2	0.9	100.0%
Creative	45.2%	54.6	0.2	100.0%	18.2%	81.1	0.7	100.0%	20.5%	79.0	0.5	100.0%
Other	56.9%	42.7	0.4	100.0%	18.3%	80.8	0.9	100.0%	22.9%	76.0	1.1	100.0%

▷ 58 percent attend church regularly

TABLE 100

Contact with Alma Mater

During the past 12 months have you . . .

	Attended a college alumni function or visited your undergraduate campus?				Given money to your undergraduate college or university?			
	Yes	No	No Answer	Total	Yes	No	No Answer	Total
All Graduates	49.8%	49.4	0.8	100.0%	47.9%	51.4	0.7	100.0%
Years Since Graduation								
Fifteen	44.1%	55.0	0.9	100.0%	51.3%	48.0	0.7	100.0%
Ten	48.7%	50.4	0.9	100.0%	48.2%	51.0	0.8	100.0%
Five	56.4%	43.0	0.6	100.0%	44.4%	55.1	0.5	100.0%
Quality of College								
High	56.2%	43.1	0.7	100.0%	60.4%	39.0	0.6	100.0%
Medium	46.2%	53.1	0.7	100.0%	44.0%	55.3	0.7	100.0%
Low	50.7%	48.4	0.9	100.0%	45.2%	53.9	0.9	100.0%
Size of College								
Small	52.2%	47.2	0.6	100.0%	54.2%	45.4	0.4	100.0%
Medium	50.4%	48.8	0.8	100.0%	51.3%	47.8	0.9	100.0%
Large	45.8%	53.3	0.9	100.0%	34.4%	64.9	0.7	100.0%
Control of College								
Catholic	52.3%	46.9	0.8	100.0%	56.6%	42.4	1.0	100.0%
Public	47.0%	52.1	0.9	100.0%	32.7%	66.5	0.8	100.0%
Private	51.3%	48.0	0.7	100.0%	56.8%	42.7	0.5	100.0%
Income								
Under $6000	55.1%	44.0	0.9	100.0%	40.6%	58.8	0.6	100.0%
6000-9999	50.9%	48.5	0.6	100.0%	43.6%	55.9	0.5	100.0%
10,000-14,999	46.7%	52.6	0.7	100.0%	50.9%	48.5	0.6	100.0%
15,000-20,999	49.9%	49.5	0.6	100.0%	62.1%	37.5	0.4	100.0%
21,000 and over	47.9%	51.1	1.0	100.0%	68.7%	30.6	0.7	100.0%

▷ Almost half attended an alumni function or visited their undergraduate college during the past year.

▷ Almost half contributed financially to their college.

▷ With the exception of visits to their college campuses, older alumni are more active in all civic and social areas than younger graduates.

▷ Contribution rates are substantially higher for alumni of Roman Catholic and private institutions than for alumni of public institutions.

10

The ROLE of MARRIAGE and the FAMILY

Primary attention in this study has been directed to the education and the careers of liberal arts graduates and to their general roles in society. This chapter presents some data on marriage and family· status to round out the picture of the graduates and to indicate the extent to which wives influence the career decisions of liberal arts alumni.

Role of Liberal Education in Preparing for Marriage

Graduates were asked whether they felt liberal education should help prepare for a happy marriage and family life. (TABLE 101) Opinions are sharply divided: 48 percent feel college should perform this role, while 51 percent say it need not. The older alumni are somewhat more likely to feel that college should provide preparation for marriage. Students with high academic records are somewhat less likely to assign importance to this objective. Only slight variations appear by type of major.

How well did their education meet this objective? Less than 40 percent of the liberal arts graduates say that their education provided preparation for marriage and family life.

Marital Status

The near universality of marriage among alumni is clear. Among men who graduated 15 years ago, 91 percent are now married, including at least five percent for the second time. Two percent now are divorced or widowed and only seven percent have never been married. Reflecting either their own college experience or the factors which influenced their original choice of a college, the highest marriage rate is shown by alumni from small and low quality institutions which also tend to be coeducational. (TABLE 102)

Graduates with strong academic records are the least likely to be married, probably because a higher percentage may still be in graduate school. Yet, science and mathematics majors, with a heavy disposition to advanced education, report the highest marriage rate. Alumni who earn the most money are more likely to be married, somewhat beyond the normal relationship between age and earnings. (Marriage rates correlate with income — from 69 percent for those earning under $6,000 to 95 percent for those earning $21,000 and up.) Men who attended Roman Catholic colleges (21 percent) are much more likely to be single than respondents from public (12 percent) and private (13 percent) institutions.

More than half of the alumni were married either before or within a year after graduation from college. (TABLE 103)   A third of the 15-year graduates, which included many World War II veterans, were married before obtaining their bachelor's degrees. Almost twice as many alumni of the low-quality colleges as of the high-quality colleges were married before graduation. The rate of marriage before graduation from Catholic institutions was 15 percent, while at the largely coeducational public institutions it was 36 percent. Early marriages characterize those who stopped at the bachelor's degree, while those who went on for a professional degree tended to postpone marriage the longest.

Even though half of the alumni were married during college or within a year after graduation, a striking number of comments advise against beginning marriage and career at the same time:

> Too many careers and marriages are ruined or reduced to mediocrity by hasty assumption of family and financial burdens.   *Washington University*

> Try to maintain economic independence for three to five years after graduation to permit experimentation with career fields.   *Fordham University*

> Soon after graduation, we began to have children and I had to take almost the first job offered.
> *Colorado State University*

While our graduates are in the middle of their marriages, as well as their careers, they support the thesis that a college graduate is a better marriage risk. In contrast to a national ratio of four marriages to one divorce, our ratio was fifteen to one. [1]

Wives of Liberal Arts Alumni

A review of the educational backgrounds of wives shows that half are college graduates. In contrast to the one-to-one ratio for husbands, only one in ten wives holds an advanced degree. (TABLE 104) Alumni from high-quality colleges are the most likely to have wives who are college graduates. A third of the wives attended the same undergraduate college as did their husbands. Income of alumni is not generally related to the educational level of wives, but it is worth noting that graduates in the lowest income bracket are more likely to have wives who are college graduates and who have advanced degrees.

Education affects the rate of divorce which is noticeably lower for husbands whose wives are college graduates or who attended the same undergraduate school. Where the wife is a college graduate, all but 5.1 percent of the husbands are in their first marriage as contrasted to 7.6 percent of the husbands of women without a college degree.

Where the wife attended the same undergraduate college, 4.2 percent of the husbands are in their first marriage, in comparison with 7.3 percent of other alumni. However, where wives hold an advanced degree, and this may have been caused by conflicting career demands, 8.4 percent of the husbands have been divorced, separated, or widowed in contrast to 6.1 percent of all men who were ever married.

The working wife is the exception rather than the rule. Only 14 percent of the graduates' wives are working full-time and only 11 percent part-time. (TABLE 105) As might be expected, wives of younger alumni are the most likely to be employed. This is true, however, only of full-time employment. Part-time employment of wives varies little according to year of husbands' graduation. Wives of graduates in the low income brackets are much more likely to be employed, full-time or part-time, than those earning high salaries. Although working wives are in a minority, some graduates are not averse to the benefits of two salaries, as this typical comment indicates:

> With my wife working, the two of us make sufficient
> money to travel (two trips to Europe) or to allow me
> to loaf every summer if I desire. I can't complain.
> *University of Denver*

Three-quarters of all the graduates have children, and 90 percent of those who are married have children. The typical family has two children, although 14 percent have four or more. Naturally, graduates of 15 years ago report the largest families — 86 percent have at least one child and 24 percent have four or more.

While graduates of Roman Catholic colleges are less likely to be married, once they enter matrimony, they report strikingly larger families.   Roman Catholics are four times more likely to have six to seven children and ten times more likely to have eight or more children.   Academic record in college does not seem to have a significant effect upon size of family, although there is a slightly higher tendency for top students to remain single or, if married, childless.

No one point in career characterizes the time of arrival of the first child.   Eleven percent had their first child before graduation from college, 13 percent within one year after graduation, 18 percent between two and three years after, 16 percent between four and five years, 11 percent between six and nine years, and six percent ten or later years.

Contrary to the myths surrounding the military veterans who finished college 15 years earlier, alumni who finished five years ago were just as likely to begin their families early. Low ranking students, from small colleges, from low quality institutions, and who stopped their own education with the bachelor's degree were the most likely to report early arrivals. Yet, a sizeable number of those who earned doctorates or professional degrees began their families before completing their undergraduate work.

Family and Career

Wives, children, and family activities play a much more dominant role in the career lives of alumni than may be generally recognized. Yet, very few employers really do much to influence the role of the wife.

The fact that jobs can disrupt families is obvious. A husband's deepest guilt feelings may come from his absorption in his work or the time which professional activities take from his life with his family. It is far simpler for a man to succeed in either his career or his marriage than it is to be, simultaneously, successful in both. To the extent that wives are satisfied with their husband's occupation and employer and accept necessary limitations upon family life, both careers and marriages are more secure.

The graduates report that only eight percent of all wives feel that their husbands should change occupations. (TABLE 106) More wives (11 percent) feel that their husbands should change employers. Wives of the younger graduates are somewhat more likely to desire these changes, especially in employers. Where income is low, wives are more inclined to feel that their husbands should change fields.

By occupation, wives of salesmen and of fiscal, office, and management workers are the most likely to favor a change. Wives of medical workers, college teachers, clergymen, and lawyers are the most satisfied with their husbands' occupations, but wives of college teachers are among the most likely to favor a change in their husbands' employers.

How do wives feel about sacrifices in family life to further their husbands' careers? One in three wives feels her husband spends too much time on his work   (TABLE 107) , especially those with husbands in high income brackets. Among occupational groups, wives of lawyers and of medical workers are the most likely to feel their husbands work too much.

Only 15 percent of the wives object to their husbands' job-associated travel. Concern about travel increases sharply with rising income. Wives of salesmen are the most likely to object to the travel involved.

Twenty percent of the wives, according to their husbands, would object if they were required for career reasons to move to another community. Wives of the younger alumni and of those in lower income brackets are less likely to object to moving.

Seventy percent of the men say they discuss day-to-day job activities with their wives, and 80 percent discuss major job decisions. (TABLE 108)   Less than 40 percent, however, say they often follow their wives' advice about their jobs. The younger alumni are the least likely to accept their wives' advice, even though they most frequently discuss day-to-day job decisions. Clergymen and college teachers are consistently the most likely to consult with and to accept the advice of their wives. The least likely are scientists and mathematicians, lawyers, and fiscal, office, and management workers.

There is a significant relationship between marriage and marital stability and attitude toward work. Among alumni who graduated 15 years ago, the percentage who liked their work "very much" varied from 74 percent of the married men to 68 percent of the single men to 56 percent of the divorced alumni. Comparable percentages for those who "disliked slightly" their work were three percent for married men, five percent for single men, and ten percent for divorced graduates.

When asked what they thought their wives thought about their jobs, the alumni replied as follows:

one-tenth feel their husbands should change occupations;
one-tenth feel their husbands should change employers;
one-sixth objected to travel required by their husbands' jobs (including one-fourth of all salesmen's wives);
one-fifth would object to a job-related move to a new community (particularly wives of older alumni);
one-third feel their husbands spend too much time on their work (including half of the wives of clergymen).

A number of graduates commented on the roles of family and career. Typical are these:

A major problem has been lack of time to spend with my family. A busy attorney must work nights and weekends. This creates a problem as my wife desires time also. The only solution is to budget your time. *Union College*

Don't bring your work problems home or your home problems to work. *Arizona State University*

The responsibility for a management position and a family are probably more severe than you can plan for as a student. The drive for personal success, the drive to help others, the devotion to family, these are often conflicting demands. Maintaining a balance in one's attempt to satisfy all these is indeed something of a challenge.   *Xavier University*

FOOTNOTE

1. *Statistical Abstracts,* U.S. Bureau of the Census. Washington, D.C., U. S. Government Printing Office, 1966, p. 47.

--- TABLE 101 ---

Role of College in Preparing for Marriage and Family Life

Evaluation of following goal of liberal education: "Do you feel that liberal arts education should prepare for a happy marriage and family life? Did your education provide this?

	Very Import.	Fairly Import.	Fairly Unimp.	Not Import. at all	No Answer	Total	Yes	No	No Answer	Total
All Graduates	17.5%	30.7	33.0	18.0	0.8	100.0%	38.5%	54.9	6.6	100.0%
Years Since Graduation										
Fifteen	19.8%	32.2	32.0	14.9	1.1	100.0%	38.8%	53.5	7.7	100.0%
Ten	17.3%	30.9	33.2	17.9	0.7	100.0%	39.2%	55.0	5.8	100.0%
Five	15.5%	29.2	33.8	20.9	0.6	100.0%	37.4%	56.2	6.4	100.0%
Type of Major										
Science-Math	15.8%	30.4	35.5	17.5	0.8	100.0%	33.9%	59.7	6.4	100.0%
Soc. Sci.	18.3%	31.0	32.2	17.7	0.8	100.0%	41.4%	52.0	6.6	100.0%
Humanities	18.7%	30.6	30.8	19.3	0.6	100.0%	39.0%	53.8	7.2	100.0%
Academic Record										
High	12.1%	27.4	39.9	19.7	0.9	100.0%	34.8%	59.2	6.0	100.0%
Average	16.6%	32.2	33.5	17.0	0.7	100.0%	38.9%	54.7	6.4	100.0%
Low	21.2%	32.3	29.2	16.5	0.8	100.0%	41.6%	51.6	6.8	100.0%

▷ Graduates are evenly divided on whether liberal education should help
prepare for a happy marriage and family life.
Less than 40 percent say their education met this objective.

TABLE 102

Current Marital Status of Graduates

	Single	Married	Divorced	Widowed	No Answer	Total
All Graduates	13.7%	84.1	1.5	0.2	0.5	100.0%
Years Since Graduation						
Fifteen	6.9%	90.8	1.4	0.3	0.6	100.0%
Ten	11.8%	86.1	1.5	0.2	0.4	100.0%
Five	22.2%	75.8	1.7	0.1	0.2	100.0%
Quality of College						
High	15.6%	82.3	1.5	0.0	0.6	100.0%
Medium	14.1%	83.6	1.9	0.2	0.2	100.0%
Low	12.1%	86.0	1.1	0.2	0.6	100.0%
Size of College						
Small	11.3%	87.2	1.1	0.1	0.3	100.0%
Medium	14.7%	82.8	1.7	0.2	0.6	100.0%
Large	16.5%	81.0	1.9	0.1	0.5	100.0%
Control of College						
Catholic	20.5%	77.9	0.5	0.3	0.8	100.0%
Public	12.3%	85.2	1.9	0.2	0.4	100.0%
Private	13.3%	84.6	1.5	0.1	0.5	100.0%
Academic Record						
High	15.0%	82.6	1.4	0.2	0.8	100.0%
Average	14.1%	83.7	1.5	0.2	0.5	100.0%
Low	11.5%	86.5	1.6	0.1	0.3	100.0%
Type of Major						
Science-Math.	11.4%	86.9	1.1	0.2	0.4	100.0%
Social Sciences	13.3%	84.6	1.5	0.1	0.5	100.0%
Humanities	18.8%	78.3	2.2	0.1	0.6	100.0%
Current Income						
Under $6000	29.3%	68.5	1.6	--	0.6	100.0%
6000-9999	14.8%	83.3	1.4	0.2	0.3	100.0%
10,000-14,999	6.7%	91.6	1.3	0.1	0.3	100.0%
15,000-20,999	4.1%	94.1	1.1	0.3	0.4	100.0%
21,000 and over	2.9%	94.7	1.2	0.1	1.1	100.0%

▷ Most of the liberal arts graduates are married.

▷ Marriage rates are higher among men who attended small or low-quality institutions, among graduates with poor academic records, among alumni who were science and mathematics majors, and among graduates from non-Catholic colleges.

▷ Married men are more likely to like their work "very much" than are single men, and divorced men are the least likely to be satisfied with their work.

TABLE 103

Timing of Marriage

When were you first married?

	Before grad. from college	Within one year after graduation	2-3 years after graduation	4-5 years after graduation	6 or more years after graduation	No Answer	Total
All Graduates	29.7%	27.1	19.0	13.0	10.5	0.7	100.0%
Years Since Graduation							
Fifteen	33.5%	23.2	17.1	11.0	14.5	0.7	100.0%
Ten	23.7%	26.8	19.8	13.4	15.6	0.7	100.0%
Five	31.9%	32.0	20.2	14.8	0.5	0.6	100.0%
Quality of College							
High	19.9%	28.1	22.0	15.3	13.9	0.8	100.0%
Medium	30.3%	26.8	19.3	12.7	10.4	0.5	100.0%
Low	34.9%	27.0	16.5	12.0	8.9	0.7	100.0%
Size of College							
Small	31.0%	29.3	18.6	11.4	9.4	0.3	100.0%
Medium	27.9%	26.5	20.0	13.4	11.4	0.8	100.0%
Large	30.4%	25.0	17.9	14.7	11.1	0.9	100.0%
Control of College							
Catholic	19.3%	26.4	23.3	16.9	13.1	1.0	100.0%
Public	36.0%	25.6	16.9	11.9	8.9	0.7	100.0%
Private	27.1%	28.3	19.6	13.0	11.3	0.7	100.0%

TABLE 103 - Continued

	Before grad. from college	Within one year after graduation	2-3 years after graduation	4-5 years after graduation	6 or more years after graduation	No Answer	Total
Academic Record							
High	26.1%	25.2	22.2	13.3	12.0	1.2	100.0%
Average	29.9%	26.5	18.8	13.2	10.9	0.7	100.0%
Low	29.6%	30.4	19.3	12.0	8.4	0.3	100.0%
Amount of Graduate Training							
None	34.0%	29.3	16.9	11.5	7.5	0.8	100.0%
Some, but no advanced degree	30.0%	27.5	18.6	13.4	9.9	0.6	100.0%
Master's	31.9%	27.9	17.7	11.2	10.5	0.8	100.0%
Professional	21.1%	23.2	23.6	17.0	14.6	0.5	100.0%
Doctorate	26.3%	25.9	20.9	12.5	13.8	0.6	100.0%

△ More than half of the graduates were married either before or within a year after graduation from college.

Holders of professional degrees were the most likely to postpone marriage until several years after graduation.

——————————— TABLE 104 ———————————

Education of Wives

*Answer the following for your wife (or if widowed or divorced
and not remarried, answer on the basis of your former wife) . . .*

	Is she a college graduate?	Does she have an advanced degree?	Did she attend the same undergraduate college you did?
	(Percent "yes")	(Percent "yes")	(Percent "yes")
All Graduates	50.1	9.6	31.2
Years Since Graduation			
Fifteen	48.8	10.6	30.1
Ten	51.3	10.1	29.8
Five	50.3	8.2	33.8
Quality of College			
High	58.2	11.5	20.6
Medium	51.1	9.6	34.3
Low	43.7	8.5	33.4
Income			
Under $6000	53.9	13.4	30.0
$6000-9999	48.1	9.1	31.2
$10,000-14,999	49.9	916	30.7
$15,000-20,999	51.7	7.8	31.5
$21,000 or more	50.5	9.1	27.6

▷ Half of the graduates' wives are college graduates, but only 10 percent
   hold advanced degrees.

Alumni of high-quality colleges are the most likely to have wives who
   are college graduates.

──────── **TABLE 105** ────────

Working Wives

*Answer the following for your wife (or if widowed or divorced
and not remarried, answer on the basis of your former wife)* . . .

	Is she employed full-time in a paid position?	Is she employed part-time in a paid position?
	(Percent "yes")	(Percent "yes")
All Graduates	14.2	11.0
Years Since Graduation		
Fifteen	12.0	12.1
Ten	10.9	9.9
Five	20.6	10.8
Current Income		
Under $6000	29.9	14.2
$6000-9999	16.6	12.8
$10,000-14,999	9.9	8.7
$15,000-20,999	4.8	7.3
$25,000 or more	2.3	4.9

▷ Working wives are a minority — only 14 percent work full-time and
   only 11 percent work part-time.

   Wives of graduates in the lower income brackets are the most likely to
   be employed.

————————————— TABLE 106 —————————————

Wives' Satisfaction with Occupations and Employers
of Their Husbands

Answer the following for your wife (or if widowed or divorced
and not remarried, answer on the basis of your former wife) . .

	Does she feel you should switch to another occupation? (Percent "yes")	*Does she feel you should switch to another employer?* (Percent "yes")
All Graduates	8.3	10.9
Years Since Graduation		
Fifteen	7.6	8.1
Ten	7.9	10.8
Five	9.7	14.5
Income		
Under $6,000	10.4	12.1
6000-9999	10.7	14.3
10,000-14,999	6.6	9.6
15,000-20,999	4.2	3.7
21,000 and over	2.2	2.6
Occupation		
Lawyer	4.1	9.7
Clergyman	3.6	4.7
Elem-Second. Teach.	8.3	12.7
College Teacher	3.0	11.9
Salesman	12.7	11.0
Social Serv. Worker	9.7	13.1
Medical Worker	2.4	8.9
Scientist-Math.	8.0	11.3
Fiscal-Office-Mgmt.	11.3	9.7
Creative Worker	5.3	12.4
Other	12.5	12.1

▷ Wives are generally satisfied with their husbands' choice of career.

Wives of younger graduates and in low income brackets are the most
likely to want their husbands to change jobs.

TABLE 107

Extent to Which Wives are Willing to Make Sacrifices for Their Husband's Careers

Answer the following for your wife (or if widowed or divorced and not remarried, answer on the basis of your former wife) . . .

	Does she feel you spend too much time on your work?	Does she object to the travel which your job requires?	Would she object if your job required that you move to a new community?
	(Percent "yes")	(Percent "yes")	(Percent "yes")
All Graduates	33.4	14.4	19.6

Years Since Graduation ▷ A third of the wives feel their husbands spend too much time at their work.

Fifteen	35.4	14.8	24.9
Ten	33.7	14.4	19.6
Five	30.8	13.9	13.6

Income ▷Wives of older graduates and of those in higher income brackets are most likely to object to their husbands' long hours.

Under $6000	35.7	8.6	8.1
6000-9999	30.5	12.3	18.1
10,000-14,999	33.7	18.7	19.4
15,000-20,999	37.8	15.7	27.2
21,000 and over	46.1	20.4	33.1

Occupation ▷ Fourteen percent of wives object to job-associated travel by husbands. Wives of salesmen are most likely to protest.

Lawyer	36.4	13.9	27.7
Clergyman	46.1	12.9	5.8
Elem.-Second. Teach.	36.7	8.5	20.1
College Teacher	37.1	10.8	14.6
Salesman	32.4	21.6	21.9
Social Serv. Worker	29.7	12.0	19.5
Medical Worker	42.3	9.1	20.4
Scientist-Math.	20.5	18.1	19.5
Fiscal-Office-Mgmt.	32.8	14.5	21.5
Creative Worker	30.2	14.2	23.2
Other	32.5	19.7	16.2

▷One of every five wives would object if her husband's job required a transfer to a new community.

Wives of younger graduates and of those in low income brackets are the most amenable to accepting relocation.

―――――――――――――――――――――――――― TABLE 108 ――――――――――――――――――

Role of Wife in Job Decisions

	Do you discuss day-by-day job decisions with your wife?	Do you discuss major job decisions with your wife?	Do you often follow your wife's advice about your job?
	(Percent "yes")	(Percent "yes")	(Percent "yes)
All Graduates	70.2	79.3	36.1
Years Since Graduation			
Fifteen	67.1	79.3	38.6
Ten	69.9	80.4	36.0
Five	74.1	78.3	33.4
Income			
Under $6000	80.1	82.8	41.5
6000-9999	73.4	80.5	36.8
10,000-14,999	65.4	78.0	32.0
15,000-20,999	64.0	75.9	34.2
21,000 and over	63.6	76.8	32.9
Occupation			
Lawyer	61.1	74.2	31.4
Clergyman	87.8	91.7	68.2
Elem-Second. Teach.	78.8	88.3	46.0
College Teacher	81.5	92.8	50.4
Salesman	73.1	78.4	34.8
Social Serv. Worker	70.0	84.3	31.6
Medical Worker	71.5	79.4	33.3
Scientist-Math.	59.0	73.9	26.6
Fiscal-Office-Mgmt.	65.1	73.9	30.0
Creative Worker	76.4	84.3	42.0
Other	67.1	71.5	30.3

▷ Seventy percent of the graduates talk over day-to-day job decisions
with their wives; 80 percent discuss major job decisions: but
less than 40 percent say they often follow their wives' advice.

11

CONCLUSIONS and IMPLICATIONS

The response from the 11,000 alumni revealed strong opinions about their education, their careers and their lives. While not unanimous on any one point, alumni opinions can be summarized into a number of general conclusions and translated in specific recommendations for colleges and employers.

Evaluation of Education

As undergraduates, the severest critics of higher education tend to be students enrolled in the liberal arts colleges. This was true in the 1940's and 1950's and is true today. For this reason, the reactions of these alumni to their education merits special attention.

> ▶The overwhelming majority of the alumni surveyed
> supported liberal education and felt that it had met
> their needs.

If they were to begin again, almost all the alumni would attend the same college and would major in liberal arts. Furthermore, 80 percent said they would advise a high school senior to take a liberal arts program.

They would, however, make a number of changes in their major field. Of every six graduates, three would repeat their original major, two would switch to another liberal arts field, and one would major outside of liberal arts (almost all in business, engineering or education).

▶The graduates felt that most of their courses had been
useful. Some sentiment was expressed for a five-year
program to provide a more comprehensive general
education.

While most would like to study more of almost everything offered
by the college, the highest ratings tended to be given to the courses
which were labelled as "required." The most useful courses in later
life tended to be English, mathematics and psychology. Rated least
useful were fine and applied art, economics and social science.

▶The graduates felt that a broad fund of knowledge about
different fields was important in later life and this had
been provided by their liberal arts training.

A continuing debate focuses on the extent to which liberal arts
is acceptable as terminal education or useful mostly as a preliminary
to graduate training. This becomes particularly significant in the
light of the report from the census that in 1972 there were 15,205,000
living college graduates in this country.

▶While not discounting the merits of liberal education,
alumni felt that additional graduate training was important. Half said that graduate work was essential
for success in their field and another quarter said it
was highly desirable.

Despite this fact, half the alumni held no degree beyond the bachelor's. Another quarter had a master's degree and the final quarter
a doctor's or professional degree (divinity, law, medicine, etc.).
Those who took graduate work viewed it as specific career preparation. Only a fourth with graduate training took it to follow their own
intellectual interests. Almost all the alumni had a specific career
goal in mind when they entered graduate study.

Interestingly, alumni in the three classes were considerably
less dependent upon their families for financial support than anticipated. Even among classes with relatively few students on veteran's
benefits, only a third of the cost of college came from parents.

Evaluation of Career Guidance and Placement Services

A major goal of this survey was to study the process of vocational development, including the selection of a career goal and the role
played by colleges and universities in occupational guidance and
placement.

▶ Most of the graduates selected their career goal after graduation from college. Even in middle age, some liberal arts alumni are still shifting their goals.

The author has passed the stage when he subscribes to the theory that twenty-two year olds should be expected to plot their career lives to age 65. However, students who graduate from college, if they expect to get a job, should have employment preferences and objectives. Competitive employment conditions demand that graduates be able to cite a goal at least during that most verbal of intelligence tests, the employment interview. The liberal arts alumni, themselves, felt it was important for graduates to finish college with a specific career choice in mind.

▶ Alumni were universal in condemning the lack of career guidance offered by the liberal arts college.

About half the alumni had tried guidance tests, occupational materials, and career counseling. Less than a tenth of these graduates found these formal guidance services very helpful. Much more useful assistance, they reported, came from faculty members, experiences on part-time and summer jobs, and advice from family members and prospective employers.

Yet, many alumni emphasized that no students need a more effective career guidance program than those in general education programs. But, too often, student counseling centers emphasize personal and academic assistance at the expense of career advising. Or, individual counselors may assume that requests for vocational guidance really mask deeper, more personal problems. The placement officer, while rich in practical knowledge of job realities, usually does not have enough time or the right kind of supporting staff for effective career counseling.

Even where attempted, career counseling generally falls far short of its mark because too many counselors limit their review of alternatives. Most of the truly interesting jobs,, those with the greatest future and opportunity for growth, are not found on job cards in the placement office (or on reports from surveys of past graduates). As a pair of critics put it: "One might imagine a present-day counselor exhorting Columbus to give up this mad confusion of sailing westward to find the East and settle down quietly in a pleasant villa on the outskirts of Genoa." [1]

▶ Few graduates received jobs through services provided by college placement offices.

In defense of the college placement officer, a high percentage of graduates who went on for advanced training may not have registered for any assistance. Also, many may have forgotten that they learned of their first job by scanning the placement office bulletin board or through an on-campus interview. Yet, this lack of alumni recall of placement assistance is disturbing. As Joan Fiss Bishop, the Placement Director at Wellesley College, says, "If you as a placement officer are really working effectively with a student, she wants to tell you about her first job offer as she 'knows' that next to herself you are the most interested person."

During the 1950's and 1960's, when jobs were plentiful, liberal arts colleges often shirked their placement responsibilities. The starker conditions of the 1970's demand improved career assistance.

▶ The greatest career crisis for liberal arts alumni
   occurred right after graduation — when they sought
   their first jobs.

Liberal arts alumni reported a number of difficulties in obtaining their first jobs. Some of this was attributed to the fact that they lacked the easy bridge from campus to career possessed by their colleagues from specialized curriculums. Some of this was caused by the lack of a career goal or a fruitless search to find an occupational field which matched their general education major. Others cited the lack of placement services, or their failure to make full use of these services.

The letdown came at a time when many of these new graduates were still depressed as a result of intense competition in college.

Career Lives of Liberal Arts Alumni

Historically, liberal education led to careers in the clergy, law and medicine. Now, liberal arts graduates report a wide range of employers and occupations.

▶ Despite the myth that liberal arts primarily prepares
   for teaching or social service, half of the alumni were
   engaged in private enterprise.

Almost a third of the alumni were employed by private, non-manufacturing organizations and over a sixth by manufacturing concerns. Two-tenths were employed by educational institutions — almost equally divided between elementary and secondary schools and colleges and universities. A tenth were in government service. Despite the fact that state and local governments employ half again as many people as do federal agencies, many more liberal arts graduates are associated with the federal government. Some consider the low percentage of college graduates employed by local governments a special cause for concern.

When academic standing in college was compared with present employer, it was learned that the top students in college are more likely to be working for a college or university, a federal agency, or in law or medicine.

Hundreds of different occupations were reported by the 11,000 alumni. When these were combined into a standardized occupational index, the largest number of graduates were found employed in fiscal, office, and management fields. Next came teaching at all levels, followed by science and mathematics. The traditional occupations of liberal arts alumni (law, clergy and medicine) account for only 20 percent of the graduates.

> ▶Among alumni 15 years after college, less than a
> quarter are still with their original employers.

Reports from the 15-year alumni class indicate that a quarter are with their first employer, a quarter with the second employer, a quarter with the third employer, and a quarter with their fourth or later employer. These figures, it should be pointed out, include the military services or employment as a teaching or research assistant during graduate study. The greatest mobility was shown by college teachers, two-thirds of whom have been employed by three or more institutions.

Sharp salary distinctions were shown between fields and between years since graduation. The highest earnings were reported by graduates who worked for private non-manufacturing concerns and for research organizations. The lowest earnings were for those employed by elementary and secondary schools and the military services. Five years after receiving the bacherlor's degree, medical workers (obviously affected by physicians in residency) are among the lowest paid alumni — fifteen years after graduation, this group has the highest average. Overall, comparing salaries for liberal arts graduates with those from specialized majors, a "tortoise and hare" theory was noticed. General education alumni generally start out with lower salaries but in ten or fifteen years they catch up and seem to surpass their counterparts in engineering and other specialized fields.

▶Most alumni work hard, often taking work home or
going into the office evenings or weekends.

Insulted during their student days by the press and by commencement speakers as more concerned with security than challenge, it is
interesting to note now that 70 percent of the graduates report that
they do extra work on their jobs. The most extra work was done by
teachers and medical workers and the least by businessmen and government workers.

▶A quarter of the graduates hold a second paying job.

The number of moonlighters was higher than anticipated — 24
percent held two jobs. This was true of half of the college professors
and a third of the elementary and secondary school teachers. The
total was surprisingly high for state and local government employees
(21 percent), federal workers (17 percent) and for private industry
(12 percent). These ratios may be lowered by the adverse economic
conditions of the early 1970's or raised by the influence of the in-
flation of the mid-1970's.

Evaluation of Career Life

Far from experiencing career difficulties, the great bulk of the
alumni are very satisfied with their occupations, their employers,
and their own progress.

▶Ninety percent of the liberal arts graduates are satisfied with their occupations.

While most graduates like what they are doing, distinctions are
shown between fields. Occupations which would attract many more
alumni, given the choice over again, are college teaching, medicine,
creative fields, and law. Somewhat more graduates would elect federal government service, research, and the social sciences than are
now employed in them. Given the chance to repeat their choice, fewer
alumni now would elect science and mathematics, fiscal-office-man-
agement work, sales, and the clergy.

▶Little unemployment was reported by the liberal arts
alumni.

Only ten percent of the graduates were unemployed for five or
more months since finishing college. For most of the graduates,
these were months spent "unemployed" anticipating military service
or waiting for graduate school to begin.

▶Most of the alumni were satisfied with their income level.

Despite public statements to the contrary, two-thirds of the alumni said they were satisfied with their income level. The greatest satisfaction was reported by older alumni and, not surprisingly, those who earned the most money. Those who liked their incomes the least tended to be employed in teaching, state and local government, and military services. Interestingly enough, the most satisfied with their salaries were persons employed by the federal government, business (particularly sales), and by research organizations. The highest earnings were for those who had majored in biological science (often used for premedical training), economics and chemistry. The lowest paid had studied English, foreign languages and fine arts.

Two-thirds of the graduates said that they expected to receive a promotion in the next three years.

▶Most of the alumni felt that liberal education had provided good preparation for career life.

Three-quarters of the graduates felt that liberal arts training had equipped them for career life. Presumably, some who said that liberal arts had not prepared them for a career made this observation because they felt this was not the role for general education.

Non-Career Lives of Liberal Arts Alumni

Advocates of liberal education often cite its values in preparing for more enlightened citizenship and increased capacity for personal enrichment. Were these goals considered important by the alumni and to what extent were they met?

▶Eighty-two percent of the graduates felt that liberal education should develop a sense of responsibility to participate in community and public affairs.

Too many critics of the college students of the 1940's and 1950's assumed that their goals were to pass from bland youth to mediocre old age. In actuality, they turned out to be the generation which provided leadership for some of the most innovative programs of the twentieth century: the Race to the Moon, the Great Society, and the War on Poverty. Most alumni reported some involvement in service activities outside of their regular job.

Organizational memberships are much more related to careers than to personal social needs. Of every ten graduates, seven belong to a professional association or society, two have joined a service club, and one a veterans' organization.

▶Politically, the graduates now are almost evenly divided between liberals and conservatives.

As college students, 48 percent were liberal and 39 percent conservative. Now, comparable figures are 43 percent and 45 percent. The remaining are in the middle, with no definite leanings. As time goes on, a continued shift toward conservatism may be anticipated.

▶Liberal arts graduates report a fairly active intellectual and cultural life.

For most alumni, formal education has been replaced by independent study and growth. The average alumnus, in the previous year, read five work-related, four non-fiction, and five fiction books. This average alumnus regularly reads eight periodicals — divided equally between work-related and general publications. Twenty-two percent of the alumni had published an article and two percent a book.

During the prior year, two-thirds of the alumni had attended two or more theatrical productions, one or more public lectures, and visited an art museum. Four of every ten were participants in intellectual or cultural discussion groups — ranging from 53 percent of those who majored in humanities down to 34 percent of the science and mathematics alumni.

Two-thirds of the graduates had given one or more public speeches during the year, including at least 60 percent of those in every occupation.

Religion has grown in importance since graduation. Six out of ten alumni attend religious services on a regular basis. The graduates feel that liberal education should enhance moral capacities and ethical standards.

Recommendations to Colleges

Their interest in the future of liberal education was demonstrated by the many recommendations made by the alumni. Some have already been cited, but a number of general conclusions may be drawn.

▶Liberal education should provide the broadest possible general training.

Experimentation and innovation in liberal education should emphasize greater breadth of knowledge and the development of the
skills required to integrate this knowledge into life situations.

Colleges might make time for this by eliminating excessive du-
plication of courses already fairly adequately covered in high school
or likely to be encountered during professional training. For example,
many students study United States history at three or four stages of
the educational process but study no geography after the early elementary years.

▶To be effective, liberal education must be taught by
persons with both intellectual breadth and interest in
their students.

The student revolts of the 1960's, while shattering some illusions
about the stability of American higher education, have resulted in
little improvement in the total learning atmosphere on most campuses. Now with a surplus of college teachers, selection and promotion committees have an excellent opportunity to encourage faculty
members with the ability and interest to stimulate student development.

▶Liberal education should emphasize maximum development of student capacities for self-expression.

At many institutions, the only attention paid the written or verbal
communication skills is a catalog requirement that students take a
freshman course in English composition.

Alumni feel strongly that writing and speaking are critical skills
in personal and career lives. Yet, increasingly, the college experience consists of listening in large lecture rooms and being tested on
multiple choice examinations. A notable exception may be the United
States Military Academy at West Point (not even a liberal arts institution) where the academic philosophy is based upon the tenet that
"every cadet recites and is graded daily — in every course."

Nor are liberal arts graduates the only ones to emphasize the
vital importance of communications. One of the country's largest
technical companies asked its engineering employees a few years
ago what they now wished they had emphasized in college. While not
discounting the virtues of technical preparation, these engineers said
they wished they had studied more English.

▶Colleges should urge their students to plan a career.

Students are prone to postpone career planning. Too often, their colleges, and particularly liberal arts colleges, encourage this lack of planning for occupational life. To some purists, delaying planning appears to support the cause of liberal education.

Actually, by not planning and by not being prepared for the twin demands of obtaining and holding a job, liberal arts graduates reflect adversely upon the role of general education in preparing for today's world.

▶The curriculum of liberal education may include
more occupationally-related materials.

The recent advocacy of career education by the U.S. Office of Education has implications for the liberal arts college. The concept says that everyone should prepare for a career while pursuing education for vocational, personal and social development. This need not threaten the ideals of liberal education.

Career education does not eliminate the role of liberal education but has some content suggestions for it. For example, is a term paper on a contemporary career field any less liberal than a paper on a contemporary social problem? Is an occupational analysis at a social agency an item which might be included in a field trip report? Can science and mathematics classes be made more interesting and more relevant by relating basic principles to their adaptation in commercial life?

Internship programs are important and successful in many fields. These programs should be considered by liberal arts colleges as possible vehicles for the career and personal development of their students.

▶Liberal arts colleges should assume that the employment status of their graduates is important and take
steps to improve it.

Private career schools cite, with some pleasure, the on-the-job success of their graduates and the lifetime placement services ready to help them. In contrast, too often the liberal arts college assumes that its reputation is enhanced by a complete lack of concern about its relationship to employment. This attitude is the more puzzling because of the lack of a clear relationship between liberal arts training and the world of work.

To aid their alumni, liberal arts colleges may wish to search out and try to eliminate barriers to employment. A clear example is the area of certification required for public school teaching. The key group in establishing teaching requirements in the various states has generally been composed of representatives of former state teachers' colleges. Their perspective is understandable. Liberal arts colleges should press for more flexibility in certification. Here it is important to note that the basic foundation for a good teacher preparation program according to James Conant is 60 hours of general education.[2]

Where groups of alumni with similar types of career problems may be identified (such as returning servicemen or displaced alumni), the colleges should assist by developing programs to help meet these needs or by serving as a clearinghouse to refer alumni to special resources. In the early 1970's when a surplus of aeronautically-trained engineers developed, technical institutions responded by providing a wide range of programs and assistance. Similar concern should be shown by liberal arts colleges for the careers of their graduates.

This fits into the concept of a lifelong opportunity for education, cited in the 1973 report of the Commission on Non-Traditional Study:

> If this recommendation were to be made a reality, the entire span of years of an individual from completion of secondary school to death would be regarded as a single period of time. Every individual would receive as a right a predetermined number of dollar credits which he could use up immediately for college, could defer for later use, or balance out his needs required for initial and deferred education.[3]

Recommendations for Employers

The role of employers in the future of liberal education should not be ignored. Too often, actions by employers create the greatest obstacles faced by liberal arts graduates. This is particularly ironic as many of the heads of industrial corporations, federal and state agencies, and other institutions come from liberal arts colleges.

▶Job hiring requirements should be reviewed to ascertain the minimum training and experience necessary.

Today, with racial and ethnic minority groups and women's liberation organizations very appropriately calling attention to undue rigidity in employment qualifications, many employers have reviewed their requirements to determine if more flexibility is possible. In a shift of philosophy, many employers have changed from looking for the fully "qualified" person to reviewing all candidates who are "qualifiable." In addition to promoting more employment of minorities, employers should use the same techniques to search for new ways to make better use of the unique capacities of liberal arts graduates.

▶Employers should not falsely cite liberal education as the reason for turning down an applicant.

Instead of honestly pointing out some personal weakness that bars employment, too many personnel officers seek to preserve the candidate's ego by saying, "We really don't consider liberal arts graduates for this type of work." To a brand new alumnus in the middle of what has been shown to be a difficult transition from the campus, this kind of comment seems like the kiss of death upon a general education background.

Perhaps the single most important conclusion I can draw from reading the 11,000 lengthy replies to our survey from articulate college graduates is: In an age which tends to worship specialization, liberal arts alumni have found both success in their careers and a deep respect for the utility of a general education.

FOOTNOTES

1. Mammarelia, Raymond and Crescimberi, Raymond, "Guidance Problems: Cultural or Cosmic?" *The Saturday Review*, Vol. 47, November 21, 1964, p. 76.
2. Conant, James B., *The Education of American Teachers*. New York, McGraw-Hill Book Co., 1963, p. 74.
3. *Diversity by Design*. A summary of the findings and recommendations of the Commission on Non-Traditional Study funded by the Carnegie Corporation of New York and the Educational Foundation of America, 1973, p. 11.

APPENDIX A: Technical Notes

Construction of the Quality Index [1]

The quality index employed in this study closely parallels the index of academic quality developed by Lazarsfeld and Thielens in *The Academic Mind.* [2] The same six components were utilized and combined in a similar manner, although the weighting was modified to fit a different time period and a differing universe of institutions.

The six items included in the index were: (1) total volumes in the college or university library, (2) number of books per student enrolled, (3) annual budget per student, (4) proportion of Ph. D's on the faculty, (5) size of the tuition fee, with different scales for public and private institutions, and (6) academic achievement of alumni. The bearing of most of these items on quality is obvious. It might be noted, however, that size of tuition, perhaps the least obvious indicator of quality, has been shown to be a good predictor by Rogoff and Mitchell[3] and by Knapp and Greenbaum.[4]

Data for the first five items were obtained from the 1956 edition of *American Colleges and Universities.* [5] This edition, based on the 1954-55 academic year, was the closest available to 1952-53, the reference year employed for other characteristics of the schools in this study.

Since the two ratios, library books per student and budget per student, would be adversely affected as measures of quality by large evening or part-time student enrollments, some adjustment was necessary to avoid penalizing schools with a high portion of part-time students. Such adjustment was made whenever part-time students comprised more than 10 percent of the enrollment.[6] For such schools, 3.5 part-time students were counted as the equivalent of one full-time student, the ratio deriving from Ostheimer, who showed that full-time students during this period carried an average of 14 semester hours and part-time students four hours.[7] These adjusted enrollments then were divided into volumes in the library, for books per student, and total budget, for budget per student.

The final indicator of quality, academic achievement, is taken from Knapp and Greenbaum's *The Younger American Scholar.* [8] These investigators prepared rosters of graduates· of the classes of 1946 to 1951 who received scholarly recognition between 1948 and 1952 in any of four ways:

1. Earned a Ph. D. from one of the 25 largest graduate schools in the nation. These schools awarded approximately 80 percent of all Ph. D. 's during this period.

2. Won a university fellowship or scholarship from one of these same institutions.

3. Received a fellowship or scholarship from one of nine private foundations.

4. Received a fellowship from the U. S. Public Health Service, the Atomic Energy Commission, or the U. S. Department of State (Fullbright Grant).

From these rosters, Knapp and Greenbaum developed indices of alumni productivity for each school, expressing the proportion of cited alumni among total graduates. Separate indices were prepared for male and female graduates. Since the present study deals only with men, the male index was used.

The final quality scores were obtained by totalling the individual quality points on the six items. A relatively detailed distribution of schools by quality points is provided in Table 112. For most purposes in the report, quality scores were grouped into three summary categories as follows:

High:	27 to 30 quality points
Medium:	19 to 26 quality points
Low:	7 to 18 quality points

One final note: There is a clear relationship between size of an institution and its quality, at least as measured by our scale. Large schools tend to have higher quality scores than do the smaller colleges. In part, this is explained by one of the quality index components: total books in the school library. However, many smaller but renowned schools also exceeded the 300,000 volumes required for the top score here. More significantly, the linkage between size and quality suggests that in many cases the larger institutions have more resources for enriched programs.

Sampling Strata and Size of Mailing Sample

As explained in the Introduction, sampling procedures differed for large schools (those with more than 100 liberal arts graduates in 1953), and for small schools (those with 100 or less).

Estimating the Response Rate

To aid in estimating the response rate and types of non-response, careful records were kept of the outcome of the mailings to each respondent. The results as of the June 1964 cut-off date are shown in Table 114.

A subject was considered ineligible if his returned questionnaire or letter from him or a relative indicated that he was not a male, United States citizen, or foreign citizen residing in the United States who graduated from one of the sample schools with a liberal arts major in 1948, 1953, or 1958.

A graduate was counted as unlocatable if questionnaires mailed to him were returned as undeliverable by the Post Office and no new address could be obtained from the Post Office or from his college or university. A graduate was classified as inaccessible if he was locatable but unable to answer because of illness or similar legitimate reason. Those classified "No response" are essentially a residual group not meeting the criteria for classification in any of the above categories. Of the 5,583 included here, 161 wrote letters stating they refused to answer or returned totally blank questionnaires.

A follow-up study was undertaken to gain additional information about the 5,583 who did not respond and to ascertain how they differed from the respondents. A systematic random sample of 555 was drawn and various approaches taken to reach them. A registered letter was first mailed to each asking for his completion of a brief questionnaire. Those not responding were next contacted by telephone if a telephone number could be obtained for them. At least three calls were made to each subject at his home or office before he was considered unreachable for the follow-up study. Those subjects without known telephone numbers were mailed a second registered letter asking for their cooperation. The outcomes of these activities are presented in Table 115.

From these figures, projections may be made to the total population of 5,583 non-respondents.

One final adjustment was made in the figures. Eligibility, as determined either from the initial records or from the follow-up study, could be determined only for those who were both locatable and accessible. However, it seems likely that some of the unlocatables and some of the locatable but inaccessibles also would have proved to be ineligible if reached. An assumption was made that this proportion would be the same as among those who were locatable and accessible. This final adjustment resulted in 21 additional cases for the ineligibles and a corresponding reduction of 19 and 2 for the unlocatables and inaccessibles, respectively. (See Table 116)

*Evaluation of Completeness of Sample and Review of
  Possible Non-response Bias*

While the study appears to have been relatively effective in gaining the cooperation of those liberal arts graduates it reached, the return rate of 62.3 percent of the eligible subjects clearly permits the operation of substantial bias in the completed sample. In this final section, three kinds of evidence bearing on the quality and representativeness of the sample will be considered: variations in return rates, comparisons with the middle group population, and comparison of responses between those who participated in the general survey and those who were contacted through the special follow-up.

The first type of evidence to be considered is the variation in return by year, control, size, and quality of school. These four variables are used throughout the analysis and are known for each subject whether or not he returned a questionnaire.

The total return rate varied only slightly by years since graduation. As indicated earlier, a larger proportion of graduates were lost or replaced in drawing the sample for the 15-year class than for other years but, of those mailed to, members of this earlier class were about as likely to reply.

The returns varied more substantially by control of the school. Graduates of Roman Catholic institutions were least likely to respond and graduates of other private institutions most likely. These differences, however, partially reflect variations in response by the size and quality of the institutions. There was at least some slight tendency for graduates of smaller and high quality institutions to respond.

The complete sample, therefore, appears to have been slightly biased toward graduates of the smaller and higher-quality schools at the expense of those who attended the larger and lower-quality schools. Graduates of Catholic institutions also were less likely to respond, although some compensation for this was built into the sample in advance by the inclusion of one extra Catholic institution.

Another check is provided by comparing the returned samples for each year with the middle group population which they were to approximate. These comparisons also provide a test of a subsidiary objective of the sampling procedures, namely, the comparability of the three samples.

Before drawing conclusions, two points should be made. First, the middle group population figures are not a perfect criterion for representativeness. They include, for example, some foreign students, some borderline cases, and some errors which could not be removed from the population figures but which were eliminated in the sample. Their agreement with the sample figures, therefore, would not necessarily be complete even if the sample were perfectly drawn and executed. Second, the crucial figures to examine are the percent of graduates, not the number of schools. The sample was designed to provide a representative sample only of graduates, not of their institutions. It intentionally over-represented schools with the largest numbers of liberal arts graduates through its probability proportionate to size sampling. The number of schools is shown only as a point of general information.

Taking the subsidiary objective first, it would appear that the three completed samples are at least approximately comparable in their proportions of graduates from schools of the various types represented. Some differences are observed between years. For example, the 15-year sample contains a larger proportion of private school graduates than does the five-year sample, 53.5 vs. 50.2 percent. These differences, however, are small and seem unlikely to have any appreciable effect on comparisons made between the sample years on questionnaire items.

The objective of having the three samples proportionate to the middle group population also seems to have been relatively well satisfied, with a few exceptions. Indeed, the return rate biases reported above appear to have had little effect on the representativeness of the samples. In part, this is attributable to the compensation provided by the addition of the extra Catholic institution.

The final comparisons are made with non-respondents. While the return rate bias does not appear to have seriously distorted the sample by school control, size, quality, and related variables, it remains possible that certain types of graduates, such as those who were more successful in their careers, were more likely to respond. Such an effect could operate across all schools and would not be detectable, therefore, by the foregoing analysis.

Recognizing this possibility, the follow-up study described on page 205 was undertaken with a 10 percent sample of the non-respondents. Some proved to be ineligible, inaccessible, or totally unlocatable, but of the remainder, 77 percent submitted to a brief telephone interview or completed a brief questionnaire sent by registered mail. By comparing this sample of non-respondents with those who completed the regular questionnaire, some indication may be gained of possible biases from selective responses among those who were reached.

The primary conclusion is that in many respects the general respondents and the follow-up respondents are quite similar. Only very small differences are observed by: (1) socio-economic background as measured by father's occupation, (2) undergraduate majors, (3) undergraduate majors they would choose if they began college now, (4) undergraduate grades, (5) current incomes, and (6) several attitudinal questions designed to measure occupational satisfaction.

The follow-up respondents do differ from the general respondents, however, in their occupations and types of employers. Almost half the follow-up respondents were employed in the private non-manufacturing sector of the economy, as contrasted to less than a third of the general respondents. Their occupations, not unexpectedly, are found to be typical of this sector, notably law, medicine, dentistry, fiscal management, creative professions, and communications. Apparently, the survey was more successful in reaching graduates who entered the public sector of the economy than in reaching at least these portions of the private sector.

There is also some evidence to suggest that the follow-up respondents may have been somewhat less enthusiastic about the value of a liberal arts education than the general respondents. While they were about as likely to believe that they personally received a good preparation for vocational life and no less likely to prefer a non-liberal arts major if they were to start over, they were less likely to recommend a liberal arts major to a high school student. This, in part, may have been attributed to the highly professional nature of the work of many of the follow-up respondents.

There is little evidence to suggest that follow-up respondents were less satisfied with their occupations, less successful in their jobs, or less likely to be earning high salaries. In fact, it appears that the most successful graduates were least likely to have replied.

These conclusions must be hastily qualified, however, as applying only to those graduates who could be reached either by the main survey or the follow-up study. There is a group of non-respondents about whom virtually nothing is known. These are the graduates who proved totally unlocatable, either because their college had no address for them or because they were unreachable through their last known address. Such graduates comprised approximately 14 percent of all graduates of the cooperating institutions who might have been included in the survey. They must remain a potential and essentially unassessable bias in the results presented.

FOOTNOTES

1. Much of this Appendix was written by William L. Nicholls II of the Survey Research Center of the University of California at Berkeley, who served as technical consultant for construction of the sample of alumni.

2. Lazarsfeld and Thielens, *op. cit.*

3. Rogoff, Natalie and Mitchell, Robert E., *College Board Members: A Comparative Analysis.* (Unpublished research report, Bureau of Applied Social Research, Columbia University, 1957)

4. Knapp, Robert Hampdon and Greenbaum, Joseph J., *The Younger American Scholar: His Collegiate Origins.* Chicago, Ill., University of Chicago Press, 1953.

5. Irwin, Mary (editor), *American Colleges and Universities,* seventh edition. Washington, D.C., American Council on Education, 1956.

6. Full and part-time enrollments were ascertained by consulting *Resident, Extension, and Adult Education Enrollment in Institutes of Higher Education: November, 1954.* Washington, D.C., U.S. Department of Health, Education and Welfare. Circular No. 454. September, 1955.

7. Ostheimer, Richard, *A Statistical Analysis of the Organization of Higher Education in the United States, 1948-49.* New York, Columbia University Press, 1951.

8. Knapp and Greenbaum, *op. cit.*

--- TABLE 109 ---

Liberal Arts Colleges and Their Graduates in the Population

Control, Size, and Quality	Colleges		Percent of Liberal Arts Graduates In:					
	Number	Percent	1948		1953		1958	
Control								
Public-state	117	28.4%	32.8% ⎫	40	34.7% ⎫	39	42.0% ⎫	46
Public-municipal	11	2.7	7.1 ⎭		4.7 ⎭		4.4 ⎭	
Roman Catholic	44	10.7	8.2	8	11.5	12	10.3	10
Private-Protestant	137	33.2	15.2 ⎫	52	16.1 ⎫	49	15.7 ⎫	43
Private-secular	103	25.1	36.7 ⎭		33.0 ⎭		27.6 ⎭	
Size								
Under 1,000 Small	168	40.8%	14.5% ⎫	30	16.4% ⎫	35	15.8% ⎫	34
1,000 - 2,499	109	26.4	15.5 ⎭		18.8 ⎭		18.3 ⎭	
2,500 - 4,999 Medium·	56	13.6	15.6 ⎫	38	16.8 ⎫	40	16.4 ⎫	40
5,000 - 9,999	52	12.6	22.3 ⎭		23.0 ⎭		24.0 ⎭	
10,000 - 13,999 Large	12	2.9	9.5 ⎫	32	8.7 ⎫	25	9.5 ⎫	26
14,000 and over	15	3.7	22.6 ⎭		16.3 ⎭		16.0 ⎭	
Quality								
27-30 High	34	8.2	23.6%	24	20.0%	20	17.7%	18
24-26	41	10.0	18.0 ⎫		15.1 ⎫		15.5 ⎫	
22-23 Medium	40	9.7	14.3 ⎬	44	14.2 ⎬	44	15.2 ⎬	44
19-21	52	12.6	12.2 ⎭		14.6 ⎭		13.4 ⎭	
16-18	72	17.5	12.1 ⎫		13.6 ⎫		13.7 ⎫	
14-15 Low	59	14.3	10.2 ⎬	32	9.3 ⎬	36	10.7 ⎬	38
7-13	114	27.7	9.6 ⎭		13.2 ⎭		13.8 ⎭	
Total = 100%	412	(412)	(59,291)		(56,075)		(71,925)	

TABLE 110

College Size and Quality by Control: Population

Size and Quality		Catholic	Public	Private
Size				
Under 1,000 } Small		32%	13%	57%
1,000 - 2,499 }		32	29	24
2,500 - 4,999 } Medium		13	24	9
5,000 - 9,999 }		23	21	6
10,000 and over Large		-	13	4
Quality				
27-30 High		-%	6%	11%
24-26 }		5	10	11
22-23 } Medium		-	16	8
19-21 }		5	15	13
16-18 }		20	16	18
14-15 } Low		20	9	16
7-13 }		50	28	23
Total = 100%		(44)	(128)	(240)

TABLE 111

College Quality by Size: Population

Quality		Under 1,000	1,000-2,499	2,500-4,999	5,000-9,999	10,000 and over
27-30 High		6%	5%	9%	15%	19%
24-26 }		5	8	16	12	30
22-23 } Medium		5	9	7	21	26
19-21 }		11	13	18	13	11
16-18 }		21	10	25	19	7
14-15 } Low		16	17	12	10	7
7-13 }		36	38	13	10	-
Total = 100%		(168)	(109)	(56)	(52)	(27)

──────────── **TABLE 112** ────────────

Distribution of Schools on Six Quality Items
(All 412 institutions in total universe)

Quality Measure and Categories Employed	Score Assigned	Number of Schools
Total volumes in school library		
Under 40,000	1 (Low)	56
40,000 - 79,999	2	130
80,000 -119,999	3	56
120,000 -299,999	4	90
300,000 and over	5 (High)	80
Books per student		
Under 30	1	49
30 - 59	2	135
60 - 89	3	101
90 - 119	4	48
120 and over	5	79
Budget per student		
Under $700	1	69
$700 - $999	2	107
$1,000 - $1,299	3	88
$1,300 - $1,599	4	61
$1,600 and over	5	87
Proportion of Ph.D.'s on faculty		
Under 25%	1	90
25 - 34%	2	109
35 - 44%	3	100
45 - 54%	4	62
55% and over	5	51
Annual tuition		
Public schools:		
Under $150	1	26
$150 - $249	2	35
$250 - $349	3	23
$350 - $449	4	29
$450 and over	5	16

TABLE 112- continued

Quality Measure and Categories Employed	Score Assigned	Number of Schools
Private schools:		
Under $300	1	23
$300 - $449	2	89
$450 - $549	3	64
$550 - $699	4	58
$700 and over	5	48
Academic achievement of alumni (Knapp and Greenbaum Index)		
No scholars (School not listed)	1	119
0.3 to 1.9% of graduates	2	70
2.0 to 3.9%	3	82
4.0 to 8.3%	4	73
9.1 to 61.2%	5	68

──────── **TABLE 113** ────────

**Distribution of Schools and Middle Group Graduates
by Total Quality Score of School**
(All 412 institutions in total universe)

Quality Score of School	Schools		1952-53 Male Liberal Arts Graduates	
	Number	Percent	Number	Percent
7 - 8	8	1.9%	346	0.6%
9 - 10	31	7.5	1,554	2.8
11 - 12	47	11.4	3,327	5.9
13 - 14	55	13.4	3,956	7.1
15 - 16	57	13.8	5,718	10.2
17 - 18	47	11.4	5,331	9.5
19 - 20	31	7.5	4,940	8.8
21 - 22	41	10.0	6,700	11.9
23 - 24	34	8.3	7,491	13.4
25 - 26	27	6.6	5,510	9.8
27 - 28	15	3.6	4,997	8.9
29 - 30	19	4.6	6,205	11.1
Total	412	100.0%	56,075	100.0%

——————————————TABLE 114 ——————————

Response to the Mailed Questionnaire

Outcome	Number
Returned, complete, and eligible	10,877
Returned, ineligible	277
Unlocatable	1,312
Inaccessible	5
No response or refused to answer	5,583
Total mailed	18,004

——————————— TABLE 115 ———————————

Response to Follow-Up Study

Outcome		Number
Unlocatable (registered letter undeliverable)		47
Contacted by phone or mail		420
Eligible and completed follow-up questionnaire	360	
Found ineligible	24	
Refused to cooperate	36	
Inaccessible (hospitalized, abroad for extended period, or classified assignment, etc. as reported by person at their last address)		17
Unreachable (registered letter delibered but unanswered, no telephone number available)		71
Total follow-up sample		555

————————— TABLE 116 —————————

**Estimated Outcomes of Mailings Based on
Re-distribution of Non-Respondents**

Outcomes

Ineligible subjects				555
Eligible subjects			17,449	
Unlocatable subjects		1,765		
Locatable subjects		15,684		
Inaccessible subjects	202			
Accessible subjects	15,482			
Returned questionnaire . . .	10,877			
Did not return questionnaire	4,605			
Totals	15,482 15,684 17,449 18,004			

From this information, three different types of response rates may be
calculated as follows:

Gross response rate = $\dfrac{\text{Number of eligible returns}}{\text{Number of subjects to whom mailed}}$ = 60.4 percent

Return rate of
eligibles = $\dfrac{\text{Number of eligible returns}}{\text{Number of eligible subjects}}$ = 62.3 percent

Return rate of locatable,
accessible, eligibles = $\dfrac{\text{Number of eligible returns}}{\substack{\text{Number of eligible, accessible,}\\ \text{and locatable subjects}}}$ = 70.2 percent

———————————————————————— TABLE 117 ————————————————————————

Comparison of Completed Sample with Middle Group Population

Geographical Location of School and Type of Student Body	Number of Schools In:		Percent of Graduates In:	
			1953	Total
	Popula.	Sample	Population	Sample
Geographic Location				
New England	28	9	12.3%	10.9%
Mideast	68	22	24.5	22.1
Great Lakes	89	21	20.5	23.8
Plains	64	11	10.0	10.4
Southeast	84	14	13.7	11.2
Southwest	28	6	4.6	4.9
Rocky Mountains	15	6	3.5	3.8
Far West	36	11	10.8	12.9
Total = 100%	412	100	(56,075)	(10,877)
Male or Coed				
All male	45	11	15.7%	13.3%
Coed	367	89	84.3	86.7
Total = 100%	412	100	(56,075)	(10,877)
Predominantly Negro or Not				
Yes	13	2	1.4%	2.0%
No	399	98	98.6	98.0
Total = 100%	412	100	(56,075)	(10,877)

APPENDIX B: Cooperating Colleges and Universities

Adams State College
Albright College
Arizona State University
Arkansas, University of

Baylor University
Bethany College (West Virginia)
Boston College
Bowdoin College
Brooklyn College
Brown University

California, University of, Berkeley
California, University of, Los Angeles
Canisius College
Catholic University of America
Chicago, University of
Cincinnati, University of
Coe College
Colby College
Colgate University
Colorado State College
Colorado State University
Columbia University
Concordia College (Minnesota)
Cornell University

Dartmouth College
Dayton, University of
Denison University
Denver, University of
DePaul University
De Pauw University
Duke University

Earlham College
East Texas State Teachers College
Emory and Henry College

Florida State University
Fordham University
Franklin and Marshall College
Fresno State College
Furman University

George Washington University
Georgetown University
Goshen College

Hamline University
Hastings College
Hofstra College
Holy Cross, College of the

Idaho, College of
Illinois College
Illinois, University of
Indiana Central College

Kansas, University of

Louisiana State University

Marquette University
Miami University
Michigan State University
Michigan, University of
Minnesota, University of
Montana State University
Murray State College

New Mexico Western College
New Mexico, University of
New York, City College of
New York University

Oberlin College
Ohio State University
Oregon, University of

Park College
Pennsylvania, University of
Pittsburgh, University of
Princeton University

Redlands, University of
Richmond, University of
Roosevelt University
Rutgers University

St. Anselm's College
St. Francis College (Pennsylvania)
St. John's College (New York)
St. Louis University
San Jose State College
Seattle Pacific College
State University of South Dakota
Southern California, University of
Stanford University
Stetson University
Syracuse University

Talladega College
Texas, University of
Tufts University

Union College (Kentucky)
Union College (New York)

Virginia, University of

Washburn University
Washington University
Washington, University of
Wayne State University
Willamette University
Wisconsin, University of

Xavier University (Louisiana)

Yale University

✳ The original questionnaire was a 20-page booklet prepared by the Survey Research Center at the University of California in Berkeley. All of the questions are reproduced in this condensation but some subsidiary questions and elaborations have been omitted to save space. Omissions have been indicated by an asterisk. (*)

A STUDY OF THE LIBERAL ARTS GRADUATE

GENERAL INSTRUCTIONS: Please answer the questions as frankly and accurately as you are able. Most of the questions can be answered by simply checking the appropriate category or box. ✳

1. List below the names, locations, dates, and degrees (if any) of all undergraduate, graduate, and professional schools that you have ever attended. List the schools in the order in which you attended them. (Exclude schools in which you attended only a summer session.) ✳

Questions 2 through 16 deal with your undergraduate education.

2. As an undergraduate student, where did you live for *the longest period* of time while in college? (*Check one*) ✳

3. Which of the following contributed to your expenses while you were in college? (*Check all that apply*)

   Scholarships .... ☐₁
   G. I. Bill of Rights .... ☐₂
   Summer employment .... ☐₃
   Part-time employment during school year .... ☐₄
   Loan funds .... ☐₅
   Other (*specify*) _____ ☐₆

4. What portion of your total expenses at college did you earn yourself? (*Check one*)

   None .... ☐₁
   1%–25% .... ☐₂
   26%–50% .... ☐₃
   51%–75% .... ☐₄
   76%–100% .... ☐₅

5. As best you can remember, what was your cumulative (overall) grade average for undergraduate work at the college from which you received your bachelor's degree? (*Check one*) ✳

6. To what extent were you concerned about how well you were doing academically? (*Check one*) ✻

7. Compared to other students in your class in college, how hard would you say you worked on your studies? (*Check one*) ✻

8. To what extent did you participate in varsity athletics? (*Check one*) ✻

9. How would you classify your participation in each of the following extra-curricular activities? (*Check one on each line*) ✻

10. How much personal contact did you have with faculty members? (*Check one*) ✻

11. To what extent do you agree or disagree with each of the following statements about your undergraduate training? (*Check one on each line*)

My professors were really interested in	Strongly Agree	Agree	Disagree	Strongly Disagree
their students	☐1	☐2	☐3	☐4
I received good training in how to express my ideas clearly	☐1	☐2	☐3	☐4
I received good preparation for my vocational life	☐1	☐2	☐3	☐4
There was too much emphasis on social life and on non-academic matters outside the classroom	☐1	☐2	☐3	☐4
The courses I took were, on the whole, quite challenging and interesting	☐1	☐2	☐3	☐4
My classmates often asked me for help in their studies	☐1	☐2	☐3	☐4
I often asked my classmates for help with my studies	☐1	☐2	☐3	☐4
I would advise a 1963 high school graduate to take a liberal arts major	☐1	☐2	☐3	☐4
I spent a lot of time discussing intellectual issues with my classmates	☐1	☐2	☐3	☐4

12. Here is a list of subjects which may have been offered in your undergraduate college. To the best of your memory, how many courses did you take in each subject, and how do you now feel about them. (Do not include courses taken in graduate school.) (*Answer both Column A and Column B*) ✻

13. Using the numbers on the left of the subjects in Question 12, please answer the following questions.

a. What was your major? ✻

b. Did you switch from any previous majors? ✻

c. If you could start college all over again, what field would you major in? ✻

d. Which *two* subjects did you *most enjoy* taking? ✻

e. Which *two* subjects did you find the *most difficult?* ✻

f. Which *two* subjects had the *best teachers?* ✻

g. Which *two* subjects have you found *most useful* in your career? ✻

14. While in college, did you ... (*Check one on each line*)

	Yes	No
Take a senior seminar course?	☐₁	☐₂
Write a thesis in your major subject?	☐₁	☐₂
Obtain membership in Phi Beta Kappa?	☐₁	☐₂
Graduate with academic honors (cum laude, etc.)?	☐₁	☐₂
Complete an advanced Army, Navy, or Air Force ROTC?	☐₁	☐₂

15. Listed below are some things which different people want to receive from a liberal arts education. (*Answer both Column A and Column B*)

In COLUMN A, please indicate the extent to which you now think that these are important.

In COLUMN B, irrespective of how important you consider each of these, please indicate the extent to which your education provided each.

	COLUMN A Importance of each objective (*Check one on each line*)				**COLUMN B** Did your education provide this? (*Check one on each line*)	
Liberal arts education should ...	Very impor- tant	Fairly impor- tant	Fairly unimpor- tant	Not im- portant at all	Yes	No
Develop ability to get along with different types of people..	☐₁	☐₂	☐₃	☐₄	☐₇	☐₈
Provide a broad fund of knowledge about different fields	☐	☐	☐	☐	☐	☐
Develop social poise	☐	☐	☐	☐	☐	☐
Develop a fund of knowledge useful in later life	☐	☐	☐	☐	☐	☐
Prepare for a happy marriage and family life	☐	☐	☐	☐	☐	☐
Develop a sense of responsibility to participate in community and public affairs	☐	☐	☐	☐	☐	☐
Develop moral capacities, ethical standards and values	☐	☐	☐	☐	☐	☐
Train a person in depth in at least one field	☐	☐	☐	☐	☐	☐

16. If you could start college all over again, would you still attend the same college you earned your degree from? (*Check one*) ✻

OTHER ACADEMIC TRAINING

17. Aside from the degrees which you now hold, do you anticipate receiving any graduate or professional degree in the next few years? (*Check one*)

    No .... ☐₁

    Maybe .... ☐₂

    ✻✻Yes .... ☐₃

    ✻✻*If "Yes," what degree?* _____

    In what field? _____
                                   (*write in*)

18. Generally speaking, do you feel that advanced academic training is important to people working in your field? (*Check one*) ✻

19. ANSWER QUESTION 19 ONLY IF YOU HAVE ATTENDED GRADU-ATE OR PROFESSIONAL SCHOOL. Please indicate the extent to which you agree or disagree with each of the following statements concerning graduate or professional education. (*Check one on each line*)

	Strongly Agree	Agree	No Opinion	Disagree	Strongly Disagree
On balance, I benefited more from my undergraduate education than from graduate or professional school	☐₁	☐₂	☐₃	☐₄	☐₅
Graduate or professional school was more difficult than undergraduate education	☐₁	☐₂	☐₃	☐₄	☐₅
Graduate school was really a waste of time	☐₁	☐₂	☐₃	☐₄	☐₅
Liberal arts was essentially preparation for graduate school, rather than training useful for my field	☐₁	☐₂	☐₃	☐₄	☐₅
Without graduate school, I would feel that my education was not complete	☐₁	☐₂	☐₃	☐₄	☐₅
Graduate study helped me avoid being stuck at a low level in my field	☐₁	☐₂	☐₃	☐₄	☐₅
I took graduate study primarily to follow my own intellectual interests, rather than because it might help my career	☐₁	☐₂	☐₃	☐₄	☐₅
I entered graduate school with a fairly clear idea of my vocational goal	☐₁	☐₂	☐₃	☐₄	☐₅

YOUR CAREER

20. List below all the organizations by which you have been employed on a full-time basis since you received your *bachelor's* degree. (Exclude periods of full-time study, short-term military service, or times when you were unemployed or between jobs.)

    List the organizations in order, beginning with the *first*. Questions 21, 22, 23 and 24 will be answered on the basis of these organizations. ✳

21. **In COLUMN A** above, classify each type of employer. Do this by writing the appropriate category number below in the corresponding position in Column A.✳

22. **In COLUMN B** above mark an "X" for each organization in which you were self-employed.

23. **In COLUMN C** above classify your primary job responsibility in each organization. Do this by using the number which appears before the job listed below.✳

24. Here is a list of reasons why people sometimes leave one job for another. **In COLUMN D** above, indicate the *one* reason which *best* explains why you left each organization. Do this by writing in Column D the number which appears before the most appropriate category listed below. ✳

25. Approximately how many offers of "solid job opportunities" did you have at the time you accepted your first and your current job? (*Check one in each "vertical" column*) ✳

26. Which was the *single most helpful* source responsible for your obtaining each of the jobs which you have held? (*Check one in each "vertical" column*)

	First Job	Second Job	Third Job	Fourth Job	Fifth Job
College placement office	□1	□1	□1	□1	□1
Faculty advisor or professor	□2	□2	□2	□2	□2
Direct personal application	□3	□3	□3	□3	□3
Private employment agencies	□4	□4	□4	□4	□4
State employment services	□5	□5	□5	□5	□5
Family contacts	□6	□6	□6	□6	□6
Personal friends	□7	□7	□7	□7	□7
Want ads	□8	□8	□8	□8	□8
Professional societies or contacts	□9	□9	□9	□9	□9
New employer contacted me directly	□0	□0	□0	□0	□0
Other (*please specify*)	□y	□y	□y	□y	□y

27. Since receiving your bachelor's degree, approximately how long have you been unemployed or between jobs?

    Write in total months ....months

28. How much do you like: (*Check one on each line*)

	Like very much	Like fairly much	Dislike slightly	Dislike greatly	Not Applicable
The kind of work you are doing	☐1	☐2	☐3	☐4	☐5
The supervisors for whom you work	☐1	☐2	☐3	☐4	☐5
The colleagues who work with you	☐1	☐2	☐3	☐4	☐5
The people who work for you ...	☐1	☐2	☐3	☐4	☐5
Your income from your job	☐1	☐2	☐3	☐4	☐5
Your employer's promotion policy	☐1	☐2	☐3	☐4	☐5

29. What was your annual salary when you began your *first* full-time job after

receiving your bachelor's degree? $................................
                                                    (*write in amount*)

30. What is your current annual salary in your present position? $...............................
                                                                                    (*write in amount*)

31. Approximately how many other people work for the total organization by which you are employed? (*Check one*) ✻

32. How many employees do you directly supervise? (*Check one in each "vertical" column*) ✻

33. Do you wish you were in an *occupation* other than your present one? (*Check one*) ✻

34. Do you wish you were working for an *employer* other than your present one? (If self-employed, would you like to become an employee of someone else?)✻

35. Please answer each of the following. (*Check one on each line*)

	Quite a lot	A fair amount	A little	None
Does your position involve speaking, reading, or writing a foreign language?	☐1	☐2	☐3	☐4
Does your work involve much writing?	☐1	☐2	☐3	☐4
Does your work involve much creative thinking?	☐1	☐2	☐3	☐4
Do you frequently take work home with you or come into your office after working hours or on weekends?	☐1	☐2	☐3	☐4

36. Please answer each of the following. (*Check one on each line*)

	Definitely Yes	Probably Yes	Probably No	Definitely No
Contrasted with your college classmates, would you say that your career had been more successful?	☐1	☐2	☐3	☐4
Would you be willing to move to another state to accept a promotion or a better job?	☐1	☐2	☐3	☐4
In the next three years, do you think you will change to another occupation?	☐1	☐2	☐3	☐4

	Definitely Yes	Probably Yes	Probably No	Definitely No
In the next three years, do you think you will change to another employer?	☐1	☐2	☐3	☐4
In the next three years, do you expect to receive a promotion?	☐1	☐2	☐3	☐4
In the next three years, do you expect to enroll as a full-time student?	☐1	☐2	☐3	☐4

37. Below are some of the characteristics often associated with occupations and professions. *(Answer both Column A and Column B)*

   In COLUMN A, please indicate how important each characteristic is to you.

   In COLUMN B, please indicate the extent to which your current job has each characteristic?

COLUMN A

Importance to you . . .
(Check one on each line)

COLUMN B

Characteristic of your present job
(Check one on each line)

Very	Some	Little	None		To a high degree	Moderately	Slightly	Not at all
☐1	☐2	☐3	☐4	Opportunity to use my special abilities	☐7	☐8	☐9	☐0
☐	☐	☐	☐	Chance to earn a great deal of money	☐	☐	☐	☐
☐	☐	☐	☐	Permit me to be creative and original	☐	☐	☐	☐
☐	☐	☐	☐	Give me social status and prestige. .	☐	☐	☐	☐
☐	☐	☐	☐	Enable me to look forward to a stable future	☐	☐	☐	☐
☐	☐	☐	☐	Leave me relatively free of supervision	☐	☐	☐	☐
☐	☐	☐	☐	Give me a chance to exercise leadership	☐	☐	☐	☐
☐	☐	☐	☐	Give me an opportunity to help others	☐	☐	☐	☐

SELECTION OF A GOAL

38. Have you set yourself a type of occupation or career line which you would like to follow? *(Check one)* ✻

39. If you have selected an occupational goal or career objective, when did you make this selection? *(Check one)* ✻

40. While you were in college, did you make use of the following sources of career assistance and how helpful was each in aiding you to select an occupation? *(Check one on each line)*

See Over →

	Did not refer to this source	Referred to this source and found it of little or no use	Referred to this source and found it somewhat useful	Referred to this source and found it very useful
Vocational guidance tests	☐₁	☐₂	☐₃	☐₄
Individual vocational counseling. .	☐₁	☐₂	☐₃	☐₄
Occupational reading materials . . .	☐₁	☐₂	☐₃	☐₄
Advice from family	☐₁	☐₂	☐₃	☐₄
Advice from potential employers. .	☐₁	☐₂	☐₃	☐₄
Advice from faculty members	☐₁	☐₂	☐₃	☐₄
Part-time and summer jobs	☐₁	☐₂	☐₃	☐₄
Assistance from college placement services	☐₁	☐₂	☐₃	☐₄
Other _____ (please specify)	☐₁	☐₂	☐₃	☐₄

YOUR INTERESTS

41. During the past 12 months have you? (Check one on each line)

	Yes	No
Worked on fund-raising drives for United Fund, or other such charitable organization	☐₁	☐₂
Worked on fund-raising for your church	☐₁	☐₂
Attended two or more theatrical productions	☐₁	☐₂
Attended two or more meetings of the PTA	☐₁	☐₂
Given one or more speeches	☐₁	☐₂
Published an article	☐₁	☐₂
Published a book	☐₁	☐₂
Run for, or held a public office	☐₁	☐₂
Attended one or more public lectures	☐₁	☐₂
Belonged to a service club (Rotary, Kiwanis, etc.)	☐₁	☐₂
Belonged to a veterans organization	☐₁	☐₂
Led, or assisted in the leadership of a scout troup or youth group. . .	☐₁	☐₂
Attended a college alumni function or visited your undergraduate campus	☐₁	☐₂
Participated in a literary, art, discussion, or study group	☐₁	☐₂
Given money to your undergraduate college or university	☐₁	☐₂
Attended two or more opera or symphonic concerts	☐₁	☐₂
Belonged to a political club or political action group	☐₁	☐₂
Belonged to a labor union	☐₁	☐₂
Belonged to a professional association	☐₁	☐₂
Held two income-producing jobs at the same time	☐₁	☐₂
Served on church or synagogue board or committee	☐₁	☐₂
Visited an art museum	☐₁	☐₂
Wrote or talked with a public official about a current program or proposed bill	☐₁	☐₂
Attended religious services on a fairly regular basis	☐₁	☐₂

42. During the past 12 months, approximately how many of each of the following books or publications did you read? (*Check one on each line*) ✳

MARRIAGE AND FAMILY STATUS

43. Are you . . . ? (*Check one*)

Single (never married) (*If so, skip to 48*) . . . . ☐₁

Married (first marriage) . . . . ☐₂

Married (second or later marriage) . . . . ☐₃

Divorced (not remarried) . . . . ☐₄

Widowed . . . . ☐₅

44. When were you first married?   19............
    (*write in*)

45. How many children do you have? ....
    (*write in*)

46. When was your first child born? 19............
    (*write in*)

47. Answer the following for your wife (or if widowed or divorced and not remarried, answer on the basis of your former wife). (*Check one on each line*)

	Yes	No	Don't Know
Is she a college graduate?	☐₁	☐₂	☐₃
Does she have an advanced degree?	☐₁	☐₂	☐₃
Did she attend the same undergraduate college you did?	☐₁	☐₂	☐₃
Is she employed full time on a paid position?	☐₁	☐₂	☐₃
Is she employed part time on a paid position?	☐₁	☐₂	☐₃
Does she feel that you should switch to another employer?	☐₁	☐₂	☐₃
Does she feel that you should be in another occupation?	☐₁	☐₂	☐₃
Does she feel that you spend too much time on your work?	☐₁	☐₂	☐₃
Does she object to the travel which your job requires?	☐₁	☐₂	☐₃
Would she object if your job required that your family move to a new community?	☐₁	☐₂	☐₃
Do you discuss day-by-day job activities with your wife?	☐₁	☐₂	☐₃
Do you discuss major job decisions with your wife?	☐₁	☐₂	☐₃
Do you often follow your wife's advice about your job?	☐₁	☐₂	☐₃

GEOGRAPHICAL MOBILITY

48. Which of the following best describes (a) the community in which you grew up when you went to high school and (b) the community in which you now live? (*Check one in each "vertical" column*) ✳

49. Use the numbers to the left of the regions listed below in answering the following questions. ✳

Write in the number of the region below to indicate where . . .

You were born . . . .

You graduated from high school . . . .

You lived immediately after college . . . .

You live now . . . .

YOUR PERSONAL BACKGROUND

50. From which kind of high school did you graduate? (*Check one*) *

51. Please check highest educational attainment of your parents (or step-parents). (*Check one for each parent*) *

52. If one or both of your parents are college graduates, were they liberal arts majors? (*Check one for each parent*) *

53. What was your father's (or step-father's or guardian's) occupation when you graduated from high school? (*Check one*) *

54. Are you . . . ? (*Check one*)

White . . . . ☐₁

Negro . . . . ☐₂

Oriental . . . . ☐₃

Other . . . . ☐₄

55. What is your current age? (*Check one*) *

56. What was your approximate family income (after deducting business expenses) from all sources during the past tax year? (*Check one*) *

57. Which of the following best represents your political leanings (a) when you were a college senior and (b) at the present time? (*Check one in each "vertical" column*) *

58. Please answer:

a. Have you ever served in the armed forces? (*Check one*)

No ☐₁ (*If "No" skip to 59*)   Yes ☐₂ (*If "Yes" complete this question*) *

59. What was your religious preference when you graduated from college, and what is it now? (*Check one in each "vertical" column*) *

60. Which of the following best represents how important religion was to you when you were in college and how important it is now? (*Check one in each "vertical" column*) *

61. What advice would you give today's liberal arts students about selecting their careers?

62. Do you have any comments on the problems you have experienced during your working career?

INDEX

(Note: An "n" preceding number refers to footnote number.)